MUSEUMS AND THE FUTURE OF COLLECTING

Museums and the Future of Collecting

Second Edition

Edited by

SIMON J. KNELL
Department of Museum Studies
University of Leicester

ASHGATE

First edition 1999
Second edition 2004

Published by
Ashgate Publishing Limited
Gower House
Croft Road
Aldershot, Hampshire GU11 3HR
Great Britain

Ashgate Publishing Company
Suite 420
101 Cherry Street
Burlington, Vermont 05401–4405
USA

ISBN 0 7546 3005 6

British Library Cataloguing in Publication Data
Museums and the Future of Collecting
    1. Museums—Collection management. I. Knell, Simon J.
    069.5

US Library of Congress Cataloging in Publication Data
Museums and the Future of Collecting / edited by Simon J. Knell.
    p. cm. — Papers originally presented at a conference organised by the
    Department of Museum Studies at the University of Leicester. Includes
    bibliographical references and index.
    1. Museums—Acquisitions—Congresses. I. Knell, Simon J.
    AM135.M864   1999   98-46336
    069'.51–dc21   CIP

This volume is printed on acid free paper.

Printed and bound in Great Britain by MPG Books Ltd, Bodmin, Cornwall

Contents

List of Figures

List of Tables

Preface

The contributions to this book review collecting practices in museums and suggest future directions. First published in 1999, in response to an international conference held in Leicester entitled 'Carry on Collecting?', the perspectives here come from museum practitioners and scholars of museums. They deal with such varied topics as the international trade in fossils, the representation of subcultures, policies for the small museum, connoisseurship, inferences from collecting studies and histories, disciplinarity, nationhood, collaborative methodologies and so on. It is a kaleidoscopic collection.

In this second edition I have made a number of significant improvements: the whole book has been reformatted, original illustrations added, subheads have been restored, notes now appear at the foot of the page, and I have produced a new index. I have also made some additions to the text: Rebecca Duclos's paper has had some content restored, I have added an innovative paper on ranking collections by Martin Wickham and a substantial new introductory chapter of my own.

Since first publishing this book, I have been fortunate enough to travel to many parts of the world talking about collections and collecting. This has given me the opportunity to talk to many academics, practitioners and students, from whom I have learned much. I have also taken over material culture teaching from my colleague Susan Pearce and produced, amongst other things, a substantial book on the simultaneous origins of provincial museums and geology in England in the early nineteenth century, which is based on a study of collecting practices, and a similar study of science and collecting culture in the late twentieth century. The chapter I have written here reflects all these experiences and, rather provocatively and like all the chapters in this book, is particularly aimed at informing future practice.

Finally, I should note that a great many contributors have moved post in the few years since the first edition, and I have not been able to contact everyone directly. I thank them again, and hope that the surprise of finding their work in paperback will be a pleasant one!

Simon J. Knell
Department of Museums Studies, University of Leicester
March 2003

1 Altered values: searching for a new collecting

Simon Knell

The collecting problem facing museums has many facets. Many believe it is simply a matter of locating an answer to the questions 'What and how should a museum collect?' But the problem is also one of aspirations and implications: unsatisfied desires mingle with full stores and over-committed budgets. And while it is possible to locate many aspects of museum context and provision that explain why museums are never entirely successful collectors, and about which museums have much to complain, those of us who undertake the collecting also cherish beliefs, philosophies and practices which contribute to our undoing. We also undertake our collecting in a changing world and it this changing world which both provides the motivation to collect and yet, as I shall explain, also questions its validity.

Were our ancestors here now, they would have no difficulty recognising this modern collecting problem, for they too had faced it, often within a few years of the establishment of their institutions. But when they began the modern phase of institutional collecting, almost two centuries ago, they felt they were, in many ways, dealing with a finite world. They were primarily collecting objects from nature, in a world designed by a God, where the meaning of the object was set almost unquestioningly in the context of scientific realism. Indeed, within 50 years, some felt they had achieved their primary collecting goal.[1] What they did not foresee, initially, was that collecting would continue as knowledge, education, entertainment, social politics, fashion and so on demanded, and as the museums' disciplinary interests diversified. Cultural change thus added to the diversity of collectables while the emergence of a pervasive museum culture instilled in

---

1   S.J. Knell, *The Culture of English Geology 1815–1851: A Science Revealed Through Its Collecting* (Aldershot: Ashgate, 2000), 294.

society a new need for public giving. Any finitude in the collecting project was surely an illusion.

Theirs was a world of discovery. Modern disciplines were formed and ways of knowing took on an empirical rigour which was made concrete in the new museum. However, by the late twentieth century this disciplinary framework had matured to a point of postmodernist deconstruction, and was now set in a world of digitisation and information networking. The 'hard fact' concept of knowledge gathering, which had underpinned earlier collecting, now became situated in a complex interconnected and overlapping jumble of media, methods and philosophies, which contributed to individual ways of knowing. Here, belief, personal meaning making and politics conflicted with, if not superseded, an earlier philosophy (however realistic in actuality) of disinterested and rational objectivity. In this new world, legitimacy and authority were manoeuvred into the arguments of one group to question the collecting and interpretive rights of another.[2] Having sensed the power relations inherent in cultural representation, museums sought preferred viewpoints determined by morality and ethics. Institutional collecting, which could now be seen as a power-ridden act of authoring social memory, called for fundamental review.

This increased disciplinary reflection has reconfigured the object in knowledge creation and representation. Even in rational science, which has for the most part been unaltered by postmodernism, the collectable object is no longer at the heart of most of its ambitions. The nineteenth-century preoccupation with order disappeared long ago. Thus, however we might wish to view it, the collected object seems no longer to be as central to knowledge creation as it was. This is not to suggest that all intellectual pursuits are now devoid of the need for objects. Some, like art history, palaeontology and archaeology rely upon them, and many other disciplines still retain a taxonomic corner where the object remains key. But whereas once the object was accepted as a source of 'evidence' leading to absolute truth, now its claims are not beyond doubt.

This, however, is just one side of the interpretive equation: the readings that are possible from the object. The other side of this equation concerns

---

2   See, for example, the essays in I. Karp, and S.D. Lavine, *Exhibiting Cultures: The Poetics and Politics of Museum Display* (Washington: Smithsonian Institute, 1991).

the use of the object in the interpretation of knowledge to an audience; the role of the object in communication. Even here the 'real thing' may seem less essential. Many activities, which once relied upon its presence, are now achieved using other media: media in which the dynamism of the living event gives an even greater sense of witnessing a 'truth' or in which levels of interactivity and interrogation permit doubts to be removed. One wonders what would have happened if the early Victorians had had access to the movie camera or Internet. Would we have had a museum culture? But then the early twentieth-first-century Web, with its free access, encyclopaedic qualities, and failing curation, is perhaps more like the museum than we realise.

If, then, museums – defined as they are by the possession of these, now often altered, objects – are to exist into the future, how should they confront collecting? How do the efforts of the collecting institution fit into the modern way of knowing? Are museums moving beyond the object and beyond disciplinary knowledge? Are they destined to become centres solely for personal meaning making, the solution of contemporary social issues, and for educational experiences? Certainly many recent changes have suggested this kind of a future, but there are others which seem to suggest a return to the core values of curatorship.

One possible future, being much discussed at this time, lies in the world of digitisation. Across Europe, for example, there are grand plans for a pervasive 'Ambient Intelligence Landscape' (AmIL) which is to be built around networked 'digital libraries' (repositories of digital material), which grow from, and echo, our physical museums and libraries. Information will come to us through our environment and via wearable technologies which are intimately linked to personal context and need.[3] With AmIL comes a plan for digital collecting which makes the encyclopaedic desires of our museum founders appear insignificant. However, the architects of this AmIL world are developing a knowledge infrastructure *exactly* like that created by museum builders in countries like Britain in the early nineteenth century. They too were constructing a pervasively networked new technology offering previously unknown access to knowledge. And just as

---

3   Information Society Technologies Advisory Group (ISTAG), *Scenarios for Ambient Intelligence in 2010* (Luxembourg: European Commission, 2001). S.J. Knell, 'The shape of things to come: Museums in the technological landscape', *Museum and Society*, 1(3) (in press) discusses this development in more detail.

in modern Europe, they too hoped to satisfy 'inclusionist' social agendas.[4] To this emerging world, then, the lessons of 200 years of museum collecting provide both a model and a warning.

A full review of digital 'collecting' is beyond the scope of this book, but I am mindful that much contemporary collecting will be replaced by activity focused on digital capture, which will be undertaken without the survival of a physical counterpart. With this will come changes in fundamental beliefs about the required physicality of evidence and the associated characteristics of authenticity, but I have already suggested that we have the capacity to accept more dynamic forms of evidence. Clearly the authority and credibility of the digitising institution will play a critical role in validating digital data just as it does in preserving and relaying data associated with material objects. In this new world, the relationship between public and expert remains the same: the expert distils a 'truth' and the public decides whether to trust in it.

What is interesting about these developments is that the fundamental drive to collect and engage with 'real things' (even if digitised) remains. The computer scientists who now lead the 'digital heritage' revolution, like many museum practitioners and the early founders of our museums, retain a firm belief in both the inherent factuality of the object and the ease with which it can be gathered up. It is social change of the kind suggested by this AmIL world which raises doubts and questions about the future of collecting but yet also suggests that in one form or another its future is assured.

Context and change

Change of the kind being predicted by the new technological visionary has been a constant companion to museum development. It was only in the last four decades of the twentieth century, for example, that a new professionalism transformed the museum's relationship with its collections. One key moment of realisation in this transformation came just a quarter century ago with the publication of Philip Doughty's report on the state and status of geology collections in UK museums. His rhetoric against a failing profession, then personified in the membership of the UK's ninety-year-old Museums Association, proved sensational and stimulated others

---

4   Knell, *Culture of English Geology*, 52.

to stand up and say 'We too have been abused!'[5] Professional standards of care and a workable system of museum accreditation were an almost immediate response.[6] But what had caused this moment of realisation? The implication was that the profession had been living a lie. Professions are, amongst other things, identified by standards, but there seemed to be none. This was, however, not the modern manifestation it appeared to be. Subsequent research revealed that collection abuse had been the norm for 160 years.[7] While academics had revelled in glorious histories, they had skirted around the realities and consequences of past amateurism, monument building and an irrationality of provision, preferring instead to document the nobler qualities of unfunded dedication, the pursuit of natural knowledge and so forth. Rather than revealing a modern failure, Doughty and his contemporaries were, instead, seeing the mirror-like reflection of their own professional expectations. As part of a large influx of fresh and idealistic graduates into museums in the 1960s and early 1970s, they, like everyone who joins long-established institutions, discovered a past disguised by myth and rumour. What they saw was real enough and did indeed speak of failure and neglect. A glorious past *had*, it seemed, been betrayed: Britain has a substantial claim to founding modern geology, a founding which also stimulated the emergence of a pervasive provincial museum culture in England. It was rather unexpectedly, then, that later

---

5   P.S. Doughty, *The State and Status of Geology in United Kingdom Museums* (London: Geological Society, Miscellaneous Paper 13, 1981). See P.S. Doughty, 'On the rocks', *Museums Association Conference Report* (London; Museum Association,1980), 12–4. G. Kavanagh, 'Collecting from the era of memory, myth and delusion' (Chapter 9) mentions some of these reports but there were many others, for example: B. Williams, *Biological Collections UK* (London: Museums Association, 1987); J.D. Storer, *The Conservation of Industrial Collections: A Survey* (London: Science Museum and MGC, 1989).

6   Museums and Galleries Commission, *Introduction to Registration* (London: MGC, 1995). Museums and Galleries Commission, *Standards in the Museum Care of Geological Collections* (London: MGC, 1993). These documents were also produced for biology, archaeology, large object, musical instrument, costume and photographic collections.

7   S.J. Knell, 'The roller-coaster of museum geology', in S.M. Pearce (ed), *Exploring Science in Museums*, (London: Athlone, 1996), 29–56. Knell, *Culture of English Geology*. S.J. Knell, 'Collection loss, cultural change and the second law of thermodynamics', paper delivered at the Society for the History of Natural History, 'Lost, Stolen or Strayed' conference, Leiden, 2000.

research revealed that the betrayal had been initiated by the very actors who had contributed to the founding of the science and museums in the first place.

'Betrayal', however, is the wrong word. Throughout their existence museums have suffered from gross underfunding. Perhaps they had had golden moments of prosperity, but for most these really were momentary. In Britain, we like to blame the government for such things as underfunding, but the fact is that most of our museums were invented by private individuals who then sought public support; most public museums began with private ideas, private collections or private societies. One cannot escape the fact that these museums were founded on the borderline between Victorian patronage and charity. 'Here are my children, please look after them!', the founders said to those public bodies which took them on, and at once the museum became an orphan under the care of step-parents. That local and national governments supported these orphans was a reflection of other evolving Victorian values: national and civic rivalry, charity, the democratisation of education, the reform of taxation and the adoption of a political philosophy in favour of public funding. At the time it was felt that these unwanted offspring could be patronised for public (and therefore political) benefit. Museums continue to be invented by the same means: a personal vision followed by the public purse. But there is a fine line here between this kind of public patronage and simple charity, and the cyclical fortunes of museums suggest that this line is often crossed. Thus the annual budget round frequently appears like a scene from *Oliver Twist*.[8]

Like most countries, Britain has lacked a strategic rationale for museums, and consequently there has always been a disparity between actual and required levels of funding. Every old plough poking its rusty metal above the roadside stinging nettles seems to be asking to become the founding piece for yet another museum. But while the desire to found museums is undiminished, the available funding for the traditional type will inevitably grow smaller as all funding bodies have available to them an increasing diversity of potential recipients for support under those worthy banners of

---

8   '"Please, sir," replied Oliver, "I want some more." The master aimed a blow at Oliver's head with the ladle; pinioned him in his arms; and shrieked aloud for the beadle.' Charles Dickens, *Oliver Twist* (1838).

'science and education', 'social and community services' or 'identity and citizenship' or 'the Arts'. External competition of this kind is just one factor which suggests that museums need to confront the resource implications of collections. There has also been much internal turmoil resulting from professionalisation of practices, and economic and political change. These, too, suggest a need for review.

Recent professionalisation, in the context of social change, provides useful insights into the world in which museums operate and within which we aim to develop collections. The process of professionalising practice can be traced back to the birth of museums when many curatorial benchmarks were established. The latter decades of nineteenth century added further innovative practices in thematic display and education. Although it is easy for museums to believe theirs are inherited problems, we should not fool ourselves into thinking that our predecessors, of even 180 years ago, were any less sophisticated when they came to consider their actions. They too, for example, had to deal with relativist philosophies which suggested that the reality of objects was an illusion. Their museums, like ours, were a key mechanism for accommodating and facilitating social change. They too had to deal, in their museums, with the interaction of secular society and religious belief, as has again become important in the setting of twenty-first-century multiculturalism, immigration and terrorism. They too had the know-how but not the funding. Theirs was, however, still a museum world dominated by the natural sciences, which from the outset gave an underlying intellectual drive and clear parameters for evaluating the worth of objects. What they did not have is modern levels of resource, and when that resource came along these disciplines were no longer at the height of museum fashion. By then archaeology had already risen to prominence, public art galleries were a civic expectation, and collecting activity in folk life (social history) was well advanced. From the 1960s, museums in Britain entered an entirely new world: museum communication became increasingly studied and incorporated into ever more sophisticated exhibition design; informal education programmes expanded; the conservation profession grew from its tiny foothold; collection management was transformed and the contents of registers and index cards were soon flowing into computers, while emerging documentation specialists struggled to keep up with rapid technological change and horrendous backlogs. More widely, specialist groups (a formalisation of 'communities of practice', now a key management concept)[9] and agencies (like the UK's area museum councils) began to provide support of a kind that overcame local deficiencies. Many of these innovations were homegrown but they were set in a world undergoing what was at first called 'Americanisation', and unsurprisingly many museum practices also came to the UK from across the Atlantic.

These late twentieth-century changes represented a concerted effort to put things right, to make a leap in professionalisation after a 150-year creep. The 1970s and 1980s were important decades in this regard but are light years away from the mobile, networked and information-ridden world of the present: relatively few families had cars in early 1960s Britain, let alone telephones; 1970s documentation efforts centred on filling in cards; and in the 1980s computer interactives in museums were still a rarity. Clearly museums were adapting but the most significant change for museums was, in the mid-1980s, to recognise the place of change itself in their fortunes, and to discover that institutions can actually utilise the opportunities of change to secure their futures. For museums, which had once so valued a monolithic immutability, this conceptual shift was revolutionary, for the museum itself became an increasingly elastic concept. The Natural History Museum (NHM) in London, for example, was by the end of the century offering a wide range of training and consultancy services. With its designed galleries and customer care policies it bore little relationship to the heavily criticised and conservative British Museum of the nineteenth century from which it had arisen. It remained criticised, however, this time for embracing change: but had it not done so its very survival would have been in doubt. It now forms the model of the twenty-first-century museum: focused, businesslike, public friendly and pluralistically funded, yet preserving its collection and research identity. This is not to suggest that its staff don't still complain, that it has not lost rare skills and scarce knowledge, that its public are perfectly happy, or that its managers don't have to paddle hard to keep the ark afloat, but this museum has certainly

---

9   These 'communities of practice' include the UK-led Biology Curators Group, Geological Curators Group, Social History Curators Group, Society of Museum Archaeologists, and the US-led Society for the Preservation of Natural History Collections, and the more recently formed Natural Science Collections Alliance. These communities are now also represented online by such specialist lists as Natural History Collections listserver (NHCOLL).

adapted to the modern context and made itself capable of embracing future change.

Other museums have been less successful at adapting to constant change. Many set themselves on a course, perhaps only five to ten years ago, with a particular staff infrastructure, which enabled them to fulfil the goals then perceived to be central to the modern museum. In the intervening period, society has moved on still further and its needs have changed. The result for some museum services has been repeated restructuring while others find themselves at a point of tension between what they are and what they need to be. Restructuring is only ever a short-term solution; the future for the museum and for collecting lies in the production of flexible systems and flexible workforces.

The NHM's path to a new identity arose in response to a crisis in public funding which came to a head during the Thatcher government of the 1980s. Indeed, the more general revolution in practice had only just begun when the first post-war recession hit in the 1970s. Recessions followed thereafter with predictable and depressing regularity. In many countries, and famously so in Britain, the onset of the 1980s meant a switch to rightwing government and the rise of economic accountability. This also brought a governmental denial of community or social action – surely a central tenet of museum provision. With this removed, all those public bodies unable to justify themselves in financial terms were destined to struggle. There were repeated crises for government-funded and independent museums as the century progressed. Few avoided cuts, many lost staff and some closed.[10] Museums which had survived on hidden costs and professional camaraderie were now faced with a new financial reality; a sense of 'corrosive cynicism' prevailed, and not just in Britain.[11] Museums *had* to change.

---

10   See, for example, D. Butler, 'French museum "in decay" fights for its life', *Nature*, 385 (1997), 378; E. Culotta, 'Mass job extinctions at L.A. museum', *Science*, 260 (1993), 1584; J. Seymour, 'No way to treat a natural treasure', *New Scientist*, 12 March 1994. For the impact of recession and cultural change on museums and collecting see S.J. Knell, 'Collecting, conservation and conservatism: developments in the culture of British geology in the late twentieth century', in D.R. Oldroyd, *The Earth Inside and Out: Some Major Contributions to Geology in the Twentieth Century* (London: Geological Society, 2002), 329–351.

11   S. Weil, *A Cabinet of Curiosities* (Washington: Smithsonian Institution, 1995).

But even in more prosperous times, such as when the British government channelled National Lottery money into a major capital programme for museums, outcomes where not always the best for collections. Revenue budgets did not increase and thus museum expansion meant job redesignation as collection-focused staff took on roles centred on the management of personnel and buildings. While the profession began a range of initiatives to keep museums afloat, the government remained blissfully unaware of what drives the swanlike museum forward. Shiny new museums, and the new brand of edutainment centre which sprang up in competition, concealed a crisis in funding which brought many long established museums in Britain to the point of collapse. The response was the return to the idea of a national strategy, but one that recognised existing provision and the need for pragmatic solutions.[12] Strategic approaches had been proposed by governmental agencies throughout the twentieth century, but only this time did it seem likely that the government would respond.

One side effect of the new financial emphasis, which arrived in the 1980s, was that the cost of maintaining collections could no longer be quietly concealed. This caused anxiety and frustration among professionals who knew that collections had never been properly funded and therefore had never had the opportunity to prove their worth. Spreadsheet accountability entered the world of museums, as it had done in other sectors, and museums adopted management techniques from industry to monitor their performance and plan for change. Such performance measurement appeared, to some, to make perfect sense for collections, and for the work done on them. This use of numerate analysis in museums appears, by its very nature, to bring scientific objectivity to processes and events which are otherwise difficult to define, summarise or evaluate. But figures do not make facts. They can be ill-conceived, wrongly used or misunderstood. They also take on a life of their own, quoted by those who do not (and perhaps do not wish to) understand them or how they came about. They hold no notion of quality (service, patrimony, community, expertise) or of the long term.[13] Those who quote them do so for political ends and thus

---

12 Re:source (The Council for Museums, Archives and Libraries), *Renaissance in the Regions: A New Vision for England's Museums* (London: Re:source, 2001).

13 Museums Association, 'Performance management', *Museums Briefing*, 5 (1994). Audit Commission, *The Road to Wigan Pier?: Managing Local Authority Museums and Art Galleries*, (London: HMSO, 1991).

numbers are reaped and weighed with the annual corn crop, or at best the political cycle, when much of the work of museums takes decades to bear fruit – on the timescale of forestry and landscape management. Figures are, indeed, politically powerful because they can be held up as sound-bite-sized proofs in a way that qualitative data cannot. The problem is not so much a weakness in the concepts of accountability, or even of number summaries, as in the frailty of interpretation and the manipulations of political practice. In this world it is not actual outcomes that come to matter but those that can be quantified.

In other ways, too, the approach can take on irrational qualities by trying to quantify meanings and values, an irrationality which echoes the 1970s' obsession with cost-benefit analysis where human and environmental costs were unrealistically quantified in monetary terms. Barbro Bursell, in this volume, complains that simple numerical definitions can have serious implications for what museums are permitted to collect, and that when number summaries are available more complex arguments remain unheard.[14] But there is undeniably a relationship between the numbers that define the things we collect and the number that appears in black – or red – at the bottom of the museum balance sheet.

In the early 1980s, environmental agencies replaced the bald economics of cost-benefit analysis with more qualitative environmental impact analysis. Similarly, in the late 1990s, a new wave of increasingly qualitative evaluation gained a foothold in the museum sector – particularly in the area of learning in museums. These more reasoned methods are what we might expect in a mature 'knowledge-based society'. Accountability is fundamental to all institutional practices, and no less so to the act of collecting, but it needs to be understood, measured and analysed using appropriate tools which bring improvement to practices rather than merely stir up a desire for political change.

Museums were invented to capture and keep against a background of change, not *to* change. Yet, inevitably the collected thing is called upon to perform in ways that were never intended by the museum at its point of collection, simply because of the impact of change. An example of this can be found at the Imperial War Museum at Duxford, England. One of the largest aviation museums in the world it once collected good examples of different types of combat aircraft; its collecting mission was technically

---

14   B. Bursell, 'Professionalising collecting' (Chapter 18).

focused. Today, the abstract histories one might construct from these objects can be perceived as projecting a clean and dehumanised interpretation of conflict. Future collecting will need to address this problem and the objects collected are more likely to carry human stories and link directly to the historical events of a conflict. It is not that the power or relevance of real objects is questioned here but rather the public, and indeed the staff, require something else of them. The audience for these objects is also changing and its 'ways of knowing' have been altered. Virtual squadrons of F-16 pilots did battle in the late 1990s using the networked game *Falcon 4*. Audiences watching the *Band of Brothers* television series also understood the heat of battle perhaps better than any non-combatants before them purely as a result of new cinematic techniques. For these audiences, the objects in the museum of war perform rather differently. Our parents almost certainly saw something different in them.

The future contexts of collecting will almost certainly change as much as they have in the last twenty-five years. Some changes, such as in available technologies, are more predictable, but where political and social forces operate change is always an unknown. However, we can expect the era of accountability to continue, so change will continue to present risks to long-term institutions. The recent past tells us that museums can expect no assurances of having a future unless they too change in order to demonstrate their relevance. Change here is not simply a matter of educational or exhibition programming, it refers to shifts in the museum's underpinning philosophy. The past is gone, and while we can attempt to hold onto its remnants in our collections and interpretations, we cannot run museums in ways that were conceived on past models. It is here, in this rather challenging world, that the future of collecting exists. And as one of our most heavily-guarded, fundamental and conservative activities, collecting will be one of the hardest to re-orientate. The fact is that the collecting policy of today will not fit with tomorrow; but perhaps the collecting policy itself has had its day anyway.

The collecting policy: saviour or deceiver?

Since Susan Pearce first suggested that the processes of collecting were not that well studied, a considerable body of research has been published. However, practice has yet to make sense of this resource. Much of this research is in the area of private or popular collecting, frequently asking why people collect, which does not necessarily resolve our institutional needs though it can explain some of our actions. Pearce and Patricia Kell, in this volume, give collector and donor profiles from both ends of a period spanning some three hundred years.[15] These collectors and donors are united by a common understanding of the collecting process: one determined by their own personal needs and ambitions. Collector profiles of professional staff would certainly illuminate internal museum practices and point to inconsistencies. This is what María García and her colleagues did in Tenerife when trying to establish a collecting consensus. They found that there were as many collecting criteria as there were staff![16]

What their museums lacked were collecting policies. The introduction of these policies into museums marked a shift towards rationalising, and supposedly intellectualising, practices. Collecting policies have laid down the local law in terms of legal issues, international conventions, national and international codes of ethics, pyramids of responsibility, and geographical, temporal, taxonomic, and financial constraints. They have thereby taken us part way along the path to professionalising collecting practice. While they do say what can be collected and how, their greatest value has been in providing a rationale for rejecting gifts and resolving internal and external arguments concerning the funding of purchases and fieldwork. Collecting policies are *the* gatekeeper documents of the collection, though there may be acquisitions committees which interpret these documents and thereby hold the keys to that gate. This type of committee interpretation becomes necessary, though it remains uncommon and imperfect, because most policies contain sufficiently vague statements to enable their strictures to be circumvented, if a really desirable, but nominally excluded, object does become available. Most policies lack a deeper intellectual rationale for collecting and, by definition and rather illogically, collecting policies isolate the object from other practices – perhaps in other institutions – which might achieve that same intellectual end.

Collecting policies continue to conceive of objects as facts which can simply be gathered up. This belief rather overestimates the inherent

---

15   S.M. Pearce, 'Collections and collecting' (Chapter 2); P. Kell, 'The Ashmolean Museum: a case study of eighteenth-century collecting' (Chapter 5).

16   M. García, C. Chinea and J. Fariña, 'Developing a collecting strategy for smaller museums' (Chapter 19).

qualities of the object and underestimates the interpretive processes which make sense of the material world. It is a nineteenth-century principle that we have failed to question.

Collecting policies do not totally release the profession from collecting anarchy. Individual museums may have 'found themselves' through the development of a policy but they will not have done so entirely,[17] for museums do not operate in isolation. In their detail, few collecting policies provide sufficient framework for defining a collecting philosophy. They focus instead on simple object acquisition and are thus engaged in a kind of object fetishism – that is a human–object relationship where the object has magical powers over us.[18] Despite statements to the opposite, and with some notable exceptions, collecting policies tend to encourage myopic parochialism, and thousands of museums pursuing their own isolated policies suggests unaffordable inefficiency. Yet collecting policies give a deceptive sense of rationalism, another illusion which separates safe practice from efficient, sustainable and meaningful activity.

So, from a holistic perspective, existing collecting policies tend to have considerable limitations as strategic documents. Moreover, at the highest resolution – that of the individual institution – we see other irrationalities. Most obvious is the direct geographical match between funding body and the area from which the museum collects. All activity is constrained by the geopolitical definition of the museum's 'community'. But is this appropriate for all disciplines and types of material: Bronze Age settlements, industrial development, bird populations, stratigraphy, or mass-produced consumables?[19] If human experience now extends globally (as it long has in many countries and will increasingly do), and the best intellectual practices (such as found in universities) engage with that

---

17   Indeed, as we know, policies such as these are often created by 'adapting' those of our neighbours. So, perhaps the museums have not 'found themselves' at all.

18   The term 'fetishism' in collecting and material culture studies is well established and does not imply a sexual or obsessive relationship. Susan Pearce, *Collecting in Contemporary Practice*, (London: Sage, 1998), 128, traces it to the Portuguese *feiticos*, meaning 'a charm', which anthropologists appropriated to refer to objects with inherent magical powers.

19   M.A. Taylor, 'What is in a "national" museum? The challenges of collecting policies at the National Museums of Scotland' (Chapter 14) gives some examples.

international context, what is the collecting role of a community-based museum? If it is simply about local identity then this needs to be realised and collecting practices may need to be altered. If it is about excellence in disciplinary areas then this is something rather different. Whereas once the local object was evaluated as being a distinctive or regional nuance in the national knowledge-base held in provincial museums, today that object might be viewed as a site of local identity making. The Victorian vision of civic pride – an earlier equivalent of identity making – was not simply built upon collecting the local but on the quality of the materials the museum held wherever they came from. The local perspective can be overplayed.

This emphasis on the local perspective creates policies which endorse a 'free market' collecting economy and the gathering of isolated tokens. In these circumstances there is no integrated understanding of the collecting mission of the museum infrastructure as a whole. This does not mean we should all sign up to a 'grand plan', adopt a single perspective or eradicate the local. But, all the same, it does not mean that there is any justification for collecting policies which merely reflect the source funding. Collecting policies need to be replaced by strategies which adopt a more long-term, holistic, inclusive, integrated, cooperative, sustainable, rational and thoughtful view of the purpose of institutional collecting. These are pervasive themes in most areas where the modern world is being restructured. They need to work their way more extensively into museum collecting and to do so museums will require a deeper understanding of how material culture works in society and how it can be made to work in the museum.

Ending perpetuity and redefining collecting

Given the history of museums – the one with the warts rather than simply the heroics – it is no wonder that the profession is deeply protective of collections. Indeed, the profession swears to a creed which makes the collection a god over it. As disciples of this god, museum professionals are indoctrinated with arguments which support growth and retention, and, using well-chosen examples, justification is simple and the collection remains largely unchallenged, if not entirely understood. These professional beliefs have led to the creation of an entity which possesses even greater immutability than the museum itself. For it is not the museum building which is protected with perpetuity clauses, but the collection at its heart.[20] What is erected is a blanket defence of collections, protecting the concept rather than examining the true nature of the collections or the processes by which they were created.[21] The result is entrenchment: religion as opposed to good questioning theology.

Perhaps the most powerful argument (politically if not philosophically or economically) for the retention of material in museums, is that it exists in the museum in the first place. The argument is obviously circular and self-justifying, and comes about for those reasons alluded to in the discussion above. If no process of selective evaluation has taken place in advance of acquisition – as has often been the case, except at a superficial level – then the implied attribution of importance is simply an illusion. These issues are important because collecting cannot move forward without examining the whole cycle of acquisition, retention and disposal, and understanding why collections are perceived as they are.

The collecting problem that needs to be resolved is insoluble not simply because of the problems of deciding what to collect, but by the unrealistic belief that when something is collected it will be kept in perpetuity. If this belief can be eradicated, as it must be, then a strategy can be achieved that is sustainable. Increasingly professionals grow less opposed to the idea that pruning will be needed, and that 'distillation' will become a key curatorial skill. While many museum professionals have been brought up to believe they are contributing to the future, and that their efforts are cumulative and enduring, this will not always be the case. The founders of the museum movement also thought this but their poets, most notably Tennyson, told them how unrealistic this was.[22]

---

20   International Council of Museums, *Statutes, Code of Professional Ethics* (Paris: ICOM, 1987), 4.1; M. Briat and J.A. Freedberg (eds), *International Art Trade and Law*, Volume 3 (Paris: ICC Publishing SA/Deventer: Kluwer, 1991); Museums Association, 'Disposal', *Ethical Guidelines*, 2 (1996), 2a.

21   J.R. Nudds and C.W. Pettitt (eds), *The Value and Valuation of Natural Science Collections* (London: Geological Society, 1997) arose through a concern that collections might be valued as financial assets. See also, for example, Society of Museum Archaeologists, *Selection, Retention and Disposal of Archaeological Collections: Guidelines for Use in England, Wales and Northern Ireland* (London: Society of Museum Archaeologists, 1993).

22   For the hopes for immortality embedded in the founding of museums and collections, see Knell , *The Culture of Geology*, 313–20.

The way to begin, perhaps, is by reconceptualising what is meant by 'collecting' and in doing so take a cue from the founding fathers of museums. They sought to improve upon the kind of 'childish' collecting seen in private cabinets but they did not mean to replace all the private collector's tricks. For them it was the museum as organised knowledge and cultural exemplar which was to be preserved for all time, but not necessarily every item within it. They copied private collectors by mining and refining their collections through sales, destruction and exchange. 'Collecting', as it was conceived at the outset, was to practise connoisseurship, to distinguish between what should be acquired and kept and what should be disposed of. The term 'collecting', rather than referring to an act of accumulation, had a more holistic meaning which encompassed every moment in the life of an object in the collection. Disposal, like the decision to repair, or to show, was an act of the collector as expert. It was an aspect of being a collector, and thus an aspect of the act of collecting. Collecting redefined in this way becomes a practice capable of rational action: material can flow in, but it can also flow out. It is not two processes, but a single dynamic act of balance. Collecting is the interaction of expert with manager, and the object is engaged in the processes of collecting from the moment it is considered for the museum to the moment when it leaves the collection. The collection then becomes rather less immutable and considerably more manageable.

Clearly this more liberal (in one sense), though actually more restrictive, definition will ring alarm bells in many quarters. Museums aren't supposed to be like private collectors, critics will say, they have a unique custodial duty – surely this is the very point of the museum. This rethinking of collecting does not oppose this view but suggests pragmatism; to set collections in concrete is indefensible and has been a root cause of museums' failure to achieve successful custodianship. Existing professional ethics have never really prevented disposals by unscrupulous authorities and, if anything, have encouraged loss by neglect as museums have been obliged to hold onto collections even when they had no prospect of resources to care for them. It is time to recognize that museum communities in many countries have reached a state of maturity with regard to professional ethics and government regulation so as to ensure that the floodgates of disposal – always the fear amongst those who have stuck to the perpetuity clause – will not open. Further safeguards can be put in place. In the US and UK there are accreditation schemes which set basic standards. In other non-museum areas of activity, such as in UK universities, all manner of activities are quality assessed. This kind of independent review can be a viable means to ensure those floodgates remained closed and that rational in-out management is maintained. The great professional concern is that collections will be sold for profit, to bail out an institution stripped of revenue funding, and that the material sold will as a result be lost from public view. There are a number of issues here that need pragmatic response rather than blind ideology. Museum professions have to, and can, deal with them. They cannot afford to hide from them.

A majority of objects held in museums will remain there in the long term, but common sense suggests that if two centuries of collecting have provided nearly all that is to be found in museums, and a single century has supplied vast collections of motorcars and aeroplanes, it is time for a serious rethink. This rethinking requires the museum community to consider what it has (and might pass on to someone else or might be lost) and what it might want (our future collecting). The next century will provide just as many opportunities to collect things that fly and things that can be driven but will there really be a doubling of the number of vehicle museums? The thought that museums will have to lose some of these things is a painful one and although to a large degree it is inevitable there is much museums can do to mitigate the worst effects of this loss. In many cases objects will simply move from one institution to another and duplication will be eradicated.

Let me demonstrate this problem with the example of the milk bottle, both to indicate how collecting has often been undertaken and raise some questions we fail to ask at the point of collection or subsequently. Some twenty years ago, I was undertaking some work for a small museum when I noticed a crate of milk bottles in the collections.[23] The response to my obvious question was, 'I doubt that anyone is collecting them, so I am.' It was a reasonable and fairly typical response. In 1982, these objects were still in widespread circulation and they are useful, perhaps, for saying all kinds of things about design, convenience foods, and the legacy of pre-motorcar shopping, though the curator gave me no such explanation. I did wonder

---

23   In Britain, milk was (and still is) delivered to the doorstep in recyclable bottles. It is a practice that has massively declined with the rise of the car, improved milk processing, and the arrival of the disposable carton.

how these bottles were to perform in the museum setting – what was their function? There are amateur bottle collectors who have their own examples, perhaps, and museums do have some obligation to those in society who share their interests in material objects and their typification. On the other hand it is unlikely that such a collection would contribute much to mainstream history making. Academic historians, if current practices in the subject area are any indication, prefer other sources. To the historian, the 'Drink a pint of milk a day' slogans of the 1970s and the Norman Wisdom film *The Early Bird* (a comedy about the rise of a large (milk) corporation and its impact on the small local trader) say much more about the socially valued aspects of any history in which milk bottles might play a part. Indeed, I doubt that milk bottle history is ever going to be that big and where it does fit into other histories other sources are perhaps more useful. Yet that crate of milk bottles is consuming resources all the time it sits in the museum store. The bottles may have nostalgic value but this, in time, will evaporate, so for how long should the museum keep them? Present rules suggest that they should be kept forever but this question should have been asked at the outset. What curators often forget is that museums preserve an infinitesimally small proportion of things made, used or known; the reverse side of this is that nearly everything is lost, and most of it without a tear. It is hard to accept that not a single milk bottle will survive, but museums have to make a choice: milk bottle, chopper bike or space hopper? In the much longer term, and measured against the limitations of national resource, the choice might be milk bottle, Spitfire or Matisse? Unlike the seemingly ordered and limited natural world (which is still far too big to fully collect), the world of production is limitless and objects from it are variably attached to activities associated with history-making or interpretation for the public. Objects certainly do have a role and do have particular powers which museums can exploit, but museums need to understand the things they do well and those they do not.

Museums, then, need to ask: for how long will this object be kept? Does it really matter if it doesn't survive? Are there things that are valued more than this object and which should be collected in preference? Do the contents of other media (books, film, and so on) negate the need to collect? Would a digital image sufficiently capture the key points of this object? How is the object likely to be used in the next 50 years? And so on. We live in a world driven by notions of progress, improvement and change, which deliver inevitable redundancy in things both big and small (from canals to snuff boxes), but museums have to be more than places for redundant things – there must be a bigger historical purpose and ideally this purpose should not, in the first instance, be set out simply in terms of collecting.

The interweaving of values

Other problems of trying to rationalise collecting result from the dynamics of human relationships with objects. Museums traditionally try to create some sense here by pursuing clearly identified aims. These might, for example, revolve around identity making, themes or disciplinary knowledge. However, objects in no sense respect even these rather abstract low-resolution boundaries. Many history museums are engaged in collecting identity. Their purpose is to construct a set of materials which resonate with a group of people who have a shared experience. These might simply be people who share a geographical and/or historical 'location', or interest. Their museums are about remembering, celebrating, and belonging, and so need certain kinds of material culture for these purposes and certain approaches to collecting it. Objects here give a sense of authenticity and concreteness to a shared identity. Collecting for this kind of museum must grow out of the community, it cannot be imposed. The subject of the museum is the people and the objects themselves are always secondary. To those outside this community, the collections and the museum are thematic, even if that theme is the identity of an 'Other'.

Whether or not museums do collect with identity in mind, a visitor can still construct identity from the experiences the museum offers but this is rather different. Indeed, in recent years much has been made of museums as sites of personal meaning and identity making. However, Bourdieu and others have written a great deal about how various contexts (perhaps all contexts) contribute to our making, so museums need to ask deeper questions about their role.[24] The fact that people can make personal meanings or construct their identities in museums does not confer on museums a special social role. Curators may imagine that the closely argued historical narrative on the gallery walls gives this sense of place and contributes to building identity but most visitors will not read it. Perhaps the museum works as a place of identity only on a romantic level (a 'dream

---

24   P. Bourdieu, *Distinction: A Social Critique of the Judgment of Taste*, (London: Routledge, 1984); D. Miller, P. Jackson, N. Thrift, B. Holbrook and M. Rowlands, *Shopping, Place and Identity*, (London: Routledge, 1998).

space'): an old building, or where visitors nostalgically remember a childhood visit, or tie some half-remembered history into the objects on display, or ponder an inconsequential local icon which is generated and retained by public demand.[25] Indeed, Bourdieu suggests that the art museum, for example, has a fundamental role in maintaining class distinctions and the distribution of power.

It is certainly possible to locate, particularly within those communities which have been conquered, colonised or vanquished, a strong association between objects, past events and present identity.[26] For several writers the notion of the community is central to effective collecting, from Tomislav Sola's vision of the 'demuseumisation' of culture to Kell's belief in the collection's uniting influence.[27] Many contributors to this book propose a sharing of the resource and an end to cultural imperialism. Such beliefs seem simultaneously to endorse and contradict the community view.

However, the term 'community' is loaded, representing a collective and an exclusive entity. As Rebecca Duclos suggests, and Graham Dominy amply demonstrates, the museum collection can sit on the boundary between communities, being for one a remembrance of home and for the other symbolic of colonisation.[28] What is representational is also confrontational.[29] Much of what is interesting in society is found at this interface between communities. Žarka Vujic's museums were keen to gather representative collections from all factions involved in the conflict in Croatia.[30] Dominy describes the remodelling of South African museums to perform a unifying role. In the past they had been symbolic of a clash of communities. This outward-looking, boundary-crossing approach is

---

25   For many years the public's favourite exhibit at Scunthorpe Museum in Lincolnshire, UK, was Joey, a red deer from a local park that was fed by the public. On its death the museum bowed to suggestions that the half-eaten carcass be 'stuffed' and an icon was created. With some local resistance it was removed from display in 1992 and the space freed up for more didactic interpretation. There are many 'Joeys' in museums around the world.

26   D.J. Parkin, 'Mementos as transitional objects in human displacement', *Journal of Material Culture*, 4(3) (1999), 303-20.

27   T. Sola, 'Redefining collecting' (Chapter 24) and P. Kell (Chapter 5).

28   R. Duclos, 'The cartographies of collecting' and Dominy (both this volume).

29   See also P.M. Messenger, *The Ethics of Collecting Cultural Property: Whose Culture? Whose Property?*, (Albuquerque: University of New Mexico,1989).

30   Ž. Vujic (Chapter 10).

important, as internalised histories of communities can create romanticised abstractions, promotional guides or histories erring on the side of propaganda. The sameness of their chosen representative material culture, when compared to adjacent communities, can also suggest other weaknesses in the community/identity-centred model.

In a completely different arena, Jim Fowler shows how a museum's discovery of its community can transform that museum's very nature and the media by which it records and represents that community.[31] In Malcolm MacLeod's West Africa, the community is alive and the 'collection' remains in use, preserved in its 'context' and its 'community'. This notion of context is key to the identity making museum. The 'collection' examined by Pearce belonging to the Straws in Worksop, and MacLeod's Manhyia Palace Museum at Kumasi,[32] are extreme examples of collecting or preserving context, of making immortal what one can of a life, a time or a place. While the Straws' collection is much like the buried past which communities around the world are fighting to preserve from looters, Kumasi has resonances with nature conservation and the ecomuseum, a preserved living entity.[33] In contrast, Bursell describes the collecting of a complete kitchen – removal of a big chunk of material context (so it would seem) and placing it in a museum. This type of preservation is rarely possible, and raises all kinds of questions about the things which museum professionals value and why, and how the scope of any object collecting never results in preserving much in the way of context at all.

Of course, the boundaries surrounding what museums should care about have moved considerably since the days when they were a representation of a handful of core, material culture- and order-focused disciplines. The civil rights movements of the 1960s transformed that world and thus we should not be surprised to see Nicola Clayton arguing that material culture can be used to break down stereotypes and social segregation, realise disability awareness, introduce informed discussion of sexuality, and

---

31   J. Fowler, 'Collecting live performance' (Chapter 23).

32   M. McLeod, 'Museums without collections: museum philosophy in West Africa' (Chapter 3).

33   Knell, 'Collecting, conservation and conservatism'. N. Brodie, J. Doole and P. Watson, *Stealing History: The Illicit Trade in Cultural Property* (London: ICOM UK and Museums Association, 2000).

involve minority and youth cultures.[34] These are surely subjects at the heart of the early twenty-first century museum, but how should they affect collecting? Currently, equality legislation can actually prevent the recording of race or sexual orientation. One also needs to ask if museums are the right medium with which to record cultures that are intentionally alternative. Though not to collect such material is conceivably an act of censorship, inevitably the actions of museums will result in omission of this kind. The risk then is that only the more vociferous groups will find themselves recorded. But social practices are also manufactured in a bewildering array, and again choices need to be made about what and who should be collected and recorded. Again evidence most practices will disappear without leaving a material trace.

Disciplinary practices and beliefs

In contrast to the identity making museum, the disciplinary museum focuses very much on an intellectual rationale, with implicit values of authorship, research rigour, connoisseurship, tradition and a range of knowledge structures. To this world, a museum built purely on personal meaning making would be entirely worthless unless it conformed to disciplinary requirements for selection and data capture. The act of collecting can then become a point of tension between the self-creation of meaning by the group which is its subject and that academic 'other' which hopes to understand that group on its own terms. Thus in museums identity can become entwined in more abstract disciplinary readings, while thematic perspectives act like scissors cutting out and removing certain readings from a tangled context.

In the disciplinary framework, the object is called upon to function in a variety of ways, and this implies that objects tend to have attributed to them sets of associated values which specify why they are worth the expense of keeping them. A more specific discussion will explain what I mean, and lest anyone should think that I fail to understand their particular discipline, I shall focus this example on that museum area on which I have expended most time: the fossil collection. I could easily have chosen coins, flints, bird skins, domestic life objects, aeroplanes, working costume and so on. Arranged in taxonomic and stratigraphic order, fossils can be perceived

---

34   N. Clayton, 'Folk devils in our midst? Collecting from "deviant" groups' (Chapter 12).

as series composed of filled and unfilled spaces. In a provincial English museum, unlike rocks and minerals, fossil collections are largely derived from local rocks. Gap filling certainly takes place but is justified as a process of establishing new local records. Collections also arise from unique collecting opportunities, and many museums have fossil collections which have arisen from the building of motorways, railway lines, gas pipelines and so on. These temporary cuts give rare insights into the landscape's inner anatomy and archaeologists and geologists are invariably soon on the scene. Still other fossils were amassed, in Lincolnshire, for example, as a result of major iron workings and less important brick and limestone workings. Like the temporary exposures mentioned above, most of these sites too have now gone. In the late 1980s and early 1990s the local museum worked with fossil dealers to enrich the collections. So, many of these objects arose out of opportunism and were acquired not as research of a kind that necessarily produced a published account but which, using the geologist's connoisseurship skills, generated materials that were deemed to hold significant potential for particular reasons.

However, to see all these specimens as local records is rather to simplify their complex significances. A few specimens in the collections of this museum had appeared in scientific publications and thus the museum had a duty to protect them. Other specimens were unique (the only known occurrences of taxonomically and stratigraphically interesting material), and because of the uniqueness of the local geological succession, were also therefore unlikely to be represented even in the collections of the national museum. They weren't published but the curator knew which ones they were. A visit by a French specialist at one point confirmed the importance of some of these specimens in another way, in the context of European taxonomy. Yet there were other specimens which had no data (though they could be identified and the rock could be fairly securely inferred) but were huge. The largest came from the local Cretaceous Chalk and was a reasonably common English fossil. It was kept by the museum because of its considerable communicative powers. The objects here then were taxonomic records, stratigraphic records, local records, objects good for explaining things, objects that were impressive or iconic or aesthetic. They included objects that were an opportunity realised and kept for those who could not be there when collecting was possible. There were also objects here associated with human history, whether in the folklore of 'Devil's Toenails' (*Gryphaea*, fossil oysters which proudly sat on the town's coat of arms), or because they came from the efforts of the hundreds of labourers who dug the ironstone, or through association with important local collectors, such as Canon Cross, or folk-hero curator's like Harold Dudley, or important scientists, like the Geological Survey's Vernon Wilson, who came to survey the ironstone during the Second World War for strategic purposes. Other specimens worked simply as reference materials – purely for communication in identification or as set dressing in display. If examined individually each fossil would have different sets of attributes which would describe its place in the collection.

All disciplinary curators should have at least this level of connoisseurship of their collections and the values I have mentioned here can be found in collections of many types. However, we should not overstate the similarities. Minerals, for example, arise from entirely different natural processes and are gathered into collections on the basis of entirely different principles. Certainly we could find the record, the icon, the historical object and so on but care is needed in extending the parallels too far. Although both fossils and minerals frequently come under the care of geological curators, relatively few specialist curators feel fully conversant with both.

Another factor in these assigned value judgements is that they are relative to other collections. Thus if every fossil collection in the country became lost, even the most common fossils in the museum collection, I have described, would be elevated. While this is, I hope, unlikely to occur, in more subtle ways, which remain unnoticed, the values are being constantly altered by new finds (locally and elsewhere), changes in knowledge, losses due to neglect or decay, the introduction of fakes and forgeries into the market place, the loss of sites, conservation restrictions on collecting, new academic research and disciplinary beliefs, and so on.

This adds to the complexity of evaluation and exposes the curator – unless deeply involved in research on a particular group of objects – to the risk of erroneous conclusions. However, the reality is somewhat more controllable. The curator can admit to working on a limited canvas which values objects against local or regional criteria. This provides a baseline for judgements because essentially this internalises evaluation – it is unnecessary to know if the museum up the road has the same specimen or a dozen of them. One classic defence here, which curators much like, is to say that the specimen is unique. But uniqueness is a quality held by all things and in itself is absolutely useless for decisions to collect or keep. One needs to ask 'How is this object unique?' Aside from its individual existence, the usual justification is that it was found, used or made at a particular time or place. This *may* be important, but perhaps it tells us nothing surprising, nothing we don't know from other evidence. So the contributory nature of that discovery is minor – it is a voucher of a discovery, but the discovery is not very important because we essentially know what it is telling us or it is simply attached to a very insignificant piece of information. So do we need the object (coin, fossil, slug, sewing machine) as a voucher to prove the point? What level of resource input can it justify? An ecological survey, for example, might lead to the collection of thousands of beetles but only some of these will become permanent vouchers. And in the case of these ecological vouchers – and excepting really rare, unexpected or cryptic species – there is a time limit on their usefulness as a record of an occurrence. A common beetle telling us that this is a particular kind of wetland habitat may not survive in the collections once the site has been drained – its usefulness may be over. While such specimens in collections do provide a history of biological and ecological diversity, we cannot value all specimens in collections in this way.

So, if a hoard of 100 coins dates a stratum in an archaeological section, how many of these coins are needed to act as a proof, and how many for the purposes of public communication, or to realise other potential uses? To many museum professionals, simply to ask this question is an act of heresy, but surely this is just the sort of question we must ask and in less obvious circumstances than this.

These questions usually prompt a response which suggests these things are not simply 'examples kept' but opportunities for verification. Perhaps someone discovers that there is a different, but very similar coin, sewing machine, beetle or fossil which is difficult to distinguish from the look-alike original. This opens up the possibility that we may have made a mistake in our earlier conclusions. Our collections will now need to be re-examined and will contribute to new knowledge or verify the previous discovery. These things happen reasonably often but only a portion of collections have this potential. An additional complication comes from the impossibility of accurately identifying some things because of the inadequacy of taxonomies (fossils being a good example of this). But the sum of this argument is that rational decisions need to be taken of the actual or potential worth of the thing. We do not value all things in the same way, and each object has a particular role and value, but if the sole justification for keeping something is that it is unique, without any further qualification, then it really is a candidate for disposal.

Of course, curators are creative people, and any curator worth his or her salt should be able to come up with something to defend their loved ones. One possible argument against this rationalism, which I have used myself, is that the object holds 'potential'. A good example of the potential of the collected thing concerns the discovery of the conodont animal. Conodonts, microscopic tooth-like structures, had been making important contributions to geology for nearly 130 years but the animal from which they came remained entirely unknown. They were one of the great mysteries of modern palaeontology. Then, in 1983, a streaky smudge of a fossil was discovered in a Scottish collection where it had lain unnoticed for more than fifty years. This was the long sought after conodont animal. This, with the other discoveries it stimulated, turned conodonts into evidence for some of the first and most successful vertebrates, of key importance to debates concerning vertebrate evolution. The discovery stimulated an explosion in evolutionary research,[35] but it is interesting to ponder how important that smudge was the moment *before* its significance was recognised. In these situations connoisseurship skills are critical.[36] The conodont (rather than conodont animal)-containing rock had some meaning before the moment of transformation: it was a stratigraphic marker, a specimen showing conodont relationships (i.e. an assemblage of conodonts), its geographical data marked its presence in a faunal realm, and it was gathered when site, time and equipment made collecting possible (often a very strong case for retaining material). It was fortuitous that the specimen survived in the collection, but it was also probably the product of considerable distillation at the point of collecting. So the

---

35 R.J. Aldridge and M.A. Purnell, 'The conodont controversies', *Trends in Ecology and Evolution*, 11 (1996), 463–8. S.J. Knell, 'The most important fossil in the world', *Geology Today*, 7 (1991), 221–4; S.J. Knell, 'What's important?', in Nudds and Pettitt, *Value and Valuation*, 11–16; P.S. Doughty, 'Through a glass darkly: value concepts and ultimate objectives', ibid., 35. Thanks to Mark Parnell. Note that fossil structures receive names even when, as sometimes happens, we don't know the animal or plant from which they come. Thus to talk of conodonts is to talk of certain anatomical parts of a particular group of animals.

36 L. Young, 'Collecting: reclaiming the art, systematising the technique' (Chapter 16).

specimen fitted into an established framework of knowledge and all that was required, and was lacking in the 1930s, was someone to study it. The specimen survived not because of its potential but because it already had value. However, there are limits to the numbers of conodonts we might want to keep – they are no different from coins or beetles.

The problem is recognising what is important: an object contains a multidimensional assemblage of possible values, but only some of these can be perceived by the viewer. To select one value over another can be a manifestation of blindness of perception or just of fashion (fashion here being a prevalent set of values in a 'community of practice' – such as a disciplinary group). It is almost certainly time limited, as we shall explore in the next section. A classic example is the political correctness of 'stuffed' – more correctly, 'mounted' – animals and whether such specimens should be retained in museums.[37] If these specimens are to be burned or consigned to the dustbin then we would need to be able to demonstrate that other methods are available to facilitate the kind of 'knowing' that is possible from viewing mounts and indeed to ask if this 'kind of knowing' is important in the first place.

Singular views of collections are dangerous, and really demonstrate how the museum practitioner is different from other experts in his or her discipline. The cutting-edge expert in ornithology may be ill-equipped to judge the value of a museum specimen. Yet a bland claim of hidden possibilities has to be tested to be credible. Evaluations of objects are complex and require the kinds of consultation already laid out in disposal guidelines. Many objects in natural science collections may have little use to modern science but are rather objects of history and culture, so even in the disciplinary collection, objects may have meanings as complex and interwoven as those associated with the more subjective realms of identity, nationhood, citizenship, ethnicity, and so on. Take the fossil collection of the Victorian 'literary geologist' Hugh Miller at the National Museums of Scotland, for example. It includes the actual specimens he illustrated in his very widely read attacks on pre-Darwinian evolution in the middle decades of the nineteenth century. The collection remains of real scientific value, but it also embodies that Victorian *Zeitgeist* which agonised over time, life, death and the universe, also encapsulated in Tennyson's *In Memoriam*, and

---

37   A good example of this is J. Harlow, 'Stuffed animals die death in PC purge of museums', *The Sunday Times*, 11 May 1997, 3.

it therefore facilitates more complex historical readings.[38] But these cases need to be made, they cannot be assumed. All museum objects acquire histories which might suggest significance but there is a danger in valuing the object just because it has been a long-term resident in the collections.

Martin Wickham seeks a numerate solution to assessing the relative merits of objects and takes the need for consensus into account and handles all this subjectivity, relativity and multidimensionality with iterative pragmatism. Here number summaries seem to work, though Wickham is keen to point out the limitations of the method, and suggests where a more qualitative approach may be required.[39] What is important here is that curators are actually having a go at evaluating individual objects and weighing one against the other. However hard it is, museums need to evaluate the functions of the object in order to determine why and how it is collected (the expended effort) and how long it will endure in the collections (its disposability). Maybe the curator who acquired it cannot answer that question now but he or she can recommend a time when a review might prove beneficial, and certainly views might change. Maybe the answer is 'until something better comes along', maybe it is 'indefinitely'.

There is yet another perspective we can take in viewing collection worth. Palaeontological curators have a particular relationship to their collections, and while taxonomies shape patterns of storage, it is the interpreted meanings of these fossils as living animals and environments, or as aesthetic or historical objects, which given them appeal to audiences. This raises further questions about the inner relationships of objects to disciplines which cannot be fully explored here. Studies of art, archaeology, palaeontology and histories of design and materials require collections of physical objects – they cannot operate without them. In contrast, most other historical research values the library and archive above the museum collection. Relatively few historians look for answers in material culture itself, even if they are writing about material culture. Indeed, in my experience, object collections often fail historians looking for evidence of the history of social practices. Unlike archival materials, objects are not

---

38   S.J. Knell and M.A. Taylor, 'Hugh Miller, the fossil discoverer and collector', in L. Borley (ed), *Celebrating the Life and Times of Hugh Miller* (Cromarty: Cromarty Arts Trust and University of Aberdeen, 2003), 156–167.

39   M. Wickham, 'Ranking collections' (Chapter 21).

good at retaining information, particularly if collection management has been poor (which has been the case in most collections at some point). In contrast, and rather ironically, the basic documentation associated with collecting activity *is* actually useful in a multitude of ways, even if one can no longer attach it to an actual specimen.

In the latter decades of the twentieth century social history was a particularly strong and well-represented discipline in museums. A burgeoning social awareness, no doubt influenced by E.P Thompson and others, politicised a field which previously used terms like 'folk life' or 'domestic life'. The social awareness, which emerged from this discipline in the 1980s, has now moved beyond it; now, for many museums, social agenda dominate and do so outside of any disciplinary framework. Gaynor Kavanagh, in this volume, captures the late twentieth-century situation of museum social history well, and raises a raft of questions about its functioning and value. Part of the difficulties for the associated collections arises from this transformation from folk life to social history. The folk life agenda arose from concern for disappearing traditions and took to collecting the settings, costumes and tools of domestic life before they were lost. Social history, by contrast, took a greater interest in historiography and understanding the life lived and the objects that performed within it. Here objects might be described as being social historical but they were only so as a reflection of practices which were known by other means: accounts, witnessing, oral histories and so on. The objects themselves tell us little by comparison. So how does the object contribute to history making? What is its relationship to other media? Does it authenticate or communicate? The answers to these questions should shape collecting. Perhaps the social history curator is simply collecting technologies; certainly this is the case if just amassing objects in isolation from any other recording practices. The stool, the christening gown, the trade union banner and the flat iron are solutions to need, technologies for a social purpose. The social practices which utilise them and invest them with value are intangible and exist outside of these objects as Kavanagh makes clear.

Archaeologists and palaeontologists have little else other than sites and material remnants and frequently turn to modern analogy to interpret their finds. In contrast, historians have access to a wealth of material that is far more useful to history making. Kavanagh is clear that the social historian should be collecting other things and using other means; that simple object collecting for the purposes of making social histories is unsupportable.

Let me give some examples which illustrate the technical/social divide. Take a 'Whites Only' sign which hung above the entrance to a bar in apartheid South Africa. Collected to signify a historical moment, this object is firstly interpreted as a wooden sign, a type of broadcast technology. Any further interpretation of its place in society and its social historical meaning can only come by placing meanings into it – drawn from the external context; it cannot come from the sign itself, even though it has words written upon it. We may now *make* the sign powerful and iconic (just as it was *made* powerful when it was in use), but on its own it is obscure. Nonetheless it appears to work as evidence backing up or authenticating the historical message because it was 'there'. We could use this sign in reminiscence work, and from that draw out rich social histories, but the histories are coming from the person and not the thing. The position of the sign is no different had we undertaken its collecting as part of an ethnological study. To take another example, the bat that Babe Ruth used to hit a homerun at the inauguration of the new Yankee stadium in 1923 – recently unearthed and dubbed 'the Holy Grail of sports memorabilia' – is first and foremost to be understood as a piece of sports technology. Its significance is that it was used by the player on that occasion but how can it aid history making? Perhaps we could weigh it, feel its grip, study the wood, and so on. More than anything this is an object into which meanings and interpretations are pumped, not the other way around. It is for this reason that it is powerful and desirable.

Historians of the twentieth century and beyond will have an increasing diversity of resources available to document the past without recourse to mass collecting. That is not to suggest that museums will stop collecting real objects but rather than there is an increasing urgency to understand collecting as a technology that has a complementary relationship to other technologies, media and methods. This has always been so – particularly in the field of history. Museums, however, often seem to carve out their own peculiar material culture centred disciplinary niche, often separate from the wider world of disciplinary practice.

Objects, then, exist within a complex web of social and disciplinary practices, both prior to collecting and once in the museum. An awareness of these facets of the object world and the ingrained beliefs of disciplines and museums is necessary to move collecting forward. Richard Dunn's 'self-conscious collecting' steps in this direction by realising and recording an underlying purpose, as do Young's connoisseurship and Samdok's fieldwork methods.[40] But in other areas, only now are disciplines recognising the social practices which underpin their subjects. John Martin argues that the inadequacy of laws controlling the trafficking of fossils feeds corruption and disenfranchises primary producers and end users.[41] The law becomes a disabling smoke screen which affects some but not others and thus disorientates the collecting process. Markets in art, and other areas of culture, do this universally. Janet Owen, in an entirely different way, shows how control of collecting remains in the hands of those who ultimately will neither curate nor interpret the collection.

Time and collecting

Just as the museum makes the past its subject, its collections inevitably become the past's product. Things in the museum grow old, and as they grow old they become rarer because once-contemporary objects have now worked their way out of society and into the town dump. So, over time, the material in the museum grows in 'value'. But is this 'value' relevant to the museum? The fact that something is old is, as argued above, no reason to keep it in a museum. Like 'potential', and 'uniqueness', 'age' and 'survival' are false idols. Objects must have other values aside from age which give them worth. There is no denying that old things have a wonderful power over us, and the last thing museums must do is lose that fascination with the past, but we must also ask, 'What else is of value in this object?'

Time is rather too big a topic to be covered fully here but a short examination will illustrate its role in collecting and the limitations it places on what is possible. Nearly twenty years ago ICOFOM[42] held a conference called 'What of Tomorrow's Needs?', which, unsurprisingly, could only conclude that the future is unknown and cannot be planned for. Society has a similar relationship with the past. As many a modern historiographer will tell us, we cannot actually *know* that past but are, instead, limited to making mere constructions of it in ways determined by modern context and medium. Things from the past only ever exist in a present – they are always

---

40   R. Dunn, 'The future of collecting: lessons from the past' (Chapter 4), L. Young (Chapter 16), and A. Steen (Chapter 17).

41   J. Martin, 'All legal and ethical? Museums and the international market in fossils' (Chapter 13).

42   International Committee for Museology, part of the International Council of Museums (ICOM)

contemporary with the viewer.[43] They are not pieces of the past as such, but pieces of the present which have a past. The ancient Roman pot may have the markings of the maker, but these are markings to be read now. That is not to deny that the object has some intrinsic physical characteristics and associated contextual data. It is because of these that it is retained, but the relationship between this intrinsic data and what we see is rather more subjective. When I see Nelson's jacket at the National Maritime Museum in London, for example, I sense that I am in touch with the past regardless of the fact that that past is entirely in my head and has come to me from school history teachers and books, romantic films, paintings, television advertisements, and so on. Moreover, while I can claim to have spent a good deal of time researching that period, I still can't claim any purity of view – there are just too many gaps and they have to be filled somehow. It is a problem with which all historians have to contend, and which causes the best of them to go to extraordinary lengths to locate evidence which might limit their interpretations and reduce the size of those gaps.

What this line of thinking initially suggests is a narrow envelope of time in which we understand practices very well, and from which we can collect reasonably well. The ancient Roman knew his present as we know ours; but he could not know ours and we cannot fully know his. We have already decided that we cannot collect for the future, other than by collecting the present. And if we look to the past we have similar problems. As the moment of origin or original use recedes into the past, the objects from that time which remain with us become increasingly less well known to us, and we increasingly fill gaps in the data using our knowledge of modern and of other periods (by analogy, for example). As time passes we are moving from a position when contemporary collecting could take place to that where we are collecting 'history'. But we should not be fooled into thinking that these objects are separated by time – all those available to us, including old ones, are, as I have said, in our modern context and nowhere else. So while some museum workers have been at pains to distinguish contemporary collecting from history collecting, the fact is that all collecting is inevitably contemporary collecting, even if we are collecting things which

---

43   As A. Gell, *The Anthropology of Time*, (Oxford: Berg, 1992), 162, puts it: '…the fact that a thing can signify the events associated with its own creation does not mean that the thing itself has temporal attributes: only the events in which it participated can be said to have these.' For wider reflection, D. Harvey, *The Condition of Postmodernity*, (Oxford: Blackwell, 1990), 55ff.

are valued because of their association with the past. Contemporary collecting is one of the most difficult of practices because of its overwhelming and multifaceted nature, and because we are collecting things that reflect our own society, which we know to be complex. Collecting historical material only seems easier because there is less of it, we know it less well, and because historians have constructed narratives which value one thing above another.

From a collecting point of view, our material culture, new and old, sits on a kind of sieve of the present. Its durability (worth, quality, and so on) is a measure of how long it will sit there before it falls through to be lost. It is from the surface of the sieve that we can collect, and clearly there is more contemporary material here than there is old, because the latter has had greater opportunity to be lost. So all this material culture exists in the same time dimension regardless of the disciplinary frameworks which utilise it. And we have better opportunities to make a good job of collecting 'the now' than we do of collecting the past. So we are better able to collect and record the digitally produced plastic pop music of Britney Spears, because she exists in the context-rich present, than from the context-stripped worlds of Beatles innovation or Frank Zappa pop-cynicism. Now just as we should not be fooled into collecting something just because it is old, we should also resist the temptation to collect something very modern just because we can make a good job of it! This returns us to connoisseurship – with all its disciplinary abstractions and biases. Connoisseurship is about establishing values: not market values but those that reflect our goal of understanding. What we are asking of the object is 'What and how will this thing contribute to our ability "to know"?'

Another shaping factor here is the resolution of the understanding we seek to achieve. What the passing of time does to our view of the past, and consequently to our collecting, is to concertina the decades into each other, encouraging us to take an increasingly macroscopic view, and thus make the heterogeneous century become a homogenous entity. So while those of us who experienced the popular music of the last five decades of the twentieth century can detect every variance, swing, imitation and value, and are able to rank one artist above another, it is also possible to generalise and select things that represent a genre – even if we know this pigeonholing is very abstract and personal (since innovation in the genre is marked by individualism and thus is not really amenable to such pigeonholing). So Spears might well epitomise the commodification of music, which is something also to be found with The Beatles and Zappa, and at which Zappa poked fun. This tendency to select the one to represent the all is itself something historians outside museums would resist. And as we move to these lower levels of resolution, the more this kind of representation begins to take on unsupportable generalisations. Yet object collecting has traditionally taken this approach: representing diversity using the singular. Zappa, The Beatles and Britney Spears exist or existed in quite different contexts, worked in different ways, constructed music using different technologies. We could easily choose a framework for studying them which would demonstrate that they are more different than they are similar. In other words, this very notion of historical representation is ahistorical when dealing with social phenomena. Yet in the world of museum collections it is a fundamental curatorial skill. Academic historians prefer to deal with particular cases and might permit themselves to use them in a limited way as examples of wider practice. Samdok achieves this level of history making by engaging in a multimedia capturing of a particular context.[44] Clearly, there are two radically different approaches to history here: which one is the correct one and for which occasion? Does the decontextualised typological history collecting to be found in past practice have any role in the modern history museum?

Let's now return to the opportunities of the present. We can make choices about what we decide to collect from the sieve: the wealth of contemporary Britney material or the declining number of context-rich Beatle-related items. Our choice should be an application of connoisseurship in the context of institutional mission. If collecting is undertaken as part of a broader programme of research into contemporary society (as seen with Samdok) – as a process of recording of which object collecting is a small part – then a data-rich record will be produced. However, we should be under no illusion that we will achieve a perfect record. Encapsulating a context in any form of record is impossible, and what we create of Britney will be preserved in a very stripped-down, individualised way. We are again confronting the inevitability of loss which is inherent in the selectivity of collecting. And anyway, regardless of our attempts to collect and record, future interpretations of our collected record will arise from the future context of the viewer, who will not be aware of all those things we took for

---

44   Discussed by A. Steen, 'Samdok: tools to make the world visible', (Chapter 17).

granted, or all the things he or she takes for granted and weaves into his or her interpretation. Indeed, the future viewer may well associate the term 'innovative' with Britney in a way that I intentionally did not. Such distinctions are simply judgements of subjective taste, even if arising from connoisseurship.

From this perspective the tangible and intangible begin to merge but each of us would probably take a different view (often determined by the perspective of our discipline) on the degree to which this is so. This doesn't invalidate the collecting and recording activity, but we have to recognise the activity's inevitable limitations. The lesson that we cannot fully preserve (either by collecting or keeping or by future interpretation) the past or the present, or know the future, actually removes some of the fear we might have about getting it right. If individuals construct their own sets of values, there is no such thing as a correct decision about what should be collected. The solution then lies in sharing responsibility for those decisions, developing an informed knowledge (connoisseurship), involving others (our disciplinary communities) and working within the constraints of the materials available to us. These latter things result in shared values and return the objects to a world of, apparently more 'tangible', disciplinary realities. This sounds like a rather old fashioned kind of curatorship but curatorship doesn't have to be conservative.

There is a moment, then (that is, 'now'), when we might maximise our collecting effectiveness: the moment of reportage contemporary with the event. But this is often very difficult. Vujic's and Dominy's curators faced great difficulties in capturing the moment and representing it fairly.[45] Sometimes change is too quick, sometimes too dangerous, sometimes too harrowing. Vujic argues that in time of war as much as possible has to be collected; the process of evaluation can take place later. Those collecting contemporary art share this view. They argue that retrospective analysis enables the discernment of objects of key art historical value. Of course, such an analysis is equally likely to create omission as it fails to understand how art historical (and other) knowledge is created. Art histories are the result of academic discourse, of which one key aim is to seek out and expose omission, to bring into the spotlight that which has been ignored or

---

45   Ž. Vujic, 'Collecting in time of war' (Chapter 10) and G. Dominy, 'The politics of museum collecting in the 'old' and the 'new' South Africa' (Chapter 11).

left unseen. Dominy shows that having to rely on retrospect is dangerous. The moment apartheid began to crumble a rapid amnesia took hold. If the moment was not seized it was lost.

From 'free' gifts to the 'expense' of collaborative recording

The act of acquisition itself may be inexpensive. Indeed, the rapid growth of museums only came about because of the role played by donation. And the key role of natural science in this development owed much to the cheapness of the objects. The practice of donation is taken for granted these days, but when modern provincial museums were first established in England in the early nineteenth century it was an extremely novel and uncertain mode of acquisition. The culture of the gift, with all its social overtones (which were a major factor in making donation successful), is another of these aspects of practice which lie at the heart of the irrational and unsustainable nature of museums. It creates the illusion that collecting is free. Clearly, it is not: the long-term costs of storing and maintaining an object have to be paid whether the object was given freely or not. The cost of acquisition is a singular cost; that of keeping is relentlessly cumulative, and with time the overall costs of collecting are the same regardless of whether the object was a purchase, resulted from fieldwork or arrived as a gift. The purpose of this point is simply to reveal the illusion; if museums collect treasure or trash, the cost, in the end, can be much the same. As a collection grows, the amount of resource available for each object – such as staff time – diminishes. Even if staffing levels rise with the growth of the museum, ultimately a financial slump or institutional reorganisation will cause a rationalisation of that staff resource, with consequent implications for the collection. This is sufficiently demonstrated by history to be beyond doubt. Money, then, and the political pressure to spend it in certain ways (such as front-of-house during a recession),[46] determines the size of the cloth and how it is to be cut. Investment in the moment of collecting – to make the best of the task – is actually one of the best uses of museum funding.

A step in this direction can be achieved by replacing the museum conception of collecting with one centred on recording. This frees the museum from the risks of object fetishism (being overpowered by objects). Objects now become part of contexts (as they long have in some disciplines

---

46   Knell, 'Collecting, conservation and conservatism'.

and in some museums), and the media available to record those contexts are opened up. The justification for preferentially collecting objects in the past has been that objects retain a multidimensional aspect in a way that no other recording medium does. Objects, the argument runs, are capable of repeated reinterpretation, which is what gives collections their importance and utility. But Victorian intellectuals had limited media available to record their world and the collecting of objects circumvented all kinds of problems associated with inadequate taxonomies and a poorly educated workforce. The object also has remarkable powers by being real and imperfect – characteristics which disappear in the photography of the art book, for example, where a faithful account is impossible. But the future looks likely to extend the role of these other complementary technologies, and a fuller acknowledgement of recording (of which limited collecting is a part), rather than just simply collecting, looks set to shape future practices.

Recording also offers new opportunities for collaboration and the eradication of much isolated and localised effort, which can otherwise lead to duplication. National registers of particular object types combined with agreed taxonomies help deal with 'types' and provide a vehicle for collaborative and complementary effort. They permit individual organisations to go in pursuit of excellence and cost-effective focused specialisations to develop. There is no reason why this collaborative framework should not also extend beyond the object-centred collecting, which makes up much contemporary practice, and towards future thematic, fieldwork-based investigations which involve recording using a variety of media, as described by Steen.[47]

This suggestion does not simply apply to thematic museums. Only together can community-centred museums encapsulate regional trends and localised traditions without duplication. This also permits museums to break from geopolitical constraints and pursue the popular ideal of 'centres of excellence' with all that that offers for rationalism and sustainability. Clearly not all partners involved in the collecting and recording of a theme need to come from collecting institutions. Many projects are enhanced – indeed, sometimes only achievable – with volunteer help, or the assistance of university academics, museum societies, amateur groups, oral history groups, students, and so on. Thematic inter-institutional collaboration is

47   A. Steen (Chapter 17).

already well established in many scientific disciplines in order to make the best use of a rare fieldwork opportunity.[48]

Collaboration, however, appears difficult where there is an active market. Sports paraphernalia, for example, attracts widespread interest amongst private collectors, which drives up prices. The ethics and rationale of the private collector may be entirely different from those of the museum, and private collectors do not necessarily provide things with long-term prospects of survival, protected contexts, or public access. Nevertheless a dialogue can be useful, and remove a little competition from the marketplace. In many disciplines private collectors become excellent volunteers capable of using their collecting expertise for museum ends, and can be trained to achieve museum standards. As collecting becomes more rigorous and intellectually focused, it is important to accommodate, rather than to marginalize, the amateur. There are models we can call upon which turn volunteers into foster parents. In Britain, for example, the National Plant Collections Scheme delegates responsibility for the preservation of historic cultivars to private gardeners.[49] Here each gardener is, in effect, holding these plants in trust in a very museum-like way, but they also reap very collector-like rewards in terms of kudos of participation and skill in maintaining the collection, and they are also assured that their efforts will be continued. Perhaps, as Paul Martin's bus collector seems to perceive, there is little difference between objects in the museum and those in the private collection, and as a result, new collaborations might be possible.[50]

Commercial collectors and dealers are another group existing on the periphery of the museum world. Again, there is great potential for ethical problems – such as when a museum shows work from an art dealer's stock (which has economic benefits for other items in his stock). But there is also potential for collaboration, such as when Scunthorpe Museum collaborated with commercial fossil collectors, reaping the rewards of previously unseen

---

48　For 'centres of excellence', see the 'Wright Report', Department of Education and Science, *Provincial Museums and Galleries* (London: DES, 1973).

49　W.R. Reid et al., *Biodiversity Prospecting: Using Genetic Resources for Sustainable Development* (Washington, DC: World Resources Institute, 1993). The National Plant Collections scheme is organised by the UK's National Council for the Conservation of Plants and Gardens. It currently has 600 registered collections covering over 320 genera, 12,000 species and 36,000 cultivars.

50　P. Martin, 'Contemporary popular collecting' (Chapter 8).

fossils, while the dealers retained financially valuable, but fairly common, ammonites which they would polish up into décor fossils, incidentally removing all vestige of scientific worth. It was the richest collecting period in the museum's history and cost it nothing other than a little staff time – and, of course, the long-term cost of keeping. Without the time, money and goodwill of the commercial collectors, and the willingness of curatorial staff to give up claims to some magnificent ammonites (of which the museum had a plentiful supply anyway), this would have been impossible, and as the rock was to be lost anyway, the alternative was to lose the fossils too.[51]

Perhaps the most obvious and least contentious link-up is with university academics. Certainly, in archaeology, biology and palaeontology the building of investigative teams is fundamental to high-resolution scientific collecting. These may then collaborate with private individuals to further strengthen collecting. Some have used collecting by the local community to drive official programmes studying biodiversity, such as Costa Rica's INBio (Instituto Nacional de Biodiversidad Heredia) programme; others have utilised local knowledge and possessions to create folk museums. In these latter examples there are issues of local community ownership, which John Martin believes should be taken into account even in scientific collecting.

Whether a participant institution in a project sees itself as a centre of excellence for expertise or material culture, or a centre for identity, or part of a wider community of supporters and collaborators, the overall outcome of this kind of collaborative exercise is the notion of distributed knowledge and perhaps a distributed collection.[52] The project to found a National Museum of Australia recognised that a distributed national collection already existed and that it needed to take this into account in its collecting. It can be a perspective less based on the possessive drive to acquire objects and more on the broader intellectual rationale of the museum, which encourages sustainability through shared values and shared collections, but which is so easily lost where local or singular perspectives dominate. This is surely another key to the future of museum collecting.

Similarly, John Martin recognises the need to ensure that collecting fossils through trade should benefit the local community, but he also strongly

---

51 P. Wyse-Jackson, and S.J. Knell (eds), 'Museums and Fossil Excavation' (thematic issue), *Geological Curator*, 6(2) (1994).

52 The notion of a distributed collection became apparent not long after early English provincial museums were established in the 1820s, Knell, *Culture of English Geology*, 75 .

believes in the internationalism of science. Science relies upon this notion of a distributed collection: objects are the property of science, and as such can only be held in trust. It does not matter who holds them provided science has unlimited access. Such views are widely held in the scientific community, but Michael Taylor and Jean-Marc Gagnon and Gerald Fitzgerald take a view which gives greater weight to issues of identity which in turn place greater emphasis on ownership.[53] Such ideas don't undermine the idea of a distributed collection, but rather suggest that it should be distributed in a certain way.

At the heart of this idea of museums acting collaboratively is the emphasis on expertise as a means to make collecting more efficient and collections more rational. More than a century ago, museum guru William Flower warned against the blinkered view of museums as simply being institutionalised collections. For him it was not the collection which formed the central resource, or most distinguishing feature of the museum, but rather its staff.[54] Despite repeated delivery, this message has not been learnt and what we have seen in many museum workforces is an undervaluing of specialist expertise and the erosion of the knowledgebase of museums. Somehow the intellectual resource of the museum must be held together, for as Flower rightly says, it is the staff which define our museums, and without expertise objects are mute.

A strategy for collection development

Discussion thus far has tried to illuminate some irrational practices, dispel a few illusions, and distinguish kinds of collecting and their disciplinary relationships to social, and collecting, desires. I have redefined the act of museum collecting (returning to an earlier conception), thrown out perpetuity clauses, suggested that we must explore other ways to record, explored a range of conflicting values and even suggested that poststructuralist material culture studies shift objects into the realm of the intangible. A range of arguments and questions have been thrown at professional notions of collecting and the collected object, simply to probe for possibilities and alternatives, and question the traditions of practice which are so easy to follow but so hard to interrogate. Museums should be

---

53   M. Taylor (Chapter 14) and J.-M.Gagnon and G. Fitzgerald, 'Towards a national collection strategy: reviewing existing holdings' (Chapter 20).

54   W.H. Flower, *Essays on Museums*, (London: Macmillan, 1898), 12.

places of creativity and innovation, and this should be as apparent in collecting practices as it is in exhibition galleries.

Table 1.1 offers a proposed outline for the strategic development of collections. I shall use the term 'collecting' here as I have redefined it (as the intellectual components of an integrated 'acquisition–management–disposal' process, a process defined by a museum-specific type of connoisseurship and focused on mixed media and collaborative recording). The left-hand column gives steps along the way to constructing a strategy and answers the questions on the right. Each step involves a process of review and (re)definition. Where a particular question arises that cannot be resolved at one level, a solution should be sought at another. The process is an iterative one, with the cycle of steps repeated until an acceptable strategy is reached. For example, a museum might believe oral history recording is critical to effective collecting but cannot undertake it due to inadequate resources. It could try to address the resource shortfall (Resource step), or seek a solution in extended participation such as working jointly with another museum in the region or with local college students, or beginning an extramural class which does this work as part of its curriculum (Participants step).

Table 1.1 A framework for the strategic development of collections

Mission	What do we want to achieve?	R	D
Boundaries	What does/does not interest us?	E	E
Methodology &	When and how do we collect?	V	F
Resources	With what do we collect?	I	I
Participants	With whom?	E	N
Targets	What specifically do we do now?	W	E

A distinction between this form of a strategy making and the imposition of a collecting policy is that the former is a framework for action, for long-term goals and proactive collecting, yet it establishes short-term targets and remains responsive to change and opportunity. In this example, the strategy is reviewed annually to set specific targets, while its more policy-oriented content will change much less frequently.

The collecting taking place must be deeply contextualised, use multiple media and be driven by a mission to understand (rather than to possess). The mission here is for collection development rather than for the museum overall, though the two will be intimately related. It needs to rationalise the role of the object in what might be termed a project of research (though I use a liberal definition) and to determine what is a reasonable level of effort for the objective in hand. Questions one might ask in formulating the mission include: Who uses the collection currently and how? What are our existing strengths? For what are we known? Are there specific areas we wish to develop as excellences? Who shares our interests? What are the geographical limits on our interests, and why? Is there a case for adjusting them flexibly to suit each individual discipline? With whom can we work collaboratively in order to rationalise what we do? As with the formulation of a collecting policy, the involvement of a wide range of staff is important, but unlike a collecting policy, the strategy is not simply a gatekeeper document but rather a statement of intent directing staff to go out and acquire material in a sustainable, rational and proactive way which sees the three-dimensional archive as only a tiny proportion of the collecting (or recording) activity aimed at this goal. It prevents collecting becoming a passive, opportunistic activity or simply becoming inactive due to limited storage space. It does not mean staff have to spend extended periods of time in the field, though it does permit time to be managed to enable a proper collecting job to be undertaken. It also enables the museum to take rational decisions about what should be collected, when, how and for what purpose. It also ties movements of objects into the collections with movements of objects out. Clearly, it doesn't mean inordinate amounts of material being added to the collection. Clearly, also, activity will depend on discipline and context.

The development of a future strategy can only begin in a co-ordinated survey of existing collections. It would be too easy (were the rules by which we play not perceived as immutable) to establish new rules, to 'shift the goalposts' and dismiss the legacy of the past as embodying an inappropriate philosophy or methodology. Jean-Marc Gagnon and Gerry Fitzgerald show, in a very practical way, how bulk statistical analysis can indicate where existing strengths and omissions lie. The Canadian Museum of Nature has considerable experience of using data in this way.[55] Users

---

55 See, for example, G.R. Fitzgerald, P. Whiting and K. Shepherd, 'A comparison of methodologies used for valuation of the fish collection at the Canadian Museum of Nature', in Nudds and Pettitt, *Value and Valuation*, 110–17.

must, however, remain constantly aware of how such data have been obtained if those data are to be used effectively. The Canadian data indicates some interesting lines for future collecting, but requires, as the authors would admit, further research to gather other important quality attributes (such as data richness, completeness, state and method of preservation and so on). Curators from other disciplines may feel frustrated at the ease with which the data were gathered and analysed, and at the strong (and apparently finite) taxonomic framework of biological classification within which such collecting takes place. However, such outsider views of disciplines can be deceptive (particularly if based on number summaries); this discipline is as multifaceted and subjective as any other.

So how would this strategic approach work in practice? Let me give a fictitious example. Under an existing collecting policy the art curator of Bigtown Museum Service aims to amass a collection of art representative of that produced in the region, and to add such pieces as might provide an overview of the major art movements of the twentieth century. Collecting, here, is driven by aesthetics and established art histories. Unfortunately, Bigtown's main industries are in decline and the revenue base for the museum has been decreasing. The art gallery already has a friends' organisation which has in the past been helpful in raising funds. However, a re-evaluation of the service as a whole suggests to the museum's staff that an important aspect of the museum's activities revolves around the town's identity (whether for its inhabitants or for outsiders) (Mission step). Consequently, it was felt that its regional thematic collections were capable of recording distinctive activities that were fundamentally important to this mission, but that its attempt to gain a representation of twentieth-century art was primarily for the purposes of context and education (even if some of those items are prestigious and in themselves contribute to civic pride and identity) (Boundaries step). Fundraising by the friends might be the key means to achieve this latter end (a new educational mission), but it should not be a priority (Methodology & Resources). The art curator who had acquired local works at local artists' exhibitions as well as through gifts decides as a consequence to take a different route. Aware that little was written about the artists she was collecting, and that the museum's awareness of them relied heavily upon personal reminiscence and gossip, she decided to adopt a more ethnographic approach to the regional art scene (Methodology and Boundaries). Collecting was to be an act of recording artistic production and interaction: interviewing artists, gaining oral data, photographs of works, the studio, exhibitions and influences, and other non-three-dimensional information. The keeper of social history had acquired funding to attend training in ethnographic research techniques (Resources) and agreed to assist in getting the project off the ground (Collaboration). The staff expect that the depth of study will encourage donations from the artists themselves, but nevertheless the museum director has pooled all purchase monies with the aim of targeting expenditure at context-rich, proactive collecting (Resources). In the first year the art curator will focus on the craft potters, and as the result of an internal bidding process, the bulk of this year's 'collecting fund' will support this activity (Target). The Director has also convened a collection development board, to review acquisition proposals and objectives. The board will include representatives from various stakeholding groups (Collaboration, Methodology & Resources) and is managed to enable appropriate input against established policy/strategy without the intervention of local politics (Boundaries). It is a requirement of this board that only curatorial staff contribute recommendations for acquisition and disposal, and that they make their arguments against established criteria (Boundaries, Methodology). It has been agreed that the museum will no longer pursue a policy of keeping objects in perpetuity but that collecting will be used to 'improve' the collection by replacing certain objects with similar ones that are deemed to better fulfil the museum's mission (perhaps through better documentation). All objects in the collection are allocated to one value category:

- A-List – Premier collection. Objects of established artistic merit and rich contextualisation, critical to the museum mission. These objects will, in particular, document artistic production in the region. Objects in this category will generally be kept in the long term as it is doubtful that they can be improved upon. These objects deserve the highest levels of resource input.
- B-List – Objects useful to the wider communicative objectives of the museum. Less critical to the museum's collecting and documentation mission. An asset to be appropriately maintained and kept in the medium to long term. Objects capable of being improved upon or commonplace.

- C-List – Objects which fulfil particular objectives but which, because they don't fully meet with museum policy, or are poorly documented, can be considered ripe for exchange, disposal or replacement. In effect this is the transfer list and it may include items that another institution would consider A-List.
- D-List – Objects which are to be disposed of by prescribed means, preferably in the current year.

A new collecting?

In this chapter I have intentionally been provocative. My aim has not been to offer a complete solution, but rather a series of ideas, point out a few blind spots, and suggest that there is considerably more scope for rational thinking and philosophical probing. Some of what I have discussed appears in the practices of certain museums or in particular disciplines but no museum or discipline is immune from this kind of review. It is a shift in thinking that is required – a reshaping of the rules that govern what we do. Museums do not need the equivalent of the Beeching Report[56] (an axe that blindly cuts without considering the social implications of the loss), but an intellectual solution which will derive social and financial benefits.

A rational and sustainable future cannot be built upon such things as mere acceptance of gifts, or policies of non-disposal, or concepts such as uniqueness, age, the local, the redundant, gap-filling, object fetishism, the popular or in isolation from neighbours, complementary institutions or technologies. It can, however, be built upon: increased investment in the act of collecting; realising the opportunities of the moment; demoting the object in the act of collecting and raising associated investigative activity; fundamentally testing the role of objects in our collecting disciplines; on-going collection distillation and 'improvement'; collaboration; objects in the collection having different roles, values and lifetimes; seeing the object as a medium amongst many with its own limitations; by developing adaptive capability; by valuing expertise and by fundamentally rethinking what we mean by 'collecting'.

We need museums to remain those object-centred oases in a world of change, but in order to achieve this they too must change.

---

56 The 'Beeching Report', British Railways Board, *The Reshaping of British Railways* (London: HMSO, 1963), led to the destruction of much of the British railway network and has been much criticised as short-sighted.

2 Collections and collecting

Susan Pearce

The theme of this chapter is best introduced by considering descriptions of two English collections, both now held by the National Trust, which have been cast in what seems to be the style characteristically used in heritage circles for collections of these, and most other, kinds.

Calke Abbey was built in the early eighteenth century, although added to and altered somewhat since. It was built by the Harpur-Crewe family of baronets, who occupied the house on the site for over twelve generations. The five generations of baronets and other members of the family who lived at Calke during the nineteenth and earlier twentieth century were all great collectors, and their collections are on show in the house.

The collected material includes some natural history including significant collections of lepidoptera and birds' eggs; some of these come from the local area and contain useful information about species ranges now much curtailed. There are also important groups of historical material, including later nineteenth-century sets of toy soldiers and other children's culture, together with furniture, pictures and Egyptian antiquities.[1]

The second example, at 7 Blythe Grove, Worksop, Nottinghamshire, is a semi-detached house, built about 1906, and bought by Florence and William Straw, local shopkeepers, about two years after their marriage. Florence, the survivor of the marriage, died in 1939 and her two sons Walter and William, both bachelors, lived in the house until William's death in 1990.

Both sons, and William in particular, were devoted to their mother and preserved the contents of the house as they were at the time of her death. Consequently, the house possesses a complete suite of pre-1939 furniture and fittings, including the then fashionable Sanderson's patterned-border wallpaper and an Axminster stair carpet featuring Egyptian motifs of

---

1   H. Colvin, *Calke Abbey, Derbyshire* (London: The National Trust/George Philip, 1985).

flowering reeds and pectorals made fashionable by the discovery of Tutankhamun's tomb in 1922.[2] The house and its contents are an invaluable source of reference for the domestic material culture of the lower middle class in the middle decades of the twentieth century, a social development which is now arousing much scholarly interest.

The descriptions of these two collections convey two quite different sorts of information. The first is concerned with the importance of the collection, that is with the visible, tangible objects which comprise it, and the information which they contain. The second kind of information is quite different. This has to do with the collectors, not the collection. It is concerned with process, not product, with biography in the widest sense, and with social practice, rather than discipline-based study.

Without taxing the reader's charity too far, I should like to draw in the metaphor of the collection as an iceberg, of which as we know, one tenth is above the surface and the rest below. The tenth which appears above is that aspect of the collection which is the product, the visible. It is in the clear element of air, able to be seen and examined, susceptible to all the so-called 'normal' processes of measurement, comparison, photography and display. But the rest is in the hidden element of water, where measurements are refracted and vision behaves oddly, where sounds are distorted, senses bemused and display difficult or impossible. Traditionally, too, in our culture, what is above the line is decent, while below it morals and manners become murky.

This is a way of saying that the study of a collection has been deemed 'decent'. It can be offered as objective, as scientific, as knowledge. As we have seen, the crucial scientific principles of measurement and comparison behave properly, or, in other words, the standard discourses of modernism work as they should: unsurprisingly, since this kind of collection study and rational, scientific modernism grew up together, with collections both giving the ideas and providing the evidence for them.

But if collections exist in the air, they also exist in the opposite element of water, traditional metaphor for the dark side, the sub-conscious, the primal world of inchoate feeling from which creation comes, intellectual creation among others. Here modernist assumptions do not apply, and study, if it takes place, must concern itself with those parts modernist understanding

---

2   National Trust, *Mr Straw's House, Nottinghamshire* (London: The National Trust, 1993).

eschews as indecent, the parts of life generally submerged: subjective understanding, questions of motive, psychological biography, and lifestyle. This sort of enquiry, concerned with the collector, has been ironed out of rationalist, modernist study which describes it in pejorative words like 'anecdotal', 'personality-cult making', and 'soft'. It has to: it cannot afford the suggestion that knowledge may be dependent on personality, that it is made rather than revealed, and that how it is constructed relates in substantial part to the temperaments and life histories of those concerned.

And yet collections, like icebergs, inhabit both elements and the end result is an intrinsic whole, which has followed its own growth pattern and taken its characteristic shape whatever this may have turned out to be. In other words, to understand any collection, we have to study both its outer importance and its inner significance, realise how these are the same substance, and see how meanings are made among them.

However, the fact is that while collection study has been the subject of intense effort over at least the last three centuries, to go back no further, collecting has been considered worth studying only in the last decade at the very most. We might set out the principal contrasting parameters in the diagram presented in Table 2.1.

Bearing this in mind, I have endeavoured to design and carry out a research project which was intended to tell us more about what collecting is like in contemporary Britain.[3] This was done through a postal and telephone survey which gathered both quantitative and qualitative information. Its results bore out the findings in North America, and the supposition for Britain, that in the Western world something around 30% of people, that is between a quarter and a third of the population, now collect something. Whatever else collecting is, it is a major social phenomenon.

The project should help to lay some stereotype ghosts. The number of women collectors slightly outnumbers that of men: 52% are women as compared to 48% men. Contrary to received wisdom, the survey shows that the standard proportion in relation to contemporary British society of these collectors are in ordinary family lives with partners, children, houses and cars. They are not lonely inadequates who turn to objects because they fail with people, and we can forget the 'hands in the pockets of a dirty mac' image. Generally, the sizes of the collections are quite small, around twenty

---

3   S. Pearce, *Contemporary Collecting in Britain* (London: Sage, 1998).

pieces, and the amount people reckon to spend on a single piece equally so, at around £5.

Table 2.1 Studies of collections and collecting

	Focus	
Collection study		Collecting study
	Rhetoric	
Assumptive / authoritarian		Reflexive / exploratory
Discipline of study (for example, history)		Field of enquiry (social practice, construction of identity)
To learn more		To discover why
Nature (of world, man, the past)		Culture (how ideas about the world, humans, the past, are made)
	Style	
Descriptive / impersonal		Explanatory / personal
Product		Process
Knowledge		Meaning
	Research	
Data accumulation		Project design
Interest in content (what?)		Interest in form and style (how?)

The survey shows that the socio-economic background makes very little difference. The same kinds of collections crop up across the class spectrum: bricklayers and doctors collect early radiograms, the wives of financial directors and farm workers collect representations of pandas, and everybody collects Coronation mugs and Victorian bricks. This came as a surprise because it is not true in any other sphere of popular culture: choice of television programme, daily newspaper, or good day out are still, in Britain, more or less directed by class and/or education, in accordance with Bourdieu's theory of *habitus*. It seems to have something to do with the closeness of objects and their role as *alter egos*: just as everybody has their same family members, regardless of class, so we all approach the object range in the same way.

The great divide in collecting practice is not by class, but by gender. Women across the social scene collect the same things in the same ways, and men do the same, but the things and the ways are opposite. Both genders collect, whether by nurture or nature, things traditionally appropriate to their sex. Men have mechanical things and military things, women have personal things like jewellery, household things like spice jars, and ornaments. Men collect in order to organise their material, and do so at special times and special places. Women collect in order to remember, and have their material in the home around them all the time.

The bulk of what is collected is junk, that is to say it is either gathered up for free, or next to nothing, on council dumps or at car boot sales, or it is bought in places like seaside gift shops or ordinary stores. It is worth remembering that in the Western world 90% of all shopping is carried out by women, that is 90% of all spending, an economic strength that is just beginning to receive the attention it deserves.[4]

These gatherings of junk are, of course, the valued collections of the future, the accumulations upon which we shall depend to show us what late twentieth-century material culture was like, and to produce displays like the Straw household and some aspects of Calke Abbey. By 2030 or so, those that survive, itself an interesting and pertinent enquiry, will have become 'history', that is discipline-based, impersonal knowledge through which students will be able to learn more of the period – in other words, they will have all the qualities which belong on the left-hand side of Table 2.1.

But they have done so through gender-based (but not class-based) urges to have and hold, to buy, to remember, to decorate a home, to organise as an activity which gives interest and meaning to Saturday mornings. They have done so, in other words, through processes which belong on the right-hand side of the Table 2.1, and their final meaning – the knowledge that they embody – is a mixture of both sets of characteristics, the one informing the other. If, to return to the iceberg image with which I began, the materials go into cold storage as collections, they retain the passionate flashes of colour and fire at their hearts which comes from their collecting, and their meaning is a matter of both.

---

4   D. Miller (ed), *Acknowledging Consumption*, (London: Routledge, 1995).

3 Museums without collections: museum philosophy in West Africa

Malcolm McLeod

Museums are expected to collect things, yet museum collecting, in some cultures, need not be a good or useful activity – it may even be an extremely bad thing, something which helps destroy a culture instead of helping to preserve it. A new museum in Africa commissioned, created and paid for by the people whose culture and history it represents provides an interesting example of this phenomenon. The museum is one in which collections and collecting play a very small part. Its creation and initial success draw attention to the fact that some cultures have ways of preserving and displaying their past which need not involve the formation of museum collections.

Even when museums in other cultures have collections, these may be of little or no use. Anyone who wants to see the stupidity and pointlessness of some collecting should visit the reserve stores of virtually any West African museum. In these stores they will find the collections rotting away, sometimes severely depleted by theft. For the most part the objects they contain are rarely looked at, either by curators or researchers. These institutions do not have current collecting policies, they do not have funds to make acquisitions, they rarely add items to their collections and, in many cases, the items already in the collections seem more an embarrassment than an asset. Most of these collections are dead; decaying vestiges of the museum's own past.

These museums are also characterised by an almost total disjunction between the public displays and the reserve collections: items rarely if ever move between them, they have completely separate existences.

In the last decade or so bodies such as the West African Museums Programme (WAMP) and PREMA (Prevention in Museums in Africa) have worked hard to reanimate African museums and to improve the care of their collections. Yet, in the end, they are still faced with the underlying problem that most of these museums are creations of the colonial era and they have not developed a significant place in the life of the local people. Many of them are visited by more tourists than by citizens of the countries they are supposed to serve. At least one new museum, that at Cape Coast Castle in Ghana which deals with the dreadful history of the slave trade, was deliberately set up, with vast amounts of US aid, primarily to inform and serve visitors to Ghana rather than local people.[1]

The underlying problem is that these museums have not acquired any significant role in local life. The objects they possess lost their meaning when they were removed from their original context of use; so far, in the museum, they have not developed new meanings. In many cases this 'semantic deficit' has come about because they cannot be used: in the past most of their significance arose through their participation in appropriate activities.

There is good evidence that those few museum displays in West Africa which do attract a fair measure of public interest deal with current areas of popular interest or, in addition, draw on local heirlooms which are loaned to the museum only for brief periods and then returned to their owners before they lose their significance. An example of the former is the exhibition of contemporary and recent textiles organised by Dr Claude Ardouin at the National Museum of Mali and then toured to several other countries in the region, of the latter the displays of family memorabilia mounted in the Republic of Benin. In these exhibitions the objects on display derive their meaning from their current roles in society but, were

---

1   The West African Museums Programme is an international development programme funded by the Rockefeller and Ford Foundations and various governments. The aim is to help museums help themselves by drawing up proper plans, arranging training and advice, and so on. WAMP does not simply provide money or assistance: the aim is always that the museums it assists work for themselves. PREMA is organised from ICCROM (International Centre for the Study of the Preservation and the Restoration of Cultural Property) and runs training courses to help African curators to learn the basic principles of conservation, good curatorship and collection use. Its courses, formerly held in Rome, are now held in Africa. WAMP and PREMA are now working closely together.

they to be sundered from those roles by entering the museum's permanent collections, their significance would greatly diminish.

Collecting, that is keeping objects till they become old, or acquiring old objects, is closely related to how we see and try to understand the past. The meaning of objects – and the role of objects in creating meaning – depends upon a people's concepts of the past and of time, and upon the various ways objects can express the past in the present or serve to deny a separate existence of the past. Objects may lose meaning in museums if their role in society is incompatible with the idea of the past that the museums are trying to purvey.

Whatever the root of the problem, we have to accept that museum collections in many parts of Africa have failed to be a useful, or a used, resource. One possible way out of the problem created by basing museums upon virtually meaningless collections is shown by the Manhyia Palace Museum, Kumasi, Ghana (Fig. 3.1).

Fig. 3.1 The Manhyia Palace Museum, Kumasi, Ghana.

New museums in Africa are extremely rare. This one was opened in August 1995 and was created as part of the celebrations marking the silver jubilee of the king of the Asante (Ashanti) people, the Asantehene Opoku

Ware II. The way this new museum was created illustrates a different attitude to collecting and different ways of bringing the past into the present.

The Asante are the largest and most powerful 'tribal' group in Ghana. They dominated the region between about 1700 and the establishment of colonial rule at the end of the nineteenth century. Their king, or *Asantehene*, remains a figure of great political, ritual and spiritual importance. In the present century the Asante nation has had only three kings, Prempeh I (who was exiled by the British in 1896, allowed to return to Kumasi, the Asante capital, in 1924 and died in 1931), his successor Prempeh II, who reigned from 1931 until his death in 1970, and the present monarch, Opoku Ware II. It was the latter who, late in 1994, sanctioned the conversion of the Old Palace, built for Prempeh I and situated within the current palace grounds at Kumasi, into a museum to commemorate his predecessors Prempeh I and Prempeh II, both of whom had lived in, and reigned from, the building.

The importance of the museum to the Asante can be judged by the fact that the project was completed in less than 9 months and that the cost, well over £120,000, an enormous sum in Ghana, was met by the Asante people themselves.

The silver jubilee celebrations in 1995 were a major event attended by hundreds of thousands of Asante, many of whom returned to their country from abroad especially to take part. The jubilee had three major events: a great thanksgiving service in the Anglican Cathedral, the opening of the new Palace Museum by the vice-president of the Republic of Ghana, and a great public ceremony, attended by the president of the republic, at which the king and all the chiefs of Asante paraded and then sat in state with their officials. The last event was attended by about 300,000 people and many more crowded the streets leading to the place where it was held.

Africa is full of dead or dying museums: why should the Asante decide to create a new museum to mark the silver jubilee of their monarch and give it such prominence? There were several reasons. Firstly there was a strong sense of local pride and a desire to mark the ruler's jubilee in some permanent way. The Asante are an intensely proud people, fully conscious of the own glorious imperial past and the vast wealth their land has produced. Even today large amounts of gold regalia remain in the treasuries of the chiefs. Many Asante regard their nation as the dominant group in Ghana. At the same time, in the present decade, many senior

Asante chiefs, businessmen and women, teachers and politicians, have begun to feel strongly that Kumasi was not well served by the National Museums and Monuments Board which maintains only a small presence in the city. The main museums in Ghana are on the coast, in the capital, Accra, and at Cape Coast. These attract considerable numbers of tourists, increasing numbers of whom travel to Ghana each year. Kumasi had nothing comparable.

The Asante are very conscious of the financial benefits tourism can bring. It was felt only right and proper that Kumasi should also benefit more from its visitors. Those taking this view also pointed out that Asante culture was, in any case, far more elaborate and rich than that of the other Ghanaian groups who were represented in the museums on the coast. Although many tourists came to Kumasi most of the money they brought stayed in the pockets of the Accra-based firms that brought them. Tourists attended the great public ceremonials at the palace in which the king sat in state but, while the tour operators charged for this, even though anyone can enter freely, the Asante court received nothing.

A museum, it was therefore suggested by those planning the silver jubilee celebrations, would be a way of getting some of these visitors to pay for what they saw. Having a royal museum would also serve to give some physical acknowledgement of Asante cultural predominance.

But the museum was also needed to serve the local community. Many senior Asante feel a need to explain their own culture and history, not only to outsiders and to non-Asante Ghanaians, but also to the Asante generation now at school, many of whom have grown up in Kumasi or other conurbations and have little knowledge of traditional life.

Finally, among those who proposed the new museum, there was a high level of understanding of how museums operate in Europe and North America. Many Asante chiefs and other senior men and women have a good knowledge of overseas museums and exhibitions, having lived or travelled abroad, and, in particular, visited the major exhibition 'Asante, Kingdom of Gold' (1984) at the Museum of Mankind in London or subsequently at the American Museum of Natural History, New York. At both venues the exhibition was opened by the Asantehene Opoku Ware II, who was accompanied by a large retinue of the most senior Asante chiefs. Other Asante made private visits from Ghana to the exhibition. These people had, therefore, a sophisticated grasp of how successful museums can be – if they have the correct ingredients.

If these were the main motives for suggesting the Old Palace should be turned into a museum, it is only proper to add that there was considerable opposition to the idea that such a public facility should be set up within the palace grounds. Many chiefs felt the area was too sacred for outsiders to enter, others worried about the safety of the king. The supporters of the project countered these arguments by drawing attention to the fact that both Buckingham Palace and the White House are open to tourists.

Once the idea of the new museum was accepted, four groups of potential visitors were identified and plans made to serve them all. These groups were: Asante who knew a fair amount about traditional life and culture, younger, less well-informed Asante and other Ghanaians, tourists and, finally, VIPs visiting the king.

The planning committee decided that, to work properly, the museum should have a number of basic elements. Firstly, all visitors, before they entered the museum proper, should be shown a short film explaining Asante history and showing examples of the main Asante ceremonies. The importance of the Old Palace, and of the kings who had lived in it, were clearly stated in this film. As the film was intended to inform both Ghanaians and non-Ghanaians, soundtracks in Twi, the local language, and English, were commissioned.

Secondly, it was agreed that the ground floor of the Old Palace should be kept just as it was when Prempeh II died in 1970. After his death virtually all his furniture, books, clothing, photographs, the souvenirs presented by visiting heads of state and other dignitaries, even the files in his in-tray, had been left exactly as they were. It was decided that these, with minimum rearrangement, were to be left so that Asante and other visitors could see how he had lived and worked. This was especially important, not only because he is immensely revered but, for many Asante, it would have been impossible to enter the palace during his lifetime: it was a far too sacred and far too frightening place.

The memorabilia of Prempeh II were to constitute almost the whole collection of the new museum. This was a handy decision because it solved the problem of what to do with these things. In Asante tradition royal property should neither be destroyed nor alienated after its owner's death, yet the things that had been left in the Old Palace had no role in the continuing life of the court.

Thirdly, and perhaps most important in the present context, the question of forming a wider collection relating to Asante culture for the museum was raised – and almost instantly discarded. Nobody on the planning committee could see any point in the museum having collections, indeed, to some, the idea was almost laughable. A museum, it was made clear, was certainly not the place to keep and display valuable old objects relating to Asante history and kingship.

This rejection of a collection as an essential element in a museum relates to Asante ideas about how objects from the past are best treated. In Asante, many such objects are carefully preserved, these are mainly items concerned with kingship or with the gods. Each chiefship has one or more officials charged to see that items of regalia are carefully guarded and maintained in good repair and, when they eventually wear out, are replaced by replicas. Many of the greatest objects, such as the elaborate gold-decorated swords on which chiefs swear oaths of loyalty, have detailed histories attached to them which are known to their custodians and other senior court officials. But, in the end, however important and quasi-sacred they may be, these are also 'working' objects, objects which exist to perform some function in the continuing operation of the system of kingly rule.

What role, if any, was there for such things in the museum? Many of the committee could see none. The objects remained in good care, the sort of care that had preserved some of them for hundreds of years, and they were regularly used. They had nothing to do with museums. Eventually, after considerable discussion, it was agreed that some of them should be displayed, but they should never become part of the museum. The reason for displaying them was the acceptance that Ghanaians, who have seen little of traditional court life, and many tourists know that gold regalia, gold-decorated swords, sandals, head bands and staffs are an essential part of the traditional system of rule. They, and especially tourists, might expect to see such things in a royal museum. The planning committee therefore agreed that the upper floor of the new museum should contain six or eight showcases in which such objects could be displayed.

Many Asante and other Ghanaians, of course, often see such things as part of their everyday life and, apart from being rather surprised at seeing them in a glass-fronted case, would show less interest in them than tourists. It was agreed that did not matter: such people would find other things to interest them in the museum.

But, if it was accepted that such objects were to be displayed, where were they to come from? Perhaps the committee should try to borrow them from the chiefs who look after the regalia used at the royal court? But the essential problem was that these items would then have to be taken off display at regular intervals so they could be used. A straightforward solution was then proposed: because a major royal object was always replicated when it wore out, further replicas should be made for displaying to tourists in order to save everyone a lot of time and trouble. Foreign tourists, it was suggested, would not be able to tell the difference between old and new items, and Asante would accept copies or replicas as a normal thing. Eventually a mixture of what we would regard as the 'old, authentic' and the 'new replica' was installed in the museum.

The fourth element in the plans was perhaps more surprising: that high-quality fibreglass effigies of Prempeh I and II and Opoku Ware II and two of the queen mothers should be commissioned and form the heart of the museum (Fig. 3.2). All those involved were adamant that this was essential to the success of the museum: they wanted effigies, and without effigies there was little point in proceeding.

The decision made, photographs of the people concerned were assembled and the firm Gems in London set about creating the figures. On arrival at Kumasi they were carefully dressed and adorned with characteristic clothes and jewellery and seated at key points in the museum. Prempeh II's effigy was placed in his old chair in the corner of the room where he used to receive important visitors.

When the museum opened, the success of these effigies was instant and enormous. They were a wonder and people were desperate to see them. Other Ghanaian chiefs inquired if they could have similar displays of their predecessors created. The Palace Museum committee quickly ordered two more effigies of other important Asante royal figures. When I revisited the museum in August 1996 it was attracting large numbers of visitors, making a substantial profit, and the figures were still the prime attraction to Ghanaian visitors.

There are two contrasting elements in this story. The first is that, in Asante, the types of objects which we, as outsiders, might consider essential for a museum intended to represent Asante culture, and especially kingly rule, are preserved in other ways and are too closely involved in local life to be very meaningful or interesting in a museum context, except to outsiders. The second is that people do want to use artefacts to conjure up the past and have some form of direct communion with it. In this case they chose life-like effigies of past kings and queen mothers to do this. Of course the

Asante museum planners who originally proposed this innovation had seen such things before, both in the Museum of Mankind's 'Asante Kingdom of Gold' exhibition and at Madame Tussauds but, back in their own land, they were giving effigies a very different role.

Fig. 3.2 Effigy of Prempeh II seated in his accustomed place within the Palace reception area.

If the Palace Museum, or any other new or existing museum in Africa, is to succeed, it will only do so if it is rooted in local culture. It will only acquire support if local people see it as having something of interest to them and being relevant to their lives and concerns. Colonial-period museums are largely meaningless to the groups they were set up to serve. The Asante decided that collecting, and the care of collections, had virtually nothing to do with what they were attempting to achieve. Re-creating the past had to be done in other ways.

Of course, it is easy for outsiders brought up in a different tradition to say that what the Asante have created is not a proper museum, and to condemn it as a mere visitor attraction made more showy with wax dummies. However to do so would be to ignore the deep seriousness of this endeavour and the thoughtful way in which the Asante have tried to learn from the failure of other museums in Africa and from what they have seen of museums in Europe and North America. They are trying to find a new way to preserve and explain aspects of their culture that they believe are important and, perhaps, they will succeed where others have failed. Certainly they have not fallen into the trap of thinking that collections are the be-all and end-all of their endeavours.

4 The future of collecting: lessons from the past

Richard Dunn

Research here explores the historical, social and intellectual forces that have brought, and continue to bring, the collections of the Victoria and Albert Museum (V&A), London, into existence and the ways in which those collections have been continuously reinterpreted.[1] By examination of the V&A's history, a series of interconnected themes can be discerned: the relationship between a museum's stated purpose and its collecting; the ways in which shifting interpretations of a museum's collections alter the status of objects and so influence future acquisition; and the ways in which acquisitions affect a museum's purpose and collecting. Though derived from the history of a particular, even exceptional, institution, these issues are central to collecting in all museums today.

A museum's collecting activities relate to the purpose the institution perceives for itself. For the V&A, however, this has never been straightforward and the evolution of its collections has occurred under the influence of conflicting notions of education and antiquarianism. In its first incarnation as the Museum of Manufactures at Marlborough House, the V&A was intended to be 'A collection of specimens, which should illustrate both the progress and the highest excellence attained in manufacture' (Fig. 4.1), for

> By proper arrangements a Museum may be made in the highest degree instructional. If ... means are taken to point out its uses and applications, it becomes elevated from being a mere unintelligible lounge for idlers into an impressive schoolroom for every one.[2]

---

1   This research was carried out in preparation for the exhibition 'A Grand Design: The Art of the Victoria and Albert Museum'.

2   Department of Practical Art, *First Report of the Department of Practical Art* (London: Eyre & Spottiswoode, 1853), 30.

This instructional aim, geared specifically towards the improvement of manufacturing standards, has been repeated throughout the museum's history, even as recently as 1992:

Fig. 4.1 A gas table lamp in the shape of a convolvulus, made by R.W. Winfield, Birmingham (M.20-1974). This was one of the objects chosen from the Great Exhibition to demonstrate poor design in the Museum of Manufactures. At the time it was described as 'entirely indefensible in principle ... the artist has embodied some extravagance to conceal the real purpose for which the article has been made' (Courtesy of the Board of Trustees of the V&A).

> The V&A ... strives to provide what society needs: fresh inspiration for Britain's designers; cross-cultural collections for a multi-cultural society; a fusion of the arts, technology and history for an educational system which has traditionally kept them apart; and a forum for public debate on the issues of contemporary design.[3]

---

3   Victoria and Albert Museum, *Education for All* (London: V&A, 1992), 5.

How, then, has this educational mission affected the V&A's collecting activities? The founding purpose suggested that the museum should contain only objects of educational benefit to manufacturers, a point Henry Cole, the first director, emphasised in 1860:

> We do not buy archaeological subjects, as the British Museum does sometimes, because they are curious, but we buy objects which we think will give suggestions to manufacturers, or which are objects of great beauty.[4]

The first acquisitions of the museum included, therefore, objects selected from the Great Exhibition for their demonstration of the 'true principles' of design,[5] their educational role reinforced by the selection of objects as counter-examples of 'false principles', the latter displayed in a gallery which rapidly came to be known as the 'Chamber of Horrors'. The first displays, then, were rigidly didactic and the objects placed there were chosen to reinforce the public demonstration and indoctrination of the principles of good design (and, consequently, of good taste).

Nevertheless, other interests soon emerged. Henry Cole had signalled a desire for 'objects of great beauty', and even before 1860 the museum had begun to acquire medieval and Renaissance objects, demonstrating an antiquarian thrust which was reflected in its displays. The museum had thus moved towards the idea of collecting as a worthwhile activity in itself.[6] The next fifty years saw no resolution to the resulting confusion and by 1908 it was admitted that:

> The Museum was originally founded as an instrument stimulating the improvement in this country of such manufactures and crafts as require and admit of decorative design. In adding to the collections, however, the precise nature of its original purpose has not been throughout rigidly observed, and while the character imposed upon it at its foundation has continually

---

4   Select Committee, *Report from the Select Committee on the South Kensington Museum* (London, 1860), para. 90.

5   C. Wainwright, 'Principles true and false: Pugin and the foundation of the Museum of Manufactures', *Burlington Magazine*, CXXXVI (1994), 357–64.

6   R.C. Denis, 'Teaching by example: education and the formation of South Kensington's Museums', in M. Baker and B. Richardson (eds), *A Grand Design: The Art of the Victoria and Albert Museum* (New York: Abrams, 1997).

influenced its development, its scope has become more extensive and less defined.[7]

This ambiguity of purpose has persisted, although a recent acquisitions policy has attempted to define the parameters under which objects can be acquired. Yet even this document reveals tensions. For example, while the sculpture collection does not acquire large-scale sculptures made after 1914 (by agreement with other national museums and galleries), the rest of the museum uses a significant proportion of its purchase grant for the acquisition of twentieth-century material. Similarly, the European collections do not collect earlier than AD 300, while no such restrictions apply to the Oriental collections.[8] Although these guidelines reflect both what the museum has and its relationship with other collections, such mismatches can create problems in acquiring objects that relate in a wider context to others already in the collections.

In addition, there is continued uncertainty as to what it is that the V&A and its collections represent. This stems from difficulties in defining categories such as art, craft and design, and the differentiation between the 'applied' or 'decorative' arts and the 'fine' arts, terms whose definitions and interrelationships are continually subject to negotiation.[9] Moreover, as fashions change, the museum has redefined the canon of works that it should contain in order to present an encyclopaedia of applied art. Yet limitations of space now cast doubt on the possibility or desirability of gathering together such a collection, even though the notion of forming an encyclopaedia remains strong.[10] Other ambiguities also exist. For example, by engaging with the performing arts, through the Theatre Museum, the V&A has encountered a set of collecting issues which do not align naturally with its central purposes, and the museum's applied arts

---

7   Victoria and Albert Museum, *Report of the Committee of Rearrangement* (London: V&A, 1908), 4.

8   Victoria and Albert Museum, *Acquisitions Policy and Collecting Plans* (London: V&A, 1993).

9   C. Saumarez Smith, 'The classification of things', *Bulletin of the John Rylands University Library of Manchester*, 77(1) (1995), 13–20; P. Greenhalgh, 'The History of Craft', in P. Dormer, ed., *The Culture of Craft* (Manchester: Manchester University Press, 1996), Chapter 1.

10 For example, Victoria and Albert Museum, 'The V&A: Towards 2000', (unpublished, 1985), 2.

emphasis has often served to direct acquisitions in this area along particular lines.

Like other museums, then, the V&A's purposes and interests have changed during its history, and no doubt will continue to do so in the future.

Changing interpretations of the collections

Change, however, is not confined to the institution as a whole. After acquisition, objects do not retain a fixed meaning,[11] and one aim of this research was to explore the lives of objects after their entry into the museum. From the stories revealed, I wish to pick out some examples which illustrate different ways in which the status of objects can change, and which lead us to examine critically the aftermath of the acquisition process and its relationship to subsequent collecting.

The first is a sculpture acquired in 1861 for £1000 on the grounds that it was a statue of Cupid by Michelangelo (Fig. 4.2), thus gaining a prominent status in displays, and frequently being mentioned in guides and other publications.[12] By the 1950s, however, it was reattributed as Narcissus, an antique statue probably recut by Cioli in the sixteenth century. It is now consigned to a corner of the sculpture galleries, although its label discusses first its former attribution, followed apologetically by its current one. Although the object itself has not changed, the change in attribution has lessened its perceived importance dramatically.

The second object is a soapstone box. Upon acquisition in 1876, it was assumed to be Roman, thus fitting into the collecting activities of the museum at that time. Subsequently, its attribution has changed several times and it is now believed to have been made in what was Nubia (now southern Egypt and northern Sudan). Since the V&A does not collect African art,[13] and similar material formerly in the collections has been transferred, the status of this object within the collections is now unclear.

---

11   C. Saumarez Smith, 'Museums, artefacts, and meanings', in P. Vergo, (ed), *The New Museology* (London: Reaktion Books, 1989).

12   M.D. Conway, 'The South Kensington Museum' (second paper), *Harper's New Monthly Magazine*, 51 (1875), 649–66.

13   The placement of African art, regarded as 'primitive', in ethnographic rather than art collections owes much to the racism evident in the nineteenth and twentieth centuries. A. Coombes, *Reinventing Africa* (London & New Haven: Yale University Press, 1994). This box underwent a similar treatment to other

So objects may alter their status within a collection, and may even slip outside a museum's interests. On the other hand, it is also possible for objects to slip into a museum's collecting area, a point illustrated through a discussion of the V&A's engagement with English material.

Fig. 4.2 The so-called Michelangelo Cupid (7560–1861), prominently displayed in the V&A's 1946 'Style in Sculpture' exhibition (Courtesy of the Board of Trustees of the V&A).

While the pattern of collecting in the early decades of the museum's development involved numerous trips to the Continent to buy medieval and Renaissance works of art, the acquisition of English objects was more haphazard. In 1865, for instance, the Sterne Cup (Fig. 4.3) was turned down on the grounds that it could not 'be considered as coming within the category of works of art'. A greater interest in the English decorative arts developed, however, during the 1880s and 1890s, a period of increasing

---

objects from Africa. In 1894, for instance, the director described it as 'a curious half savage work' in his revision to the register which reattributed the box as African.

emphasis on national identity that witnessed, for example, the foundation of the National Trust and the Tate Gallery as well as the first publication of *Country Life*. By the time the new Aston Webb building was opened in 1909 (whose façade displayed statues of English practitioners of the decorative arts), the museum was deeply involved in the acquisition of English material. When the Sterne Cup was offered again in 1923, it was judged that 'this is just the kind of art which we must increasingly aim at supporting'.[14]

Fig. 4.3 The Sterne Cup (M.103–1925) (Courtesy of the Board of Trustees of the V&A).

In other words, the motives for acquiring – or not acquiring – particular objects may not correspond to the subsequent ways in which those objects relate to the collection, to the displays, to the museum's mission and to wider interests. Rather, such motives are the product of changing fashions in scholarship, and internal politics. It is not possible to guarantee, then, that the objects acquired now and in the future will always be the 'correct'

14 C. Saumarez Smith, 'National consciousness, national heritage, and the idea of "Englishness"', in Baker and Richardson (eds), op. cit.

or 'most representative' ones, or that the ones not acquired will not later be judged important.

Acquisition as an agent of change

The final point concerns the way that acquisition itself, in particular of large groups of material, can cause change. Throughout its history, the V&A has benefited from the acquisition of numerous large preformed groups of material. As separate collections in themselves, each group has arrived with its own history of accumulation and underlying purpose, which need not necessarily coincide with the museum's own mission. Such acquisitions can, therefore, alter or undermine the museum's mission and collecting activities.

This issue arose as early as 1857 with the formation of the South Kensington Museum and the resulting incorporation of the Sheepshanks collection. This group of oil paintings, watercolours, sketches, drawings and etchings, mostly by British artists, was initially presented as 'The Gallery of British Fine Arts'.[15] This immediately signalled a problematic relationship with collections aimed at providing examples of industrial art. Fifty years later, the Committee of Rearrangement report revealed an awareness of the difficult status of this group of objects within the museum.[16] Indeed, the status of the fine arts elements of the V&A's collections remains problematic; some believe they have no place in the museum. Nevertheless, the fact that the V&A has major Constable holdings – perceived as a crowd-puller – and is designated as the national collection of watercolours, makes it unlikely that any radical reassignment of such material will occur.

Not all acquisitions have been problematic, however. The V&A's holdings of Far Eastern art, for instance, were radically transformed by the acquisition of material from the collection of George Eumorfopoulos (1862–1939), which was divided between the British Museum and the V&A in the 1930s. As first president of the Oriental Ceramic Society, Eumorfopoulos was influential in the formation of canons of taste among connoisseurs in the West. In contrast to typical collections accrued until then, his centred on vernacular, rather than on imperial art, and on works of an earlier date.

15　South Kensington Museum, *Guide to the South Kensington Museum* (London: Clowes and Sons, 1857).

16　Victoria and Albert Museum, op. cit. (1908), 12–5.

The impact of his collection was to alter the ways in which the V&A and the British Museum studied and collected Chinese art, notably with a shift away from the artefacts of the Qing period (1644–1911), with its imperial resonances, to the art of early China.[17] This shift complemented the exemplification of early Chinese art for its spontaneity and vitality and within a generation the types of ceramic championed by Eumorfopoulos and shown at South Kensington were being emulated by potters like Bernard Leach.

Similar processes also occur in the acquisition of single objects. The events surrounding the V&A's joint acquisition with the National Galleries of Scotland of Canova's *Three Graces*, highlight the controversy that can arise over the attribution of 'significance' to particular objects in the applied arts. The justification of the expenditure of £7.6 million on what to the public was a work by an unknown sculptor, engendered great debates over Canova's role in the art world of his age and over the status of this object in relation to his other work. The result has been to alter the way in which similar objects, in particular works by Canova, will be studied and collected from now on, a process in which the sale rooms are an important element.

This incident also illustrates the role of museums in the formation of public perceptions of which objects are valuable (intellectually or financially). On a similar note, for instance, a donor of ironwork to the V&A recollected at the beginning of this century:

> At the time I was collecting, many people did not fail to express their scepticism as to the value of all 'the old rubbish', as they called it, which I was getting together; but I am glad to say that my judgement has been completely vindicated, and today, instead of 'old rubbish', I am told it is a 'valuable collection'.[18]

Acquisition, then, is a process which affects the way existing material is perceived, the way an institution perceives itself and the material it collects thereafter.

---

17   C. Clunas, 'Oriental antiquities/Far Eastern art', *Positions: East Asia Cultures Critique*, 2(2) (1994), 318–55.

18   R. Nevill, ed., *The Reminiscences of Lady Dorothy Nevill* (London, 1906), 256–7.

Self-conscious collecting

Through this analysis of the V&A's history, I have tried to illustrate some of the factors that affect a museum's collecting activities. In particular, I have sought to show that the determination of a museum's acquisition policy, the interpretation of its collections and the act of collecting itself, continually influence each other.

It is not possible to lay down for all time one fixed, objective and unbiased collecting policy. Rather, we should adopt an approach that I would call 'self-conscious collecting'. By this I mean that we should be open about the processes and immediate motives involved in the acquisition of particular objects, and record these as far as is practical. Indeed, this act of justification for the acquisition of objects would in some ways justify for all time the presence of that object in a collection – at the very least as a record of which objects were considered significant at a particular point in a museum's history (although this is, admittedly, an introspective justification). Conversely, I would argue that the failure to provide such a justification can lead to a very common situation – the presence of objects in a collection with no knowledge of what they are doing there or of how and why they got there in the first place. By adopting such an approach, I believe that museums could avoid the perceived need to justify with respect to current aims the existence of collections which, because acquired in the past with very different motives, fit awkwardly with those aims. After all, these motives may change; the objects may be reappraised.

5 The Ashmolean Museum: a case study of eighteenth-century collecting

Patricia Kell

Within the history of collecting in Western Europe, the bulk of activity has remained in the private sphere: individual collectors have acquired things of interest or value to them. The advent of public museums in the late seventeenth century created, for the first time, the need for coherent institutional approaches to the selection of objects. While formal collecting policies were not initially explicitly articulated, institutions clearly had to take decisions regarding the acquisition of single objects and existing collections.

The implications of functioning without an articulated policy will be examined here in the context of the early Ashmolean Museum. While it might be expected that the net effect of this non-policy was to disenfranchise the general populace, which museums in their mandates were intended to serve, this was not the case. There were not two separate spheres of activity, one in the galleries which was broadly accessible to the public and one behind the scenes at the museum which remained the purview of a privileged intellectual elite. Acquisitions were not a locus of intellectual hegemony and popular exclusion.

Some who contributed to the growing repository did indeed come from within the university, pursued learned professions, and collected and gave complete collections. However, there was a second set of individuals who had no formal affiliation with the university, who had no academic pretensions and indeed often no social pretensions, and who gave only one or two items. Yet both groups of collectors and types of donation were accepted by the museum, both were recorded in the illuminated *Donors Book*, and both on occasion were the source of 'treasures' and less valuable items. Rather than two competing publics, there was a single diverse public, which ranged in its level of academic interest and accomplishment, merging to create in the museum a co-operative entity devoted to the achievement of goals set apart from external social or political agendas. This unique situation stemmed from the museum's roots planted simultaneously in the rarefied confines of the virtuoso cabinet and in the public exhibition of freaks and curiosities. The cultural miscegenation which fostered the public museum, which I argue elsewhere was evident in the galleries,[1] was also embodied in the museum collection itself.

The Ashmolean Museum grew from the collection of natural and artificial rarities of John Tradescant the Elder (d. 1638) and John Tradescant the Younger (1608–62), which the latter agreed to give to Elias Ashmole (1617–92), who in turn presented it to the University of Oxford. When the museum was institutionalised in 1683, the possibility of future additions to and deletions from the collection was not ignored. From the time of its foundation, the repository was not expected to remain static. When Ashmole first sent the rarities to the university, he reserved to himself the right to add 'such further Gifts and Endowments as may be ornamental & useful'.[2] Again in 1684, in the document which appointed Visitors to oversee the museum, he referred to the diligence required to preserve the objects, particularly citing that they were 'lyable to be imbezelled and utterly dwarf'd from Growth by Negligence & ill Treatment'. However, he equally pointed to the possibility that the repository might 'receive daily Improvement'. Indeed, one of the powers which was given to the Visitors was to consult 'for the improvement thereof by new accessions'. These acquisitions were to consist of 'whatever the Friends and Patrons of Learning shall give to the Store of natural and artificial Rarities of the University'.[3] The museum was therefore intended, not only in the research which it promoted but in the collections themselves, to remain actively engaged in a perpetual cycle of renewal and improvement.

The view of the collection as fluid remained in effect throughout the eighteenth century. Almost a hundred years after the founding of the museum, its keeper, William Huddesford (1732–72), redoubled efforts to bring greater order to the collection, which meant in practice establishing a

---

1   See P.E. Kell, *British Collecting, 1656–1800: Scientific Inquiry and Social Practice,* D.Phil. Thesis (Oxford, 1996), Chapter 7.
2   E. Ashmole to Dr Lloyd, Vice-Chancellor of the University of Oxford, 26 May 1683, Ashmolean Museum, AMS 1, f. 1 (a copy).
3   E. Ashmole to the Vice-Chancellor, 1 September 1684, AMS 1, f. 2.

balance between the accession of new specimens and the elimination of decaying material. Not only was he to 'reduce the several Articles in the Musæum into proper Classes', he was also given authority 'to remove the decay'd & trifling things which will shew the valuable ones in a much better light'. Most importantly however, this exercise in collections management would 'be a means of their daily encreasing.'[4] The congruity of new acquisitions and institutional health gelled in the popular imagination. News of fresh acquisitions brought pleasure to Edward Wright, while he hoped that the museum would 'continue to flourish & still more & more invite curious people to contribute to its increase'.[5] The healthy collection expanded through time, with occasional excisions of degraded items.

The statutes drawn up for the governance of the museum reiterated these concerns and potentialities. A catalogue was to be drawn up of the objects, and the holdings of the museum were to be compared to it at the time of the annual visitation. In this catalogue were to be entered 'all the additions made in the precedent year'. For the better preservation of natural objects, those which were rare and 'apt to putrifye and decay with time' were to be depicted in water colours in a folio volume, with a description of the body and a mention of the donor (which was to come from the catalogue). The catalogue itself was to be kept 'under lock and key'. The money for figuring items was to come from the excess revenue generated by entrance fees paid by visitors to the museum. This profit could also be spent in 'buying more rarities'.[6] By 1714, this provision for figuring items had already been erased from the statutes, as had any mention of excess profit from fees. Indeed, the accounts of the museum indicate that there never was a profit and instead by 1773 the keeper was owed over £885.[7] The sections of the statutes regarding the expenditure of excess revenue were replaced with ones outlining in more detail the sums to be levied from gallery-goers. In limited cases it was permissible to deaccession objects: when many examples of the same object were owned, one could be exchanged for something wanting 'or to make a present of it to some person of Extraordinary Quality'; or

---

4   S. Lethieullier to W. Huddesford, 12 March 1756, Bodleian Library, Ashm. 1822, f. 25.
5   E. Wright to W. Huddesford, 5 February 1760, Ashm. 1822, f. 81.
6   *Statutes, Orders & Rules for the Ashmolean Musæum in the University of Oxford* (Oxford, 1686).
7   Receipts, etc. 1735–94, AMS 6.

anything which grew 'old & perishing' could be removed 'into one of the Closets or other repositorys and some other ... substituted'.[8]

The museum's statutes therefore focused on taking care of the objects it owned, preserving information about those which were deteriorating, and allowing controlled growth. The statutes did not, however, give any guidance about the kinds of gifts which would be most appropriate or indeed at all acceptable to the museum. There were no limits imposed on the range of types of things which might be acquired, nor were there areas identified as desirable for expansion. The accession of objects in practice, therefore, was bound to depend on the cumulative professional experience of the keepers and visitors, in whose hands decisions about what might be kept and what rejected rested.

From sources at the museum, 97 donors were identified. Of these seven made more than one benefaction. Benefactions which included many objects were more likely than those of few to be reported in more than one source but there was no preferential reporting of natural versus cultural items or indeed donations which included both. The *Donors Book*,[9] in keeping with its image of valorisation, was more likely to include donations of many objects (especially of natural items), while mid-sized benefactions were under-represented there. Cultural objects were grossly over-represented in the *Donors Book*, to the detriment of small and moderate gifts of natural history specimens. In only one case was there evidence of anything being offered to the museum which it declined.

Donations to the Ashmolean were composed of a combination of single objects, a few objects together (which might or might not relate to one another), or groups of objects of varying quantities, from a few dozen to several thousand. The largest single gift contained 2000 objects: plants in a *hortus siccus*, given by Edward Morgan, the retired keeper of the Botanical Gardens at Westminster, in 1689. Sixty of the 113 gifts (53 per cent) consisted of a single object. Lone objects ranged considerably in their import: The *Porci Pedes monstrosos* of William Corne, or the single medal retrieved from a wreck and donated by Thomas Creech in 1699, might be convincingly characterised as of no great scientific or social importance. On the other hand, the Alfred Jewel, donated by Thomas Palmer in 1718, or the monstrous human skull bone of Laurence Homer, or the piece of the true

---

8   *The Orders and Statutes of the Ashmolean Museum* (Oxford, 1714).
9   Illuminated volume containing entries for 1683–1719 and 1743–66, AMS 2.

cross in a gold box given by Samuel Butler in 1688 might be argued to have been of contemporary or even lasting cultural importance. A larger number of items in a donation increased the likelihood that it would contain both natural and cultural material. However, large collections were rarely composed exclusively of cultural items, while moderately sized donations of only natural specimens were also uncommon.

Who were the people who gave things to the museum? Were they people intimately associated with the university? Were they part of the broader scholarly community? Or perhaps they were just people who happened to live near the museum?

Many of the donation records list college affiliations of the donors. Of the 97 benefactors, 40 (41%) are known to have had a formal academic connection with the university. Those who had been to college were more likely to give natural history specimens and less likely to give cultural artefacts. They also preferentially gave larger rather than smaller numbers of objects. Indeed, while influenced by the qualities and value of the objects themselves, donors were explicitly moved to give to the museum out of a sense of loyalty to the university. George Scott identified himself as being 'always very ready to embrace every Opportunity of expressing my Regard for my Alma Mater'.[10] Similarly Samuel Butler's gift was given 'As a sign of his affection for this University'.[11] Indeed, Ashmole himself in his original gift began by noting 'It has of a long time been my Desire to give some testimony of my Duty and filial Respect to my honored Mother the University of Oxford.'[12] The museum adorned the university; it was an attractive and admiration-inspiring token of the value of the institution. A source of pride in itself, it also permitted the expression of a more generalised enthusiasm for the university.

Benefactors came from a wide range of occupational groups. Physicians, lawyers, and antiquarians are listed alongside fishmongers, sea captains and merchants. The single best-represented occupational group is clergymen (12%), quickly followed by those who are recorded merely as 'esquire' (11%), merchants (9%), physicians (8%), and women (7%). If the collectors are grouped into categories, 9% worked in businesses with no

---

10   G. Scott to W. Huddesford, 29 March 1759, Ashm. 1822, f. 38.

11   *Donors Book*, 1688.

12   E. Ashmole to Dr Lloyd, 26 May 1683, AMS 1.

academic association,[13] 18% in fields concerned with knowledge about cultural and natural history,[14] while 24% were engaged in what might be considered gentlemanly activities.[15] Those who worked in business almost invariably gave small donations of cultural items to the museum and never presented large collections. Those from the academic sphere gave relatively fewer cultural items, concentrating most heavily on large collections of natural history. The gentlemanly caste focused on small numbers of cultural items.

Those who had some affiliation with the university and those from the scholarly professions shared a pattern of donations centred on large collections of natural history objects. However, when profession was compared with college membership, only about half of physicians and, indeed, half of clergymen had a known association with Oxford. The common pattern amongst university members was shared more widely within an educated community. A sample of social groups with no link to the university (merchants and those known as 'esquire') indicates a complementary focus on cultural items and small benefactions. Women also generally donated in this pattern.

Finally, on the issue of residency, donors to the museum lived in a wide variety of places. There was a core in Oxford (29%), while this, in conjunction with those in Oxfordshire and the neighbouring counties, accounted for 50% of benefactors. Several benefactions came from the Continent, including runic objects from Johannes Heysig in Sweden[16] and a seal from the Dutch consul in Turkey, Ioannes Gosch.[17] Those who lived in or near Oxford were more likely to give small numbers of objects than those who lived farther afield, perhaps indicating a more opportunistic donations strategy.

The population which gave objects to the Ashmolean divides repeatedly into two groups. Approximately half belonged to a college at the university; half lived in the vicinity of Oxford. Approximately half gave only a single item; almost half gave only cultural objects. Indeed, two

---

13   These are captain, carrier, fishmonger, locksmith, sea captain and ship's purser.
14   These are: antiquarian, keeper of the Ashmolean, naturalist, pharmacist and physician.
15   These are: diplomat, gentleman, lawyer, politician, Sir and esquire.
16   *Donors Book*, 1683.
17   *Donors Book*, 1701.

groups emerge fairly distinctly from this analysis. On one side, the largely university-educated, often Oxford-affiliated, members of the scholarly community collected substantial numbers of objects – often natural history specimens – on their own and donated them en masse to the museum. On the other side, those engaged in business, with no formal tie to the university, and often more distant, gave a single item or a very small group of primarily cultural artefacts. Between these two extremes lay a continuum of individuals from a range of social positions and with varied orientations towards collecting.

It would be useful to compare these findings with the profile of visitors to the museum. While account books are extant recording money received from visitors, the amount of information about the people themselves, apart from the size of group in which they came, is inconsistent and strictly circumscribed. People from a variety of backgrounds saw the rarities, ranging from foreign gentlemen to country lasses. Some of the curious were members of the university: commoners, freshmen, fellows and the proctor. Some noblemen are identified by name. Sex was no barrier, as women came singly and in groups, nor was religion.[18] Both visitors to the galleries and those who contributed objects to the collections, therefore, came from a range of social stations and occupational categories, and both sexes.

By incorporating the gifts of large collections and the smaller presents – both of which, it would appear from their inclusion in the prestigious *Donors Book*, were valued by the institution – two classes of things came to be held in the museum. There were those of explicit use in research which, indeed, often arose from a research project. Many of the gifts of fossils received by Huddesford were prompted by his endeavours in the preparation of his published works. As William Borlase wrote to him in 1759: 'If you find any chasms, or want of Specimens to elucidate any theory ... take a memorandum and send it to me, and I shall think my self oblig'd to supply you.'[19] Secondly, objects were given which were found to be curious by their owners, such as the Countess of Westmorland's gift of a very large magnet in 1756 and many individual donations of foreign idols. These two types of benefactions broadly assort by donor according to

---

18   Account books of the museum, mainly recording monies received from visitors. These examples are taken from the period 1714–17, AMS 5/2.

19   W. Borlase to W. Huddesford [1759], Ashm. 1822, f. 27.

relationship with the university, place of residence, and the degree of integration into the scholarly community.

People gave things to the museum often out of a fairly ill-justified sense that they were appropriate there. In donating a crucifix in ivory in 1781, the Rev. Dr Wilson noted that he had 'formerly shewn it to some of our most celebrated Anatomists in London, who pronounced it the greatest curiosity of the kind they had eer seen'.[20] Similarly, William Borlase, who gave many mineral samples to the museum, particularly recommended a specimen of native tin as it was 'so very scarce that the existence of it, is questioned and often denied by the most celebrated Fossilists'. He therefore 'thought it might not be unacceptable to you to have one demonstrable proof of it among the Cornish Fossils in your Museum'.[21] The value placed on the museum was reflected in the treatment of objects offered to the collection. Smart Lethieullier, for example, sent a collection of specimens in spirits 'so few in number that I beg you would place them wherever you please & not let my name appear as ye Benefactor of them'. Any desire for personal recognition was subsumed into the larger common project of the institution. 'It will be sufficient satisfaction to me', Lethieullier continued, 'if I can any ways oblige you, & in some measure contribute to shew your Labour is not in vain'.[22] An entry appeared in the *Donors Book* the same year acknowledging a gift of 16 bottles of specimens from him. Cultural objects underwent a similar process of evaluation, as for example Jared Leigh's claim to space in the repository for Carracci's *Christ*, which was predicated on it 'being in the best condition possible considering the time when the Carrache's painted.'[23] More pointed social motives were also possible, as was the case with the 'pseudo-protestant whip' given by Gervase Wilcox,[24] which had been used 'to punish wicked zealots who had threatened the Monarchy, the Church and the Universities with ruin so that they might (in the name of God) prosper less.' He donated it 'in perpetuation of the shame and dishonour of men of that kind.'

These motivations paralleled those of private collectors. Intellectual curiosity, an inherent sense of the value of the objects, and the social prestige associated with them were the principal moving forces. However,

---

20   Extract of a letter from Rev. Dr Wilson, 12 May 1781, AMS 1, f. 18.
21   W. Borlase to W. Huddesford, 4 November 1765, Ashm. 1824, f. 16.
22   S. Lethieullier to W. Huddesford, 8 May 1756, Ashm. 1822, f. 25.
23   Jared Leigh to W. Huddesford, 14 January 1758, Ashm. 1822, f.36.
24   *Donors Book*, 1683.

the nature of the museum as institution, the lifespan of which stretched on infinitely from the moment of the original benefaction, meant that while the motivations for collecting resembled those of private collectors and indeed the objects themselves recreated the range found in personal cabinets, the collection which resulted was rather different. Where the private collection reflected a more or less consistent range of interests on the part of an individual, the museum, as an accumulation of such whims, manifested some degree of incoherence. However, the mixture of objects responded to the requirements of a variety of interests. There were things which held immediate interest for researchers, others that attracted attention in the galleries, while a further set embodied unexplored research potential. The conjunction of objects from sources beyond the reach of any single individual underpinned the unique and invaluable resource which the museum became.

The *ad hoc* collections policy of the museum effectively kept its holdings at the centre of academic debate (which might well have been the primary intent of a formal written policy, had there been one). The statutes to the museum began by pointing out 'the Knowledge of Nature is very necessary to human life health and the Conveniencies thereof'.[25] The museum was to serve as a locus for the generation of such knowledge, an enterprise aided by the donation of complete collections which had been dedicated to this same goal when in private hands. The number of large natural history collections which came to the museum were the fruit of researchers' private investigations. William Borlase, for example, gave at least eight benefactions relating to his work on Cornish minerals.

William Cole of Bristol set out at great length a proposal to give his substantial collection of natural material to the museum in 1695. He described the way in which his objects fitted into his scholarly agenda and made it a condition of the gift that the university support the completion of the plates for the natural history he was preparing based on the specimens. He had spent years, he noted, 'in ye search & observation of things naturall wth aboundant & careful experiments on them'. His attention focused 'espetially in the generation & transfigurations of ye lesser Animalls wth observations of their oeconomic properties & wherein ye perfections of ye

---

25   *Statutes*, 1686.

divine wisdom is no less admirable then in ye greatest.'[26] Cole envisioned his natural history both as an international research tool, once translated into Latin, and as a guide to the galleries 'for the information of Inquirers especially ye more ingenious,' whose curiosity he felt should be 'satisfied in any things they shall see among my Collections, and find them figured & describ'd therein wth observations on them.' Here again is the acknowledgement of the collection resting between the world of the researcher and that of the gallery-goer, and providing useful knowledge to both.

Beside the demand for support in his publishing project, Cole set out a number of other conditions with his gift, not the least of which was that it should be housed in its own repository: '[M]y Collections do onely consist of things Natural and nothing of humane art' which he dismissed 'tho most exquisitely curious ... being so extreamly inferior to ye other (especially when passing ye test of a Microscope)'. This led him to 'desire that mine may be preserved in a distinct Repository, and not swallow'd up in that wch beares an other mans name and Memory'. His reluctance to add his collection to the Ashmolean was not solely the result of *amour propre* but emerged from a sense of the merit of his specimens which 'in things Natural exceed it in number and quality, excepting those additions made unto them since their first donation, among wch are some of mine.'[27] Cole saw his collection as a valuable asset, and one which reflected positively on himself; it was a source of prestige he was loath to see subsumed into another man's museum.

The university ultimately viewed the expense of his demands as greater than the worth of the contents and declined the proffered gift. Lhwyd's report on the collection noted that the specimens 'in respect of number and Rarity are at least half as valuable as those now reposited in the Ashmolean Museum.' Furthermore 'being all of his own procureing from their native places, he is able to give account (for the most part) whence each particular came; which few masters of Collections can pretend to, tho it be very material in Natural History.'[28] However, concerns about the cost of the plates for the natural history, the timing of the benefaction and the degree

---

26 Proposals for surrendering Mr Cole's collections, Bristol, sent to Edward Lhwyd, March 1694, Ashm. 1820, ff. 57–62.
27 Proposals, 1695, Ashm. 1820, f. 68.
28 'Dr Lloyd acct of Mr Coles Museum read before ye Delegates' [n.d.], Ashm. 1820, f. 71

to which Cole was willing to provide money for the support of a keeper dissuaded the university from accepting the gift. Nonetheless, Cole's sense that his collection, used actively in the generation of knowledge about natural history, belonged in the university museum, and the keeper of the museum's equally sincere consideration of the gift, confirmed the enduring entrenchment of the museum in the prosecution of research.

In the historiography of collecting there has been a tendency to privilege the experience of those who formed large collections, who were by definition wealthy and often of the social and political elite, and of those who gave their collections to institutions. Books such as *Lives of the Founders, Augmentors, and other Benefactors of the British Museum*[29] serve to emphasise the importance of those who formed only a small fraction not only of the collecting population but also of those who gave objects to the museum. While museums have acquired many important items as part of major benefactions, the influence of those which contained only a few things should not be underestimated. On occasion treasures, such as the Alfred Jewel, were given to museums as solitary items by men with little or no other contact with the institution and no further collection. Similarly, there can be little doubt that while some groups of objects given en masse to the museum were valuable individually and as a group, other objects which arrived bundled together were of little significance. Objects of great and of little worth came into the museum through both channels.

While it is possible to divide collectors broadly into two groups – the academically enfranchised and the academically disenfranchised – this artificial division serves only to underline the continuity across the social spectrum. The museum collection was not a place to play out well-defined roles of inclusion and exclusion. Instead, perhaps because of its want of a prolonged and well-defined cultural tradition and perhaps because of its genesis as the synthesis of popular entertainment and private study, it liberally accepted all those who wished to contribute to it. And while there might be some expectation that those who came from other than the scholarly cabal would not consider themselves appropriate donors, in other words that there would be self-selection in favour of those who felt culturally at ease with the university environment, in practice the process of self-selection did not exclude those who did not share this background.

---

29   E. Edwards, *Lives of the Founders, Augmentors, and other Benefactors of the British Museum, 1570–1870* (London, 1870).

The combination of a view of the museum as the cultural inheritance of a broad segment of society, and the acknowledged importance of objects for the improvement of society, prompted the transmission of such things to the museum regardless of the status of their original owners. It was a duty as John Coakley Lettsom observed in 1774 not only to collect for 'private gratification' but 'to be useful to by distributing happiness amongst our fellow creatures'.[30]

The traditional paternalistic obligation of the elite to care for the people was extended in the collection to all those who might own signification objects. No better place for the proper keeping of these sources of communal good existed than the museum itself. The reformulation in a public institution of the pursuit and presentation of this knowledge enlarged the number of those who could feel that they were participating in this important work, even if it was only by surrendering a single object into its care. The museum united the socially disparate into a single common quest for the improvement of mankind.

The early history of the Ashmolean therefore has rather subversive things to say about collections policy. Collecting was driven by research, a notion which is anathema for many today who see the primary, if indeed not the only acceptable, role for the museum as a place of education. Further, in an atmosphere considerably more socially attenuated than that of today, scholars and common folk were able to co-operate in the creation of important collections without the benefit of guidelines. Their shared convictions about the importance of the museum and the objects which belonged there permitted the pursuit of a common goal, without its formal articulation. Perhaps, then, we need concentrate our efforts on defining the importance of the institution as a whole, rather than quibbling over policy, and let those with an interest in the concerns it adopts join freely in their prosecution.

---

30   John Coakley Lettsom, 1774, *The Naturalist's, and Traveller's Companion, Containing Instructions for Collecting & Preserving Objects of Natural History, and for Promoting Inquiries after Human Knowledge in General*, London (2nd edn), vii–viii.

6 The cartographies of collecting

Rebecca Duclos

Picture two children returning from a romp which takes them across fields and hills, along a stretch of beach, through a dense forest, and on back home along rocky tracks and well-worn paths. From a bird's eye perspective their route is a terrestrial line of flight wriggling its way through a wilderness below. Their travels are punctuated by a staccato beat of stop-and-go as they take every opportunity to add to a stock of treasures gathered along the way. How might these adventurers tell their tales of travelling? Perhaps they will extract from their pockets a collection of flowering things and sweet-smelling grasses, odd bits of bird's eggs or moth's wings, snail shells and skipping stones which will become part of their story's unravelling. Back home on the kitchen floor a map of a journey may be dramatically drawn – not with the usual cartographer's tools, but with objects and stories, artefacts and narratives. Through their attentive presentation and excited commentary, the children not only describe their circuitous route, but illustrate it, qualify it, prove its material existence while also emphasising – even exaggerating – certain of its more memorable aspects.

This simple scenario invites us to see the practices of museology and cartography as more closely linked than we have traditionally imagined. As one eight-year-old summed it up: '... all my special things make me feel like I'm part of the world'.[1] To create a collection of objects and a compendium of supporting narratives is, for these children (and for ourselves), an important means of mapping all manner of journeys. Although the assemblage of things gathered in our story may not have followed a decisive pattern of collecting at the time, the group of objects brought together serves as a testament to experiences undergone. The

---

1   M. Csikszentmihalyi and E. Rochberg-Halton, *The Meaning of Things: Domestic Symbols and the Self* (Cambridge: Cambridge University Press, 1981), 130.

collected items are not only physical specimens corresponding to points on a landscape, they represent a more abstract and infinitely expandable language of symbols which enables the children to create an endless set of prosaic and poetic maps of their adventures for others and for themselves.

In many respects the act of curating a collection is similar to that of drawing a map or creating a travelogue: each effort attempts to make what is not immediately perceivable perceivable – at least in the mind's eye. Collections and maps are both documentary and anecdotal travellers' tales, which in Stephen Greenblatt's words, are caught between the 'undifferentiated succession of local moments and a larger strategy toward which they can only gesture.'[2] As they gesture toward these other realms, museologic and cartographic endeavours use physical and narrative evidence to push the limits of a culture's 'representational technology' by referring symbolically to things beyond their own tangible presence. The configurations of mindscapes and landscapes brought forth through these practices offer traces of discovery and movement which, while given a tangible presence, derive from and give rise to intangible worlds of experience.[3]

As two- and three-dimensional entities struggling to transport us into the deeper dimensions of time and space, both the map and the collection-as-map oscillate in representational limbo. They are message-bearing entities that operate metonymically (having a direct relationship to a specific body of material or a landscape), but also metaphorically (acquiring symbolic value related to, but not necessarily representational of, their origins).[4] This duality gives these entities a solidity of form with a fluidity of function. When orienting us through exhibition or atlas to destinations of an aesthetic or geographical nature, museological and topographical 'maps' allow individuals to journey uniquely through physical and metaphysical territories of their own choosing. This ability to configure intellectual as well as emotional routes of travel is a characteristic shared by museological

---

2   S. Greenblatt, 1991, *Marvelous Possessions: The Wonder of the New World* (Oxford: Clarendon Press, 1988), 3.

3   See G. Kavanagh, 'Objects as evidence or not?', in S. Pearce (ed), *Museum Studies in Material Culture* (Leicester: Leicester University Press, 1989), 125–37; S. Pearce, *Museums Objects and Collections; A Cultural Study* (Leicester: Leicester University Press, 1992), 36–67.

4   Pearce, ibid., 26–30.

and cartographic productions, a linkage which may be fruitfully explored by practitioners in the two fields.

Although many contemporary studies of collections incorporate a diversity of outside sources in their analyses, writings from the field of cultural geography rarely make an appearance in museum studies bibliographies. Such authors as James Clifford, Edward Said or Mary-Louise Pratt draw upon this discipline in their work, but it is in the context of anthropology, more than museology, that these authors meld theoretical traditions.[5] In museum studies, specifically, associated fields such as cultural geography could be used more readily to examine topics relating to the 'cartographic power' of imperial assemblages, as well as critically questioning the relationship between topography and taxonomy in the collecting of natural history specimens.

When approached from a cultural geography perspective, future museological studies may be directed toward any number of research areas. For instance, we might question how the ownership of colonised lands was cartographically secured through the mapping of territories, production of travelogues and publication of anthropological tracts, while simultaneously asserted through the material seizure of artefacts, cataloguing of specimens and display of collected objects. Another area of inquiry for museum scholars and post-colonial theorists pertains to the foreign importation of topographical and taxonomic analyses, often articulated in museum settings, which forever altered indigenous relationships toward the land. And finally, an unrealised project of some depth would be the comparative study of disciplinary developments in museology and cartography to see how these two practices of 'surveillance' have shaped the ways in which we have come to know our world.

Cartographies of collecting

This sweep of topics from the political to the aesthetic, in which museology and cartography have the potential to intersect, can only grow larger as our understanding of collections and our definition of mapping expands. This chapter looks at some aspects of the 'cartographies of collecting' and

---

5   J. Clifford, *The Predicament of Culture: 20th Century Ethnography, Literature, and Art* (Cambridge, Mass.: Harvard University Press, 1988); E. Said, *Orientalism* (New York: Pantheon Books, 1978); M.-L. Pratt, *Imperial Eyes: Travel Writing and Transculturation* (New York: Routledge, 1992).

questions how the aesthetic, taxonomic and symbolic value of objects is used in constructing a notion of place, and how place is, in turn, integral in creating a sense of identity.

Our opening story of the two children and their object-laden adventure has encouraged us to think of collecting as a form of mapping, but it also invites more complex readings which may be subsequently investigated. Three themes will emerge in the pages that follow: (1) collections have historically created their own topographies of space, externally generated, but often internally explored and re-visited; (2) collecting and mapping have a darker side, sometimes being used to assert a powerful presence in a foreign land through practices of displacement and replacement; and finally (3) assemblages of items map out what we might call landscapes of desire – real or imagined destinations to which we can travel using objects as our symbolic guides.

These themes will be paired with source materials ranging from history, to installation art, to poetry. The discussion moves from the contained worlds of early display cabinets to the relatively unexplored terrain where contemporary art and museological principles converge, resting finally in the more metaphorically open spaces of literary landscape. Whether we speak of displays that strive to map the unknown and possess the exotic in eighteenth-century Europe, or visit museological critiques which upset the taxonomical regimentation of colonial Australian collecting, or focus on one writer's attempt to poetically chart the imagined topographies of an Arctic landscape – we do so in order to find correspondences between collecting and mapping. The diversity of examples chosen is quite purposeful in order to illustrate the many areas of human thought and creativity in which objects, materially and immaterially, hold a uniquely 'cartographic' power to secure a sense of place and situate our notions of self.

Flowering things and sweet-smelling grasses

Topography, much like mapping, is becoming a signature word of cultural theorists as they describe the various 'contours' of argument; intellectual 'vistas' of thought; or twists and turns, peaks and valleys of disciplinary growth. The metaphorical potentials of geographical terminology are being quickly exhausted and museologists should certainly exercise some caution before jumping into the fray. Having said this, however, there has already been a natural adoption of geographical references in museological parlance, especially when discussing parallel 'explorations' of cartographers and museologists in the sixteenth to the eighteenth centuries. As James Welu writes in his catalogue essay, 'Strange new worlds: mapping the heaven's and earth's great extent':

> It should come as no surprise that Europe's obsession with the marvellous closely paralleled the great age of exploration ... Maps of this period presented the opportunity to trace the routes of important voyages and to share some of the wonders encountered by the explorers themselves.[6]

It was not only through maps, charts, and travel accounts that Europeans came to know the strange and exotic lands abroad, but also through the unique collections of 'marvellous' things brought back from exploratory voyages. With the subsequent creation of special cabinets, and later, galleries, to contain these objects, displays played a part in the mapping of new lands using artefactual rather than cartographic symbols to make accessible what would otherwise remain inaccessible to the domestic viewer.[7]

The natural world was physically contained, allowing the cabinet to express the 'world as a view', not only symbolically, but materially as well. As John Barret-Lennard argues, the development of technologies for classification and cataloguing subsequently allowed the natural world to be both archivised and textualised within institutional settings. With reference to the collecting and recording practices of the Museum of Economic Botany in Adelaide, Australia, Barret-Lennard speaks of the Museum 'reconfiguring the environment' using the 'textual tools' of an already accepted language which would '... describe and interpret things which remained unseen, or whose context of origin was unknown to the final writer and reader'.[8]

The territory of Australia was thus renamed and repackaged for consumption and distribution beyond its borders. As the melange of specimens and objects expanded, so too did the opportunities to

---

6   J. Welu, 'Strange new worlds: mapping the heaven's and the earth's great extent', in J. Kenseth, ed., *The Age of the Marvelous* (Vermont: Stinehour Press, 1991), 103.

7   T. Bennett, *The Birth of the Museum: History, Theory, Politics* (New York: Routledge, 1995), 33–47.

8   J. Barrett-Lennard, 'Projects for two museums', in J. Barrett-Lennard and C. Barnes (eds), *Peter Cripps: Projects For Two Museums* (Adelaide: University of South Australia Art Museum, 1993), 16.

reconfigure the natural world. Collections reached for that infinite and yet unattainable capability to map the world; their ordering principles gave abstract concepts and unfamiliar cultures a degree of tangibility which allowed their viewers to act as explorers – in a sense, as artefactual cartographers.

In identifying collecting with exploration we are able to suggest certain affinities between the two practices, affinities which help us to posit links between mapping and collection making. At the centre of the pairing we might place the concept of 'wonder', that which in Stephen Greenblatt's words is: 'thrilling, potentially dangerous, momentarily immobilizing, charged at once with desire, ignorance and fear – the quintessential response to what Descartes calls a "first encounter"'.[9]

Wonder, Greenblatt writes, was an almost inevitable component in the discourse of discovery, as was 'the marvellous' or 'the curious' in the discourse of collecting. We might assume that wonder was most profoundly stimulated by those 'first encounters' explorers and collectors shared alike as they gazed upon an unprecedented array of objects in cultural context, many of which had never before been seen or even imagined.

In its mediating role, the collection became both a map of discovery and a catalyst for psychic travel; it was able to arouse in its spectators similar feelings of astonishment and desire as felt by the explorers. Given the sixteenth-century interest in apocalyptic associations, focused through the curation of the supernatural, the natural, and the artificial,[10] collections assumed both the status of symbolic messengers from mysterious places and of material icons representing lands and peoples never before encountered. In terms of the collector's cabinet, an assemblage of objects was marvellous in its ability to excite a plethora of feelings: fear, delight, confusion, the magic of curiosity, and a desire for the unknown.

Krzysztof Pomian points out that collections encouraged the self to encounter the world through external means (artefacts and specimens) which were bound up with the internal, emotional responses of the collector. He describes the ideal 'topographies' of the private collection as it attempted to map the world. Its physical layout, influenced by sixteenth-

---

9   Greenblatt, op. cit., 20.

10   J. Kenseth, 'The age of the marvelous: an introduction', in J. Kenseth, ed., *The Age of the Marvelous* (Vermont: Stinehour Press, 1991), 25–55.

and seventeenth-century geographic conceptions, was intimately tied to that which was metaphysical and cosmological. For geographers of the period the four continents, which represented 'the whole of the inhabited world', were embodied through allegorical figures, but also by examples of the continents' native peoples, animals, plants, minerals and artefacts. This coupling of the symbolic and the actual represent, in Pomian's view, 'all the main categories of objects', an entire series which 'presents us with a sort of pictorial inventory of the world intended to be exhaustive not only in a geographical sense but also in the way objects are apportioned to different categories'.[11]

In this passage, Pomian significantly links the two notions of embodiment and exemplification. To be properly understood, the four continents needed to be embodied by an allegorical figure and represented by examples of peoples, animals, plants, minerals and artefacts. Early on, it seems, the spatial arrangement of collections was intimately tied to both its museological and representational effectiveness. Not only was the categorical arrangement in the cabinet central to the creation of a desired microcosm of artificialia and naturalia, but symbolic properties of objects had to then relate to even more complex orders of the macrocosm. As Eilean Hooper-Greenhill argues,[12] the 'assembling of the world' within the confines of the cabinet had everything to do with the collector making that world graspable and controllable. Operating on many levels, the presentation of the collection worked in a map-like way to construct the world by first ordering it and then interpreting that order so as to create a sense of place within the uncharted expanse of the cosmos.

Joy Kenseth's curation of the Hood Museum exhibition, 'The Age of the Marvellous', associates the collector's intense fascination with the marvellous with '... those things or events that were unusual, unexpected, exotic, extraordinary or rare.'[13] In the sixteenth and seventeenth centuries especially, it was expeditions returning from the Americas, the Orient, the Middle and Far East, as well as Africa, which brought both new objects into the European cabinet and new life to the European imagination. The tangible proof of cartographic claims appeared in the form of artefacts,

---

11   K. Pomian, *Collectors and Curiosities: Paris and Venice, 1500–1800* (Cambridge: Polity Press, 1987), 51.
12   E. Hooper-Greenhill, *Museums and the Shaping of Knowledge* (London: Routledge, 1992), 82.
13   Kenseth, op. cit., 25.

artworks and specimens which were avidly sought by European collectors and museums. As this imported exotica moved from geographical to museological sites, diverse worlds were brought together and significantly linked. Within this shifted framework, where contexts of origin and display radically diverged, collections were forced to take on entirely new geocultural orientations. For those with access to the melange of objects assembled, collections challenged viewers to acknowledge foreign peoples and places. Seen as the three-dimensional tools by which the art of the cartographer was visibly enriched, museological displays became the key to bringing topographical surveys to life by transforming them into cultural encounters.[14]

As the exchange of information and artefacts increased, and as cabinets and private museums became more numerous, ordinary individuals and extraordinary collectors could participate, at least to some degree, in the discoveries of the explorers. They witnessed places already visited and events previously transpired but were able, in their engagement with transplanted objects, to recreate the wonder of contact for themselves. Theirs was a removed interaction, but one no less potent in its effect. As demonstrated by the children who share their treasures with all who gather in the kitchen, 'what matters most takes place not "out there" or along the receptive surfaces of the body where the self encounters the world, but deep within, at the vital, emotional centre of the witness.'[15] Greenblatt compares the vigorousness of this response to a 'heart in terror'. So strong is the experience of awe and amazement that, like the heart skipping a beat, it cannot be marginalised or denied. 'Wonder', he writes, 'is absolutely exigent, a primary or radical passion.'[16]

And so, as this primary, radical passion progresses in cartographic terms, museological practices follow suit. In making inroads to an emotional centre through collecting activities, a rite of passage and a right of way are simultaneously granted to a collector. Like the children who carefully select and then gather up their flowering things and sweet-smelling grasses, a collector may scan their store of precious items and visit or return to places existing outside of their everyday experience. Perhaps this is the most impressive cartographic quality of collections: that geographical and

---

14   Barrett-Lennard, op. cit., 16–17.
15   Greenblatt, op. cit., 16.
16   Ibid., 17.

psychological topographies can be seen in the mind's eye and marvelled at whenever the mood strikes. In this sense, the viewer of the collection is accorded the same privilege as the student of maps: '... to contemplate at home and right before our eyes the things that are farthest away.' To excite a sense of wonder, to collapse the boundaries of time and distance, to travel between the present, the past, and future – we have made and will continue to make use of the cartographies of collecting in order to steer our way through a myriad of actual and imaginative worlds.

Birds' eggs and moths' wings

The collection's power to generate imaginary topographies through which a viewer may travel has indeed been used to create images of worlds whose true landscapes are unreachable. This power can, however, be a very volatile, very persuasive power, one used to focus a viewer's eye only upon carefully selected aspects of a land's natural diversity. In every projected landscape full of flowering things and sweet-smelling grasses there are other unsightly parts – the broken bird's egg or tattered moth wing – which may have been weeded out of the presentation. Considered as exclusive rather than inclusive sites, the controlled cabinets of curiosity represent reinterpreted landscapes whose natural roughness and threatening mystery has been suppressed or exaggerated in order to quell a collector's anxiety or pique a society's fantasy.

The desire to know, to understand and to control our environment has always been a very strong one and our various attempts to master nature are well analysed in nearly all disciplinary traditions. In museology and geography, especially, it is the tools of our management – taxonomic definition, classification schemes, topographic grids and cultural surveys – which receive the brunt of criticism. In our efforts to contextualise and make hierarchical, the world around us we rely not only upon our powers of observation, but also, many critics have shown, upon our powers of manipulation and domination.[17]

---

17   See M. Foucault, *The Order of Things: An Archaeology of the Human Sciences* (New York: Vintage Books, 1973); Said, op. cit.; K. Walsh, *The Representation of the Past: Museums and Heritage in the Post-modern World* (London: Routledge, 1992); J. Duncan and D. Ley, *Place/Culture/Representation* (London: Routledge, 1993); Bennett, op. cit.

For the children, a particular landscape was encountered and, in a way, tamed by their having passed through it – by their having extracted elements from it which serve to record their movement. This form of mapping, as we have said, helps chart a route but, more importantly, it asserts a presence by memorialising an event and capturing an ephemeral experience for posterity. Echoing Pomian's earlier use of the word 'embodiment,' Jonathan Smith implies that museological and cartographic acts are ultimately about concretising and preserving events through the creation of a language of transformed symbols. Smith writes: 'we might say that the recorded or embodied event is more real than the unrecorded event because, transformed into symbols, it is able to exist beyond the time and the place of its original enactment'.[18] This is a second aspect of the children's cartographic collection: it exists physically and is lasting whereas the day's journey has been lost to a temporal and spatial past. The environment encountered by the adventurers exists now only in its re-presentable form as embodied landscape, not as landscape itself. However, with their collected objects the children possess the necessary symbols to make their travels in nature as real as they can be for others because they can name, order and re-present the elements of the landscape in very decisive ways. Since others were not present during the original enactment of the collecting process, a great deal of trust is placed in the children's account told through the symbols they have brought back home. Although the curation of the children's artefacts and narratives is hardly what we would call manipulative, the example of their interpreted objects suggests that the tripartite relationship between the land, its collected specimens, and their interpreted exhibition has not always been an easy one.

This issue, within a very specific historical and geographical context, has been the subject of a recent installation in the Museum of Economic Botany in Adelaide, Australia. In 1993, conceptual artist Peter Cripps staged 'Projects For Two Museums', a double exhibition, with one project being an intervention in the Adelaide Museum's 1870s display of botanical specimens.[19] Cripps's aim was to demonstrate that colonial institutions were a powerful and decisive (if not politely ignored) force in what Australian historian Paul Carter has called the 'rhetorical settling' of land.

---

18 J. Smith, 'The lie that blinds: destabilizing the text of landscape', in Duncan and Ley, op. cit., 80–1.

19 Barrett-Lennard and Barnes, op. cit.

Cripps's artistic intervention echoes Carter's historical interrogation of the taxonomic urge which informed all manner of colonial initiatives. 'How', queries Carter, 'does exploration differ from that other great eighteenth century naming discipline, botany?'[20] Uncovering the ways in which the ownership of a new found Australia occurred, in part, through the naming and classification of its topographical features has been a strong research area drawing upon the expertise of scientists, historians and cultural geographers. Added to that list are now artists and museologists whose work moves the research into the sphere of cultural and exhibiting institutions.

In an effort to understand the strategic renaming of the land deemed 'Terra Nullus' by Europeans, early land surveys, exploration narratives and government documents of colonial Australia have been the most common sources of information. Cripps's artistic questioning of the museum's role in the process adds an important and complex layer to this inquiry. In its subtle effort to be interdisciplinary through a combined use of archival, architectural, visual and museologic evidence, Cripps's critique is reminiscent of that produced by other conceptual artists from Marcel Broodthaers to Fred Wilson.[21] With Cripps, we have further proof that a new style of museo-centric art is continuing to evolve, and with it, the potential to have curators, museologists and artists produce exhibitions with a unusual critical edge and visual potency.

The Museum of Economic Botany is one of those rare institutions whose display area remains much as it was when first built. Set up in the late 1800s, the museum had a number of official purposes: to provide enjoyment, act as a research institute, and facilitate economic development. However, it also signalled more imperialistic pursuits. It was, as Cripps's catalogue points out, '... not just a colonial institution, one that in its grace and solidity signalled the achievements of the colony, but an agent in the process of colonisation and colonial development'.[22] For Cripps to interpret the Adelaide Museum collection in terms of agency was to see it not as a static map listing Australia's botanica, but as an applied tool in the surveying and re-naming of a colonised land.

---

20 P. Carter, *The Road to Botany Bay: An Exploration of Landscape and History* (New York: Alfred A. Knopf, 1988), 18.

21 L. Corrin, *Mining the Museum: An Installation by Fred Wilson* (New York: New York Press, 1994).

22 Barrett-Lennard, op. cit., 13.

Although Australia's natural features and plant life were already mapped out by the Aborigines within their own complex understanding of the environment, these indigenous conceptions of the land did not conform to those of the white settlers. The newcomers were not so much interested in learning about the space in which others lived as they were in claiming an idea of place which they themselves could describe, possess, and soon inhabit. They did this through means such as collecting, labelling and arranging external elements within internal frameworks of order as justified by the motherland. Such activities were part of transforming 'spatial extension into a spatial text' by creating a colonial map of Australian place-names, property boundaries and geophysical realities which would establish the new settlers' dominant position within the landscape.[23]

Cripps uses a combination of inserted objects, mirrors, archival text and built forms such as seed pods and shell-like encasings to draw attention to the museum's own form of rhetoric. Using these devices the artist attempts to relate the museum's internally controlled topography to the desire for control of the outside world. Cripps's strategic interventions in the gallery space serve to both interpret and interrupt the visitor's journey through the display's carefully mapped-out progression of thought. To walk around the space is to physically experience the scientific discourse of empirical classification: knowledge is revealed across a horizontal field of glass cases; our view is punctuated by upright cabinets impeccably ordered; supervising our passage are the watchful eyes of eminent founding fathers. Into this landscape, Cripps brings mirrors which reflect hidden parts of the museological regimentation. Underneath cases he provokes investigation through objects, text and lights. Up above, he replaces the authoritative stares of ancestral statues with self-reflecting glass. Along the aisles he deposits casings with interior lists of terms equating order with power, economy with botany. The overall effect is to make our interaction with the space a charged one. Our physical, museological experience is infused with a more metaphorical insistence that museums, like maps, must be read as representational entities which do not simply reflect the world but actively conceive, articulate and structure our relationship to its elements.

As Cripps illustrates, the physical space of a gallery and the psychical relationship we have to objects are very powerful forces. When these forces

---

23   Carter, op. cit., 50.

are harnessed in the form of publications or exhibitions to promote particular visions – visions of exotic places kept at a safe distance, economically exploitable environments, or pristine landscapes supporting a life of naive innocence – museum productions can have a profound effect upon public consciousness. In this example, where the creation of an Australian national identity was encouraged by exhibitionary strategies we can see how the collection of specimens was just another way to map the land and contain its natural features within a recognisable and repeatable format. As exhibitions became part of the claiming and mythologising of the new-found land, surveyors and scientists, landscape painters and topographers legitimised their visions through a vast network of representational outlets including both cultural institutions and geographic publications.

These troubling reminders of our tragically ambitious taxonomising are crucial to confront. Through their critique and reinterpretation, historical displays reveal much about the ways in which we have both displaced and replaced ourselves and others in an effort to make sense of where we stand in an ever-changing world. The acts of collecting and mapping are, by definition, decisive, selective interventions into our surrounding environment and it is through these practices that we attempt to mark a presence. Like the children who select and save precious evidence of their journey, we too want our presence to be acknowledged and perpetuated long after we have travelled elsewhere. What is left in the end, however, are not so much lines of movement but traces of thought which are subject to the tides of time washing in new readings and shifted interpretations.

Snail shells and skipping stones

There is a children's game called 'Snail' which is played on the beach when the tide is low and the wide expanse of sand running down to the water's edge hardens in the sun. The game begins when an enormous spiralling snail shell is inscribed and its interior space divided into squares – much like a hopscotch game which tapers concentrically inward. The object of the game is to pitch stones into various squares where an opponent must retrieve them while hopping on one foot. With each retrieval the hopper must stay on only one foot, avoid toppling over, and continue all the way into the centre square of the snail before they are finished. If the hopper is successful they keep the retrieved stone, if not, they must forfeit two of their stones to their opponent, whose turn is then taken. Whoever is the first to hold ten stones wins the game and claims the rocky cache as proof of victory for that round. The greatest prize of all is to be able to keep the precious playing pieces which had originally been chosen with great care by each of the contestants. The collecting of the playing stones is a crucial element in the pre-game ritual, with a beach-wide search producing a fine array of specimens which, through the act of collecting, become transformed into valuable keepsakes. The degree of a stone's perfection gives the opponents extra incentive to capture and keep it as a token of the game, but also to admire it as a beautiful object in and of itself.

To this day we can imagine small collections of these rocks hidden away in closets everywhere, perhaps accompanying other bits of seaside memorabilia whose significance is known only to the keeper. These stones are more than just stones since they hold sensual memories within them: the screech of a gull overhead, the itch of sand between the toes, the sighing of the ocean as it gives itself up to another sunset. Although this childhood stash represents a rather typical example of a nostalgic collection, the game of 'Snail' does have particular literal and symbolic significance for discussing a third aspect of the cartographies of collecting.

In its physical aspect, the collection of snail stones demonstrates how even the most motley assortment of objects may be tied to special moments in our past; how, when discovering that box in the closet, we may be brought back to a beach where we spent many summers as children, or as adults watching our children play. We might yearn for that playful physicality or wish that competition could always be so innocent. Collections such as these allow us to travel to another place, to another time, perhaps even inhabit another body. We are able to navigate our way between the reality of what is present to the remembrance of what has passed.

Symbolically – with its inward spiralling curves and discreet spaces marked off within a larger, unified form – the 'Snail' game is a map of our memory. In touching the smoothness of our skipping stones and making a mental pitch into the spiral of the past we set psychic landmarks to help us reach back to our individual and communal histories. For this inner rehearsal of memories the map in hand is a familiar one; we know how to use objects as navigational tools to move between worlds of experience, between the external and the internal. As we travel towards the centre in the game of 'Snail',

> we are in a poetic world of myth and metaphor where each of us can live with the chaos of experience and turn it into a little personal sense through the

transforming power of collected objects. These offer us an enclosed and private world, where collections mirror and extend our bodies and souls.[24]

As stimuli for geographic imaginings or catalysts for a 'cartographic consciousness', objects have an immense amount of emotional, locomotive power. They are able, especially, to arouse memories of being in a particular place at a particular time and to resituate us within those memories in present and future contexts. In this way, collected objects both 'mirror and extend' our images of self as that self is continually reviewed during the cycles of life. Susan Pearce's comment suggests that these images and cycles are intimately connected to enclosed and private worlds and passages through life which are in turn shaped by the transforming, but also transporting, power of collections.

Finding words to discuss the relationship between objects and abstract concepts such as transformation and transportation is not easy. Museological language is continually reaching for a more poetic tone when attempting to describe the psychic spaces which objects help us to reach. Many collectors, curators, and writers struggle to find ways to articulate how collections work in terms of memory, nostalgia, or sentimentality, but, in their struggle, they often lose sight of what is most magical about the way in which memory itself functions. Cartographers face similar difficulties as they, too, are given the task of rethinking how maps work upon us, how topographic plans translate complex messages about space and time and distance while also acting as triggers for remembrance or instigators of desire. One quality common to both collections and maps (perhaps a linking theme for museologists and cartographers) is their ability to move their viewers so passionately between the visible and the invisible, between what is here and what lies there, between presence and absence.

For John Moss, the author of *Enduring Dreams: An Exploration of Arctic Landscape*, the world he imagines in his wandering mind is often configured through objects. In one poem included in the section, 'The Cartography of Dreams,' the writer's memory works through the *inukshuit*, the stone constructions whose recognizable forms and graceful solidity are the 'Arctic's vivid language in rock,' that are able to '... save a traveller's life,

---

24   S. Pearce, 'Collecting as medium and message', in E. Hooper-Greenhill, ed., *Museum, Media, Message* (London: Routledge, 1995), 21.

lead a hunter to food, and offer solace to a spirit seeker'.[25] When Moss conjures up the presence of these structures, he uses image and metaphor as a way of translating both the intimacy and expanse of an arctic landscape in which he travels. His thought and his memory take on a decisively cartographic quality as he reminds us: 'You do not imagine yourself without imagining where in the world you are ...'

With these words Moss insists that memory and imagination are inevitably situational, that our dreams and visions take place in a location which is integrally bound to our sense of self as it is perceived within that situation. But Moss also cues us to acknowledge the transient quality of memory, especially as it is mediated by language and by objects. His stone figures are both artefact and symbol in his poem, offering themselves as navigational icons which mark out the liminality of our remembering selves:

> one:
> inukshuk.
> Now imagine two:
> inukshuuk,
> the length of perception between them, on rocky promontories
> separated by indeterminate terrain ...
>
> you are nowhere, neither there
> nor where you are. You are
> on one side or another
> of the line between the stone figures in your mind,
> within a field defined
> only by the limits
> of what you see.[26]

We are always 'on one side or another – of the line between the stone figures' in our minds. This is both the frustration and the enticement of memory and the fascination we have with objects and their ability to transport us to another place. Darting from object to image, from reality to sentimentality, the mind is a constant traveller. We feel the wholeness of presence with an object which, strangely enough, is a reminder of absence –

---

25   N. Hallendy, 'The Silent Messengers', *Equinox*, January/February (85) (1996), 36-45, 37.

26   J. Moss, *Enduring Dreams: An Exploration of Arctic Landscape* (Ontario: Anansi, 1994).

of those places accessible only through imagination. This is also the paradox of looking at a map which creates a rigid image of landscape at the same time it invites us to move through its intangible, ephemeral, and ultimately unmappable parts.

We are, though, as Moss writes, constrained within a field defined 'only by the limits' of what we can see. If we were to fixate on the physical presence of the stone *inukshuik* alone, or travel through territory known only by its mapped out web of red and blue road lines, we would indeed be constrained by our lack of vision and imagination. Fortunately, we neither see nor remember in so literal a way, but instead, allow for a 'permutation of pairings' to surface where reality and memory can interplay and physicality finds a way to fade into poetry.

> Imagine many: inukshuit.
> Each stone figure centred in its own terrain;
> from each to every other
> a line extends and taken all in all
> the permutation of their pairings
> like a topographic grid
> holds the landscape in place,
> a dreamscape fixed like a holograph
> approaching perfection
> in the wandering mind.
>
> You do not imagine the world
> unless you imagine your absence
> among its particulars.

We experience the world through a rich combination of the graspable and the ungraspable – at times longing for the presence of things most deeply when we are absent from them. Although a feeling of placelessness may overwhelm us in the midst of an object-inspired reverie – being 'neither there nor where you are' – we still have a need and desire to have our spirit travel to places which have been important to us. It is objects like our snail shells and skipping stones which ultimately help us to reach destinations inside ourselves. Akin to the stone figures centred in their own terrain, the physical and psychical presence of objects in the terrain of a collection combine to form a symbolic grid of memory coordinates which give an assemblage a metaphysical cartography of its own. In Moss's poetic language, which is perhaps the only true way we can get across the transformational and transportational power of objects, the collection gives us a sense of presence, even in absence.

Mapping all manner of journeys

Like the map, the collection offers itself as a tangible entity for contemplation, its particular arrangement helping to orient its viewer towards specific themes, chronological sequences, geographic, aesthetic, or cultural points of view. But at the same time, the collection operates on another dimension. It has a metonymic, representational power that allows a viewer to move beyond it, as a traveller moves from the dot on the map into that vast, uncharted landscape of personal encounter which the map is said to represent. To study the cartography of a collection is, then, to study it as if it were a game of 'Snail' – acting as a complex entity that functions on both physical and metaphysical levels to continually pull us toward an unknown centre. As an intentional creation, the collection provides a mental compass by which a person attempts to locate themselves, spatially, temporally and psychically, in relation to other people and other places.

The map of identity in Pomian's seventeenth-century cabinet was one which melded the material with the cosmological to create a pictorial inventory of the world. Peter Cripps's intervention in a museum's taxonomic topography revealed the complex relationship between certain regimes of display and man's desire to create a supremely ordered map of his environment. These examples suggest strongly that collecting and assembling are, in the broadest sense of the word, about mapping. If we understand mapping to be a representational practice which defines a physical notion of space but also creates a more metaphysical memory of place, we have succeeded in moving ourselves beyond standard geographic definitions. Likewise, when we are able to interpret objects in terms of their transportational and transformational powers, we will add a significant dimension to our museological analyses by recognising that collections have their own inherent metaphorical cartographies.

7 From curio to cultural document

Barbara Lawson

Collections of ethnographic objects sit uneasily in storage or on display in museums around the world – many with stories long forgotten, others with pasts shamefully remembered. The global estimate of cultural materials held by museums is over 4.5 million artefacts; more than 80% of these objects are inadequately documented.[1] Recent concerns with representation, repatriation and deaccessioning accompanied by the realities of shrinking budgets, reductions in curatorial staff and increasingly crowded storage facilities make maintaining existing collections, as well as continued collecting, controversial topics.

Before the question of continued collecting can be addressed, there is a need to assess the state of present ethnographic holdings in museums. Since documented collections are less problematic in terms of their continued support by museums, they will not be included in the discussion that follows.[2] The aim here is to provide an overview of past ethnographic collecting, chiefly nineteenth-century practices, and to examine the potential of resultant collections for study and use. The focus is a collection

---

1   W. Sturtevant, 'Does anthropology need museums?', *Proceedings of the Biological Society of Washington*, 82 (1969), 619-50; B. Reynolds and M. Stott (eds), *Material Anthropology* (Lanham, Maryland: University Press of America, 1987), 8.

2   Less than 20 per cent of ethnographic collections are documented. See W. Chapman, 'Pitt Rivers and his collection, 1874–1883', in B. Cranstone and S. Seidenberg (eds), *The General's Gift: A Celebration of the Pitt Rivers Museum Centenary 1884–1984* (Oxford: JASO, 1984), 6–25; D. Cole, *Captured Heritage* (Vancouver: Douglas and McIntyre, 1985); C. Hinsley, *Savages and Scientists* (Washington, DC: Smithsonian Institution Press, 1981), 194–200; Sturtevant, *Op. Cit.*, 622–3; G. Stocking (ed), *Objects and Others* (Madison: University of Wisconsin Press, 1985), 6–8; D. van Keuren, 'Museums and ideology: Augustus Pitt-Rivers, anthropological museums, and social change in later Victorian Britain', *Victorian Studies*, 28 (1984), 171–89.

of 125 objects from the New Hebrides,[3] donated to a Canadian university museum around 1890. Historical research provided valuable contextualisation for this undocumented collection, and its unique nature was recognised. A visit to Erromango, the remote South Pacific island where this material had been collected over a century ago, provided an opportunity to exchange information about these objects.

Examination of undocumented collections assists in distinguishing objects that can contribute to an understanding of the past or have value for the present from those candidates for potential deaccessioning. The relations between historic ethnographic collections and communities will then be considered to determine whether these objects have a place in contemporary museum practice. These deliberations may offer useful criteria for addressing the issue of contemporary ethnographic collecting.

Nineteenth-century curios as potential cultural documents

Before the emergence of popular photography, objects provided an important means of representing exotic places and peoples. The practice of collecting ethnographic materials prior to the twentieth century for 'cabinets of curiosities', and later for museums, has been well documented.[4] Objects were gathered and placed in museums in connection with the large-scale historical processes of economic development and nationalism in Europe and North America, especially those relating to colonial domination.

The early decades of collecting coincided with a period of rapid, intensive culture change in many non-Western societies. Early collectors of ethnographic material included sea captains, sailors, traders, naturalists, missionaries, military personnel, administrators and travellers. Collecting was a two-way process, with local concerns and collecting interests working occasionally in concert, but often in opposition to one another. The exchange of goods was mediated by a variety of local factors and collecting interests, including seasonal cycles, remuneration, aesthetic fashion and individual bias. Objects were received as gifts, in exchange for trade goods

---

3   Now the independent Republic of Vanuatu.
4   See, for example, E. Carpenter, 'Collectors and collections', *Natural History*, 85(3) (1976), 56–67; Cole, op. cit.; A. Kaeppler, *'Artificial Curiosities' being an Exposition of Native Manufactures Collected on the Three Pacific Voyages of Captain James Cook* (Honolulu: Bishop Museum Press, 1978).

or cash, or occasionally taken as souvenirs of hostile or pleasant encounters. They were also stolen. Yet thefts were likely to incur more in the way of risk than advantage, since collecting endeavours prior to the twentieth century were generally subordinate to other activities, which might be placed in jeopardy by the unethical removal of objects. Most items removed by early collectors were replaceable; however, there were many local manufactures that became obsolete as cultures were transformed by extensive contact.

Ethnological objects in museums are not merely tangible evidence of an 'other' reality, but also strong and revealing indices of intercultural processes.[5] The very lack of disciplinary methodology in the gathering of these objects has resulted in a natural layering of material goods, corresponding in kind and quantity with successive cultural encounters. A cross-section of these deposited cultural symbols reveals articles that were discarded as they were being replaced by non-indigenous materials, goods that were sold or exchanged to participate in an increasingly cash-oriented economy, or items intentionally rooted out by those with plans to alter local behaviour such as traders, missionaries, and colonial administrators.

Collection history has been used as a means of determining the authenticity of objects and the soundness of details regarding provenance, age, and other supporting documentation.[6] Specific consideration of the context in which a collection was made, however, imparts information about the manufacture and use of objects, offers insights regarding the relation between local and introduced material culture, and reveals the historically contingent, intercultural relations that made collecting possible. It also exposes the types of foreign, local, cultural, and individual influences at work when certain items were selected, while others were left behind.

---

5   A. Appadurai (ed), *The Social Life of Things* (Cambridge: Cambridge University Press, 1986); J. Clifford, *The Predicament of Culture* (Cambridge, Mass.: Harvard University Press, 1988); N. Thomas, *Entangled Objects* (Cambridge, Mass.: Harvard University Press, 1991).

6   A. Kaeppler, 'Anthropology and the U.S. Exploring Expedition', in H. Viola and C. Margolis (eds), *Magnificent Voyagers* (Washington D.C.: Smithsonian Institution Press, 1985), 119–47; D. Waite, *Artefacts from the Solomon Islands in the Julius L. Brenchley Collection* (London: British Museum Publications, 1987).

The case of the Robertson New Hebrides collection

The Redpath Museum is a natural history museum founded in 1882 by Sir William Dawson, a well-known palaeontologist and McGill University's fifth principal. The museum's holdings include palaeontological, mineralogical, zoological and ethnological collections. The Ethnology Collections of the Redpath Museum have been selected for this examination of museum stratigraphy because they reveal a virtually undisturbed pattern of Canadian contact with 'exotic' peoples.[7] Although these collections have endured their own particular history of isolation and obfuscation, very few alterations to the original corpus have occurred. Their geographic scope is global and reflects Canadian national and commercial endeavours of the late nineteenth and early twentieth centuries. These sparsely documented and idiosyncratically gathered collections are typical of those found in museums that came into existence during the last century when nationalistic ventures and economic development facilitated Western contact with a variety of distant lands and peoples. Doctors, missionaries, geologists and travellers, many of whom had been enlisted to participate in various British imperial or commercial endeavours in different regions of the world, were among the museum's early donors. Although most of these early supporters were affiliated with McGill University, the Redpath's ethnological and archaeological collections, being neither systematic nor the work of professional anthropologists, were not acquired or displayed in a manner that accorded with the museological principles of the emergent discipline of anthropology.

This case study begins with a typically undocumented nineteenth-century museum collection lacking in all but the most rudimentary contextual data: no collection dates, no donor information except for a name, occasional geographical locations, and a description of the object – often limited to a word or two.[8] The collection was donated between 1883 and 1896 by the Reverend H.A. Robertson, address unknown. It consisted of 125 objects: barkcloth, clubs, bows, arrows, spears, skirts and ornaments. Labels

---

7   The Redpath's ethnology collections comprise over 16,000 ethnological and archaeological artefacts with particular concentrations from central Africa, Oceania and ancient Egypt.

8   B. Lawson, *Collected Curios: Missionary Tales from the South Seas* (Montreal: McGill University Libraries, 1994) provides more in-depth discussion.

indicated their origin in the New Hebrides, islands situated some 2200 kilometres north-east of Sydney, Australia. Although noted as being on display in the Redpath's *Guide to Visitors* (1885), there was little to explain the presence of these objects in Montreal, roughly half way round the world from where they were manufactured and utilised.

I checked a variety of local sources and archives for additional information thinking that the path from the New Hebrides to Montreal was rather an unusual one for the 1880s, and convinced that some clear indication linking these two distant locales would be forthcoming. Unfortunately, nothing materialised until I came across a footnote in a work discussing the mid nineteenth-century sandalwood trade in the south-western Pacific. This trade supplied China with large quantities of sandalwood in exchange for the tea that British settlers in Australia were very fond of drinking. Mentioned in this footnote was a Robertson, missionary on Erromango, an island in the New Hebrides, and a name noted on the objects in the Redpath Museum. This eventually led to a group of 14 missionaries associated with the Presbyterian Church in Nova Scotia, Canada, who had established the first colonial foreign mission in the southern New Hebrides. These islands had been enthusiastically ceded to the Nova Scotians for missionary activities by the British-based London Missionary Society which had lost one of their most famous members, John Williams, killed within hours of setting foot on the island of Erromango. Williams's death attracted missionary fervour to the area, and Erromango, before long, came to symbolise the nadir of human spirituality.

The negative view of Erromango held by outsiders had been established years before by Captain James Cook, the first European to visit the island in 1774. Although his stay was brief, it was typical of encounters that followed into the next century, with misunderstandings leading to exchanges of musket fire and arrows, darts and stones. The impression of Erromangans passed on to posterity by Cook was that of an untrustworthy and hostile people and the island was avoided by European ships until 1825, when Peter Dillon, a South Seas trader, discovered a large stand of sandalwood. Dillon's experience of Erromangan indifference to trade goods, inter-tribal hostilities, unprovoked attacks and the island's unhealthy climate resonated in the frustrated accounts of traders and missionaries throughout the century.

Difficult times continued on these islands, both for local islanders because of disease and degradation brought by the sandalwood trade, and for the missionaries, who were not well adapted to life on the malarial isle, with their zealous messages hopelessly out of touch with local needs and desires. Out of five missionaries who tried to establish contact on Erromango, four were killed as a result of local misunderstandings, and one died from poor health. These 'martyrdoms' were followed by the arrival in 1872 of Hugh Robertson, donor of objects to the Redpath Museum, who with his wife Christina raised a family and remained on Erromango for the next 41 years.

The historical contextualisation of Robertson's collection was based on an examination of descriptions made by early observers of Erromangan material culture. These works were used to corroborate provenances indicated by Robertson and to determine possible provenances for unidentified objects. Robertson's own narrative of his missionary endeavours, *Erromanga: The Martyr Isle* (1902), was used extensively for its descriptions of Erromangan material culture. Although his account adheres closely to the missionary conventions of the day, his residence of thirty years on the island at the time of its writing and his extensive contact with the local population provide invaluable descriptions of the manufacture and use of a variety of objects. Robertson's written work devotes particular attention to the physical appearance of Erromangans and includes descriptions of clothing, barkcloth and ornaments. Weapons are also given special attention, as is the construction of canoes, houses and fences. Of particular fascination to Robertson were sacred stones, which is not surprising given his vocation.

Although not from a very well-known island, nor including Pacific Islands material most familiar to Western audiences, Robertson's collection is important because it gives evidence of specific intercultural relations during a period marked at one end by intensive but very limited contact and at the other by considerable depopulation and large-scale conversion to Christianity. Although this material belongs to the genre of idiosyncratic rather than systematic collections, it appears to represent a cross-section of utilitarian and ritual objects, including material used by both men and women. Upon more careful examination, however, Robertson's professional and personal biases come into relief, providing insights into potential areas of emphasis and exclusion in the material he collected.

Robertson's existence on Erromango and his missionary activities there were part of a continuing exchange of European and Erromangan goods that had served as the primary language of contact between these two cultures from the time of the first European visitors. For him and many of his colleagues, the missionary work was accomplished by systematically replacing aspects of traditional culture with those of Europe. The goods in Robertson's collection reflect the primary targets of the missionary. A majority of them are related to Erromangan appearance, reflecting the missionary emphasis in establishing a dress code. Although traditional dress and ornaments were permitted, and even admired in the case of women's garments, most incentives for local individuals to participate in mission activities consisted of presents of cloth and clothing. That European clothing was a major criterion in distinguishing Christians from 'heathens' on Erromanga is made explicit in Robertson's account. Another focus of missionary endeavour was the elimination of local warfare. Erromangans were required to leave their bows and arrows and clubs behind when attending mission activities. Finally, but not less significantly, are those objects that were the focus of traditional spiritual beliefs, such as sacred stones.

Traditional clothing, ornaments, weapons and ritual paraphernalia are all items of material culture commonly donated to Western museums by nineteenth-century missionaries, both because they were being removed locally by missionary practice, and by virtue of their effectiveness as evidence in the home countries of evils that missionaries were busily eradicating.[9] Personal and professional biases typical of non-systematic collections, as illustrated with this case study, can be balanced by consideration of the historical context of particular collections and also by descriptions of material culture from contemporary observers. Historical sources can be used to gather valuable data regarding manufacture and use of objects and also to evaluate the soundness of existing documentation. A vital aspect of the contextualisation process involves comparing material with other known collections of similar circumstance. Consultation with experts in the original community is the best way of documenting objects.

Erromango revisited

Erromango is the fourth largest of Vanuatu's 80 islands, with an area of approximately 900 square kilometres. Its population is sparse (1400 people). The island is not very well known by the outside world and not an

---

9   Ibid.; N. Stanley, 'Melanesian artifacts as cultural markers', in S. Riggens, (ed), *The Socialness of Things* (Berlin: Mouton de Gruyter, 1994), 185–90.

easy place to visit. Intense missionary activity and depopulation have deflected the anthropologist's gaze from the time of Humphreys's short stay in 1920.[10] Artefacts collected by visitors during their limited contacts with Erromango are scattered in museums around the world, usually in very small numbers, as single donations or as part of larger collections, and consistently without documentation.[11] In the Vanuatu Cultural Centre, located in the national capital of Port Vila (Efate), Erromangan objects are hardly to be found. The centre, opened in 1961, comprises a library and museum with some 2000 objects and an archive of films, tapes, and photographs which form a very active component of the collection. At the time of my visit in 1995, a new Vanuatu National Museum was nearing completion. A few of the artefacts exhibited were accompanied by newspaper articles describing their repatriation. Among these was the only Erromangan artefact I saw displayed, a piece of barkcloth from the Australian Museum. In addition to the displayed barkcloth, I noted only 24 Erromangan objects in the centre's accession records.

Erromango displays an interesting mixture of modern and traditional ways. In Dillon's Bay, there are thatched-leaf houses as well as wooden ones roofed with corrugated iron. Dress is modern, with married women wearing 'Mother Hubbards', the loose-fitting cotton prints in vogue throughout the Pacific from the time of early missionary settlers. Young women wear T-shirts with cotton skirts and men and children wear T-shirts with shorts or trousers. Although grass skirts are worn in many Vanuatu villages, I did not see any in Dillon's Bay or Port Narvin. They are, however, a familiar item of dress to all but the younger members of the community. I showed illustrations of four Erromangan barkcloths from the Redpath Museum's collection, which were greatly admired but not recognised as a local production.[12]

10　See also A. Elkin, *Social Anthropology in Melanesia* (London: Oxford University Press, 1953), 131.

11　Notable exceptions being Humphreys's collection of 21 objects at the University Museum of Archaeology and Anthropology, Cambridge, and 150 objects (plus 70 samples) at the Australian Museum (Sydney) from Robertson and his family members and other donors.

12　In the early 1980s, James Nobuat Atnelo, one of the Vanuatu Cultural Centre's two fieldworkers on Erromango, began collecting information on barkcloth from the last three surviving people who had knowledge of its production, decoration, and use. These experts died in the mid-1980s and

Subsistence gardening is the mainstay of village life. Women do much of the work; the main implements being a hard wood digging stick about one metre in length and a long bush knife, perhaps the most frequently used import in rural areas. Pit ovens heated with stones are used for cooking the national dish, *lap-lap*, a pudding made of manioc, taro, yams and grated coconut variously combined with accents of meat or fish, all wrapped in a banana leaf. Wooden sticks are used to manipulate the cooking stones, and plaited leaf fans identical to the Redpath's example are used in tending the fire. Pandanus baskets and mats are still made and in use everywhere, intermingled with an assortment of imported cutlery, dishes and cooking utensils. I was told that locally-produced arrows made from tree ferns as in the old days are used by some men for hunting, but did not see any during my visit. Although Dillon's Bay has at least one truck and a motorised dinghy available for hire, dugout canoes with outriggers are used for river crossings and fishing.

The above impressions are offered to contrast my experience of objects in the museum setting and through historical accounts with things of everyday life in present-day Erromango as encountered during my visit in August 1995. One Sunday, following services and a supper in the church hall, I was asked to say a few words about my research; a copy of my book had been circulating in the community during my stay. The few photographs of people included in my work, most of them recognised even if taken over a century ago, raised the most interest, as did the illustrations of local objects now in the Redpath Museum. I explained my research as a collection of outsiders' observations about Erromangan material culture from the last century. Comments were invited from the small audience, and the following three questions came forth: What do people in the outside world think of Erromango? Would you send us a small piece from one of the barkcloths? Why does Malekula (a large island in central Vanuatu) have so much traditional culture and Erromango so little? To the first question, I replied that the outside world knew very little about Erromango. The second had me torn between my institutional responsibilities and what seemed a compelling request; my answer that the cloth did not belong to me personally satisfied the moment but left much for future consideration. One of the local elders intervened regarding the final question, offering that

Nobuat Atnelo's research was discontinued. See K. Huffman, 'An exhibition of bark cloths from Vanuatu', *COMA*, 16 (1985), 49–50.

Erromangans had less traditional culture than other people of Vanuatu because their traditional ways were responsible for the ill-treatment of the early missionaries. My impression was that this question and its response reflected a division in local attitudes, some having great enthusiasm for the past, others seeing former material culture as vestiges of a best-forgotten age of darkness.

Collaboration and continued collecting?

Museums are being challenged to divest their image as nineteenth-century repositories of exotic objects.[13] The most important trend to emerge in museum anthropology in recent decades is the movement toward accountability and relevance.[14] Much controversy has focused on the public domain of museums, especially regarding the politics of representation, sponsorship, and curation of exhibits.[15] Questions regarding legal and ethical ownership of collections have gained international attention.[16] In the case of the United States, repatriation issues have achieved legal recognition with the passage in 1990 of the Native American Graves Protection and Repatriation Act (NAGPRA), which provides a strong incentive for incorporating native perspectives in museums. Relations between museums and the people whose ancestors and material culture constitute their collections have become increasingly complex as artefact-related dialogues give way to fundamental concerns about control. Kaplan describes the interest in repatriation as a desire for engagement, with the objects themselves having less importance than the opportunity to negotiate with the dominant society from a position of strength.[17] These intensified interactions have produced an increasing number of successful

---

13 J. Haas, 'Power, objects, and a voice for anthropology', *Current Anthropology*, 37 (1996), S1–12, S18–22, 88.

14 A. Jones, 'Exploding canons: the anthropology of museums', *Annual Review of Anthropology*, 22 (1993), 201–20.

15 M. Ames, *Cannibal Tours and Glass Boxes*, (Vancouver: UBC Press, 1992); I. Karp and S. Lavine, (eds), *Exhibiting Cultures* (Washington, DC: Smithsonian Institution Press, 1991).

16 See, for example, J. Specht, 'The George Brown affair again', *Anthropology Today*, 3(4) (1987), 1–3.

17 F. Kaplan (ed), *Museums and the Making of 'Ourselves'* (London: Leicester University Press, 1994).

projects based on collaboration and consultation.[18]

Haas suggests that this restructuring of power relations raises questions about the mission of museums and the central role of collections in all museum activities:

> Once the very lifeblood of anthropology, ageing collections have become in some ways an oppressive burden on museum anthropology, holding back the field and not allowing museums to assume a leading role as centres of public learning for all anthropology.[19]

Although it is true that very few museums can afford to keep their ethnographic collections current by adding modern material culture, possibilities for sharing resources and collections have become more numerous. Collections data are increasingly available internationally as more museums computerise their holdings.[20] Although documentation is often crude, revision and upgrading of information is much facilitated once automated. Sharing collections data can further research; it can encourage dialogue and collaboration between museums and the communities from which collections originated, both at home and abroad; access to collections information may also assist with the repatriation of significant objects. In terms of continued ethnographic collecting, questions of accountability and relevance remain in the foreground. If institutions are able to meet the considerable demands required by existent collections or redistribute their holdings to those willing to accept such responsibilities,[21] then contemporary collecting of objects and information might be a productive joint venture for some museums and communities.

---

18   G. Abrams, 'The case for wampum', in Kaplan, op. cit., 351–84; D. Doxtator, *Fluffs and Feathers* (Brantford, Ontario: Woodland Cultural Centre, 1988); Haas, op. cit., S8; T. Nicks, 'Partnerships in developing cultural resources', *Culture*, 12(1) (1992), 87–94; R. West, 'The National Museum of the American Indian perspectives on museums in the 21st century', *Museum Anthropology*, 18(3) (1994), 53–8.

19   Haas, op. cit., S8–9.

20   See, for example, P. Gathercole and A. Clarke, *Survey of Oceanian Collections in Museums in the United Kingdom and the Irish Republic* (Paris: UNESCO, 1979) and the Canadian Heritage Information Network (CHIN).

21   P. Gathercole, 'The fetishism of artefacts', in S. Pearce, ed., *Museum Studies in Material Culture* (London: Leicester University Press, 1989), 73–81.

8 Contemporary popular collecting

Paul Martin

In this chapter, I manifest the thoughts of a collector, in this case of model buses, and relate the meaning they have to the individual from a post-modern perspective. I write from that area of the mind that is activated when the insignificant and singular is perceived as symbolic of something of far greater depth; where the real is understood through the vapours of the hyper-real it gives off. The collector's thoughts as projected here, are neither fully conscious nor sub-conscious, but surface and dive between the two.[1]

In the dentist's waiting room, see a softly lit tank of water. Tropical fish silently lure the eye. They calm us. Their seemingly effortless movement, the shimmer of their scales in the light, serve to tranquillise, harmonise, reassure. No fillings needed after all.

See the collection, spectacle supreme. A light coating of dust betrays its stillness. And yet, and yet ... contemplation activates the logarithms of the mind.

Cyberspace is not a geographical location, but for those who can enter it, work the hardware and software, attain the know-how, it is the place to be. So much information floats within it, but is rendered invisible by turning off the monitor, yet we know it is still in there, waiting to be accessed.

We carry our values and principles in the collection. The enormity of its meaning cerebrally, aesthetically communicated, every time we engage it with our contemplation. It counteracts our uncertainties and reassures our anxiety. A spiritual console in melancholia or means of empowerment. Constant companion when goalposts move, rules change or self-confidence dissolves. A friend with which to share good news and celebrate hope. See the collection and computer screen, the gatekeepers of our dreamtime ... ready to download:

---

1   P. Martin, *Popular Collecting and the Everyday Self: The Reinvention of Museums* (London: Leicester University Press, 1998).

In the beginning, I used to go door to door. I had no money and my husband didn't speak French, and he wasn't interested. But I would take the tram or the train, I'd look at the map and say: OK what small village can I do from Montreal? I'd go from door to door. I had maybe eight or ten dollars in my bag, no more. I'd take paper shopping bags along with me ... It wouldn't take me long to fill them. I'd catch the bus home in the afternoon, around four or five o'clock and get out at Dupuis, the big department store. From there I'd take the 3A to go to Notre-Dame-de-Grace. I'd have my two bags full of this and that. I'd be laughing, I was happy.[2]

Reclining in his only chair, he allowed his eye to roam freely over the spectacle of his model bus collection. It was a themed collection. They all bore the liveries of the towns in which he had lived. Encased in a mirror-backed, wall-mounted, display cabinet, the miniature feats of precision engineering held for him a full-scale presence.

The collection condensed and compacted time and space into one surveyable display. His life, he knew, had always lacked direction, nothing inspired him. He had drifted from town to town, seemingly at the behest of fate. The collection, through its sameness, he decided, somehow represented coherence and a kind of linear symmetry. It brought together the numerous towns he had temporarily inhabited in one small array. In this way, he psychologically owned the geography it alluded to, closure was found. Through it, he saw his uncoordinated life story retold as a purposeful fable. It enabled him to view his past as something other than a pointless series of random occurrences, there was some kind of internal, abstract logic to it after all. It was like free-form jazz.

The repeated, generic, serialised symbol of the model bus presented his past in an aesthetically encapsulated form. The models seemed to be saying with a collective voice: 'Behold us – we are the reasoning of your life.' He didn't believe them, of course. The fact that they carried no correspondingly miniature passengers, but were empty, as empty as he felt himself at times to be, proved to him the shallowness of their surrogacy. And yet they were important to him.

It was model buses that had attracted him, rather than cars, because buses

---

2   Nettie Sharpe interviewed by Pascale Galipeau in 1993. Sharpe moved to Montreal in the late 1940s and began seriously collecting the folk art of Quebec in 1950. Her collections are now in the Museum of Canadian Civilisation. P. Galipeau, ed., *Les Paradis du Monde: L'art Populaire de Québec* (Quebec: Musée Canadien des Civilisations, 1995), 37.

were public transport. In this way they represented a civic ethos and the values of co-operation rather than competition. They projected public and civic collectivism as personal beliefs and principles in a society seemingly devoid of them. Parallel with this was his own history as a non-driver and user of public transport. This invested the models with the bitter-sweetness of remembrance and use. This was spliced with the geography of the towns represented and his memories of them. The poetic conciseness of the collection recoded the haphazard nature of his past into temporal certainty and purpose. This reasoning made the collection imperative. And running through it all, like a spinal column, was a perception of cohesion and symmetry. It was his safe-deposit box in which he kept his principles, and only he had the combination. He did not so much look at, as visually inhale the vista.

He felt an urgency, an insistence to imbue more meaning into the collection as he once again neared the end of his stay in this particular town. That which had become familiar and lived, was soon to become history and memory. It felt important to him to pack these memories into portable symbols. Most people did this through photographs, of course; he, however, needed something more materially solid to act as a psychic storage battery, the charge of which would be needed later on in order to reify the inadequacy of his past as rich experience.

The collection, he concluded, was the agency which legitimised his past and this became more keenly felt as the present dissolved into it. He found himself wondering whether it was healthy or not, would it be tolerated by others? He remembered the hesitancy with which he had bought his first model. Model vehicles, toys, were for kids surely? Then he had visited the Museum of British Road Transport in Coventry. He had seen there the Tiatsa collection of model vehicles belonging to Tiber Riech, the renowned textile designer, in the museum's 'Model World' gallery, there on a ten year loan. He had thought to himself then: 'If it's OK for a museum to collect them, it must surely be OK for me to do so?'

He was still thinking of the museum collection when he found that he had drifted into a model collectors' shop. He picked up a model gift box absent-mindedly and began reading the information on the prize it held within; a Leyland PD2 Highbridge bus and Bedford OB coach, in the Southdown livery. It read thus:

The model displays the familiar 'Southdown' green and cream colours in a transitional layout applied between 1957 and 1960. Prior to this date, dark green lining was applied between the cream and green and below the windows, whilst after 1960, the green between decks was extended to immediately beneath the upper deck windows. Until 1957 an additional destination display was located above the platform, but (number) 348 was amongst the first to have this facility removed in 1957.[3]

He paused for thought. This information was part of a corporate livery scheme. When originally conceived, it formed part of a corporate decision-making process on real buses, therefore it was important. He wondered if the same information ceased to be important, and became instead mere obsessive detail when used in the context of a scale-model reproduction for collectors. But if so, he wondered, thinking of the museum collection, would it be made important again if it appeared as a textual panel accompanying the same models in a museum display?

He had been browsing through the 'antiques and collectables' section at Dillon's bookshop when his gaze alighted on a price guide to collectable kitchen accessories of the 1950s. Then it struck him, the thought that if anything or everything was collectable then nothing made sense any more. What, he pondered, is an eggcup for? Of course, he knew as well as anyone else that an eggcup was a small receptacle from which boiled eggs could be conveniently eaten, it was obvious. But was it? What, he asked himself, if the eggcup was manufactured for a collector? What if that eggcup was never destined for any functional purpose at all, never to grace the breakfast table, but whose destiny lay in the sanctuary of the display cabinet, the subject of adoring eyes as it was lovingly contemplated? What then, he again pondered, was an eggcup actually for?

His contemplation was broken as he noticed a glossy coffee-table book on classic die-cast models, and he was once again reminded of his own collecting 'habit'. He walked home. He would no doubt buy representative models of the next town he became resident in, to add to the collection, and he would once again contemplate his life reflected in the glass-fronted display cabinet.

He arrived home. Turning the key in the front door, he was all at once seized with an overwhelming feeling of optimism. The position he had secured in the next town he was to move to was a good one. Should it prove permanent, should he feel he had found somewhere he belonged, he

---

3   B.W. Jackson, Southdown Enthusiasts Club, notes on a presentation box containing a pair of limited-edition Southdown model buses.

would stay there. This, he felt, would allow him to enjoy his collection anew. It would become a smile instead of a frown; it would be transformed from an optic of forlorn melancholia and sadness into a triumphant cornucopia of commemoration and celebration. Laughing to himself at the fickleness of 'meaning', he began to pack his suitcase.

9 Collecting from the era of memory, myth and delusion

Gaynor Kavanagh

The distinguishing feature of making history in the museum is the act of collecting. Most other forms of historiographic practice are intent only on the capture of evidence; once it has been used, its preservation becomes a matter for others – archivists, librarians, family members. Historians working in museums must not only work with and through material and oral evidence, but also take responsibility for its long-term survival. It is a commitment which can be both enabling, in that such responsibilities give effective curators opportunities to think more carefully about the evidence they are dealing with, yet disabling because if acquisition and collection management processes are seriously flawed, very little of solid worth can be achieved.

It is useful to consider how our understanding of the past has been constructed by historians and to compare this with the different ways in which curators in the history field have also constructed histories through their approaches to acquisition of evidence.

In the past, historians tackling the history of the nineteenth century somehow seem to have had it all sown up. Their principal primary source, often the only source recognised and used, was the written or printed document, and until relatively recently the histories created from them seemed safe enough. Such evidence was created by the literate and empowered, and there appeared no need to look further. A.J.P. Taylor, for example, had little trouble with the idea that the history of Europe could be told in terms of the biographies of Napoleon, Metternich, Bismarck and Hitler.

Yet, the silences in the historians' record of the nineteenth century were eerie. The absence of first-person testimony left the histories devoid of individual perspectives and alternative accounts. The histories of ordinary people had been largely unrecorded and therefore unwritten. Later generations of historians, taking their inspiration from the Annales school and later Marxist theory, and adapting methods from other disciplines including sociology and anthropology, set themselves the task of opening up the past to scrutiny. They scoured everything from chapel attendance records and ballad lyrics to the small ads in contemporary newspapers in an effort to construct some form of understanding of individual, social and cultural experience. Because of this, the categories of what counts as the historical record have changed. Things not seen, or simply not seen as being relevant, were reassessed and revalued.

In contrast, the histories of the twentieth century are produced from a very different evidence range. They are in many respects oral histories. Some historians of the old school, while admitting the need for non-literary sources, found the expansion difficult to deal with. Taylor was a case in point, calling oral history 'old men drooling about their youth'.[1] Notwithstanding this, we are now at ease with the knowledge that this is the century of the telephone, the sound bite and memory. The histories we have are in good part derived from and illustrated by narratives which spring from verbal, rather than written accounts given of firsthand experience. The advance of recording technology, the acceptance that there is history in everyone's life story and the simple truth that people live longer are factors which have contributed to this century's record. Moreover, this material can be intrinsically interesting, and gives rise to popular television and radio programmes, as well as a small and thriving industry in the publication of personal remembrances.

History is more accessible than ever before, because its very material lies within the span of human encounter. But things are not so clear-cut and care has to be taken. Because of the dominance of oral history as a primary source, history, the record of the past, becomes (unintentionally) positioned closer to fiction, to the preferred stories. The power of the historian as narrator is challenged and even overtaken by the power of the narrations. Yet neither is pure nor innocent. Each has an agenda, whether of control through construction or personal empowerment through control. Each, therefore, is problematic.

History is distrusted (not least by historians) because objectivity is ultimately unobtainable, because it has occasionally been prone to

---

1   P. Thompson, *The Voice of the Past: Oral History* (Oxford: Oxford University Press, 1978), 62.

theoretical faddism, because at some point it has to place a limit on the sources consulted, and because it asks some questions while neglecting others. Yet, memory is equally faulty. Events and feelings are conflated, images and narratives from films and novels get subsumed into and appropriated within it, and only that which is self-enhancing or self-justifying is remembered or admitted to consciously. Moreover, within the public domain, as the historian selects the memories to be used, the fault lines merge and the land slips away into even more confusion. Histories through memories, as much as through documents, are reliably unreliable.

This is a much simplified analysis of the approach to studying the past that might be found within mainstream historiography. How does it differ from the making of history within museums through the formation of collections? The answer is not straightforward. Intellectually, there is very little to suggest a direct correlation in trends between history in the museum and that created outside of it, although, practically, there is much in common.

In terms of collecting, there are two principal trends. The first is evident in the work of the antiquarian societies and men such as Dr Kirk of Castle Museum, York, fame,[2] and indeed much passive collecting that goes on today. This centres round the drive to collect for its own sake, to complete sets, to assemble the curious and bizarre, and to create an assemblage of that which tide and time have rendered redundant. The individual lives and testimony behind an object, its provenance and association, are of little import. The meanings an object had when in use are allowed to be forgotten. The object is the thing, the curatorial obsession, the plaything of the imagination, the handy device in whatever displays are going up. But, for many, this approach has neutered the historical record and denied the survival of a tremendous richness of evidence, often of the nineteenth century.

This approach to collecting rests on a range of values about ownership and order, justified under the false god of the Object Which Speaks For Itself. Yet, as has been pointed out: 'the problem with things is that they are dumb. They are not eloquent, as some thinkers in art museums claim. They

---

2   G. Kavanagh, *History Curatorship* (Leicester: Leicester University Press, 1990).

are dumb. And if by some ventriloquism they seem to speak, they lie.'[3] Objects do not speak for themselves, unless on some psychic level to which few of us are attuned. People do the talking for them. The antiquarian collectors were often talking about themselves in the ways they collected. The collection in York says far more about Kirk's psyche than it ever does about nineteenth-century life. By the same token, people also do the forgetting for them. By not remembering the individual choices, preferences, uses and experiences behind the material, in all their confusion and often contradictions, exclusions are shouted in the full volume of total silence.

The second trend in collecting is evident within the work of Hazelius and the Nordic folk museums, the inter-war regional ethnologists working in museums in Ireland, Wales, the Isle of Man, and in more recent years in museums as far apart as Northern Ireland, Croydon, Hull and Glasgow. Careful, multifaceted fieldwork is the route chosen to acquisition. Within this approach, collecting is at its most useful only when part of a documentary process which values as much the oral testimony and photographic record as the object which comes from within the process. Much of it has been about the histories of the twentieth century. The approach has swung ever closer to recording the life and the object as evidence of it, rather than the object within the context of a life. The difference is subtle, but profound. As Julia Clark has pointed out,[4] museums collect egg-beaters, but when was the last time someone introduced themselves to you through their egg-beater or anything else for that matter: 'Hello this is me, meet my flat iron.' Instead, life stories are told through the medium of the memory of personal experience, within which objects appear in ways often totally at odds with the display techniques of many museums. In the absence of the museum's ability to think laterally, or at the very least in human rather than object terms, we have to employ resistant readings to disrupt the blandness – flat irons as door props, or mantlepiece decorations, or dirty, hot, horrible things to use, or offensive or defensive weapons in domestic disputes, or something tossed away in a wartime scrap metal drive.

---

3   S.R. Crew and J. Sims, 'Locating authenticity; fragments of a dialogue' in I. Karp and S.D. Lavine (eds), *Exhibiting Cultures: The Poetics and Politics of Museum Display* (Washington, DC: Smithsonian Institution Press), 159.

4   J. Clark, 'Any old iron?', *Museums Australia Journal*, 91–2 (1993), 57–62.

These two trends in museum collecting have led to a body of museum archives not dissimilar to the forms of history making outlined above. The antiquarian-based collecting (although it might masquerade under a more up-to-date name) has edited out the testimony of the people behind the objects, whereas the fieldwork approach has prioritised detailed remembrance.

In museums where the antiquarian approach has dominated, our record of the nineteenth century is largely mute, and the same can be true of later material. For example, at the Museums Association Conference in September 1995, Oxfordshire Museum Service highlighted the dilemmas they faced when reviewing their collections on moving them to a new purpose-built store. In particular a washing machine collected in the 1970s with no formal record other than a very basic entry in the museum's collection documentation. Here is the museum's 'document', stripped out of all associations and neutered of the meanings attached to it while in private hands. This is typical of the dilemmas that passive collecting precipitates. What should or could the museum do with it? More time can be spent in puzzling out the worth and meaning of an undocumented object than ever would be involved in effective fieldwork and recording at the point of collection.

When curatorial standards slip so low that objects are acquired without useful data, means other than referring to museum records have to be used to recover something of the human experience behind the objects. For example, the Ulster Folk and Transport Museum has experimented with nineteenth-century farming techniques and technology (for example in respect of ploughing), and in so doing has tested the assumptions that lie behind its agricultural collection. Through the study and use of the collections, or if need be replicas, generalisations and stereotypes can be confronted. In the case of the Ulster Folk and Transport Museum they were able to challenge the notion that rural society was unthinkingly conservative, and can now argue through the evidence of their experimentation and experience that it was instead given to ingenuity and adaptability.[5]

In contrast, it is reasonable to assume that a proactive approach to collecting gives rise to much more detailed and personal records, a

---

5   J. Bell, 'Making rural histories', in G. Kavanagh, ed., *Making Histories in Museums* (Leicester: Leicester University Press, 1996).

documentation base rich in information about associations and meanings. But it has to be admitted that there are nevertheless many risks associated with this approach. The context is one of preferred memories, both in terms of the selection of the informant and the content of the informant's memory. Documentary recording and collecting has, for example, centred the farm worker and ignored the farm manager or supplier, or centred the family in poverty rather than the rising (or risen) middle class. By choosing to remember one, the other has been forgotten and comparison is lost through lives made invisible. This may also be true of the various roles individuals play in life. A museum may record a woman in her home or kitchen, but not her other lives, say as Friday night dancer, or bingo player, or cashier, or daughter, or closet Tory, or lay preacher. Clearly, this narrows the enquiry to just a vague silhouette of someone's existence. In these ways, selecting from the selected haul of memory has its costs. In such circumstances, would this woman's bread knife or mantelpiece clock be enough to say who she was and what her life was like? What will be the value of this tunnel-vision record in twenty, thirty, fifty years time?

Collecting in history museums is further complicated by dynamic changes in the market values of material, a heightened sense of the past (whether personal or social) and the sheer cost of maintaining a collection in anything like a good order. It has to be questioned whether the old tenets of collecting still hold good, whether models such as Croydon Museums Service, London – which places the capture of detailed information from integrated sources above the importance of retaining the physical presence of the object – point the way ahead, and whether museums operating within the social history field can afford to take established practices with them into the twenty-first century. In the case of Croydon, all of the objects have firm provenance, and 74.5% of the objects on display are on loan and will therefore be returned to their owners as the exhibits change. The aim of the museum is to build a small collection of objects, but a very strong and detailed record through oral history, photographs and other means. In other words, something eminently manageable within the museum's medium- and long-term budget, yet consistent with its commitment to produce a detailed and inclusive archive of people's lives in Croydon which can be used effectively to construct histories.

Croydon also supplies us with some indicators about the difficulties and possibilities of gathering objects to create an account of life through past decades. The museum explores its histories of life in Croydon through six sets: each covers a span of time and contains within it objects representing 25 themes such as sex and love, travel and transport, work, dying and bereavement. The overall approach is diachronic, yet holds within it the synchronic. It allows memory and diverse personal accounts to erupt through the narrative, being not concerned with the 'tidy edges' of history, but instead more interested in the textures of experience these accounts reveal. This approach is facilitated by the use of computer stations which empower the visitor in the interrogation of the objects and the meanings and associations ascribed to them. The approach is questioning, laterally moving, open-ended, and rich in evidence derived from extensive fieldwork. None of this would have been possible had a passive or antiquarian approach to collecting been adopted.

Table 9.1 Analysis of objects on display in the 'Lifetimes' exhibition, part of Croydon Museum Service (figures given in percentages).[6]

Source of Lifetimes Objects	Set 1 1830– 1880	Set 2 1881– 1918	Set 3 1919– 1838	Set 4 1939– 1955	Set 5 1956– 1970	Set 6 1971– 1996	Mean
Original collection	41	25	14	12	0	2	16.0
Other museum collections	18	22	4	9	4	5	10.0
Models and reproductions	18	10	7	8	7	7	9.5
Local people	17	33	57	64	75	65	52.0
Local firms and institutions	6	10	18	7	14	21	12.5

Further, Angela Fussell, the research manager for the museum, has analysed the sources of the objects used in the first round of 'Lifetimes' (the exhibit will change at regular intervals to reveal other themes and experiences). From Table 9.1 it is clear how the availability of objects judged as relevant alters according to the period being studied. In the earliest display, covering 1850–1900, it was possible to find about 41% of what was needed from the established collection, a further 18% had to be tracked down in other museum collections. Where no material was available,

---

6   Data compiled by, and used with permission from, Angela Fussell, Research Manager, Croydon Museum Service.

models had to be used (18%) and 23% of the objects were borrowed from local firms and institutions. In other words, the established collections could not meet half their needs when it came to this period of history, although using museum collections together, 59% was found safe in 'public hands'. This contrasts with the last period (1970 to the present), where the established collections could meet only 2% of their needs and 86% had to be gathered from local people and firms.

In terms of its collection, Croydon in many respects is not untypical of many urban-based museums. Developed from a traditional museum collection, with limited funds, space and resources, Croydon Museum Service inherited a range of material fairly typical of what some perceive as social history. These figures are interesting from a number of different points of view. They demonstrate that established collections are rarely sufficient for the type of people-centred, visitor-aware history exhibitions that are now essential to effective provision. They also show that the nearer we get to contemporary experience, the less likely it is that a museum will have a collection adequate for current purposes.

The experience at Croydon also demonstrates the degree to which acquisition is driven by research generated through exhibition needs. Acquisition for its own sake, possibly part of a long-term research project leading to an article in a folk or cultural journal, has been long since left behind. 'Own-sakism' is arguably a self-indulgence which few museums can now afford or are prepared to indulge. Passive acquisition of someone's collection of plastic bunnies, bin liners, sweet wrappings or material gathered without regard to geographic or cultural boundaries (as was the case with Kirk) is much removed from the modern practices and imperatives of history museum work. It may only be relevant where antiquarian traditions not only continue, but are also cherished: the number of history museums so committed is very much diminished.

If the scope of museum collections is open to question, so too are the standards of collection management. The question is a simple one: can museums care for the collections they hold? If they cannot, is a detailed record in sound, image and the written word just as effective? Is a collection that is unprovenanced, profoundly imbalanced and already in an advanced state of decay always worth saving, worth being a 'museum'? In planning for the future, we have to accept the experiences of the past, and historians are usually the ones who remind us of this. The history of collecting and collection management in museums has been, to say the least and to put it politely, a very chequered one. We would like to believe otherwise, as the rhetoric of much museum-based literature makes clear. However, the evidence is disheartening.[7]

In his introduction to the survey on social and industrial history collecting, conducted by Janet Kenyon on behalf of the Yorkshire and Humberside Museums Service, Stuart Davies considered that in the region studied the full range of collection management excellence and inadequacies was represented:

> While the region has had its heroes and heroines where collection management is concerned, it does have to be said that some of the problems in social and industrial curatorship have been caused by the curators themselves. Lack of discipline in collecting, intellectual inadequacy, poor professional quality and indifferent motivation have all contributed. At the same time the senior management of many museums has hardly been blameless. Poor leadership, the absence of clear objectives and under-resourcing have done nothing to help the situation. But then neither has the indifference or even hostility, of some governing bodies. Particularly in local authorities, museums are often misunderstood, undervalued and consigned to a very low priority by senior officers and elected members themselves.[8]

There has never been a time when a clear, well-articulated and viable approach to museum practice (and especially history practice as a now dominant discipline) has been more needed. Curators can indulge in curatorial rhetoric and convince themselves that they can get by on established museum tradition. But there is a choice – either to remain content with the way things are, quietly witness the decay and politely ignore yawning gaps in the record, or to become much more certain of the criteria for and worth of collecting, and more confident in doing it well. This is as much, if not more, a matter of approach and competence as it is a matter of resources.

---

7   See, for example, J. Kenyon, *Collecting for the 21st Century: A Survey of Industrial and Social History Collections in the Museums of Yorkshire and Humberside* (Leeds: Yorkshire and Humberside Museums Council, 1992); B. Lord et al., *The Cost of Collecting: Collection Management in UK Museums*, (London: HMSO, 1989); B. Ramer, *A Conservation Survey of Museum Collections in Scotland*, (London: HMSO, 1989); J.D. Storer, *The Conservation of Industrial Collections: a Survey*, (London: Conservation Unit of the Museums and Galleries Commission/Science Museum, 1989).

8   S. Davies in Kenyon, op. cit., ix.

Whether museums concentrate on the maintenance of a physical record or elect to take the more adventurous route with the capture of integrated information, there has to be a conscious procedure and a demonstrably high level of achievement. Without a coherent and committed approach, many museums will have nothing much to offer the public, except dust and dilapidation and an awful lot of hollow promises.

10 Collecting in time of war

Žarka Vujic

This chapter concerns the collecting of objects during the war in Croatia. It is about the need to overcome the shock and astonishment felt in these circumstances, and to examine this new reality through the eyes of the museum professional.

Discussion of the nature of the military conflict in Croatia is beyond the scope of this chapter, but as people preoccupied with the country's heritage, we comprehended quickly that Croatia, and later Bosnia and Hercegovina, had been exposed to a kind of systematic destruction of natural and cultural identity unseen in Europe since the Second World War. Churches and cultural monuments destroyed; wildlife and landscape devastated. The mining of the Plitvice Lake District, the burning of the thoroughbred Lippizaner horses near Lipik, added to the terror which accompanied the killing of people.

During the first months of the war, having experienced the air raids and life in shelters, I became aware that our relationship with objects had fundamentally changed. Previously, we amassed and accumulated objects, often unnecessarily. Now these things became a burden – we only took into the cellars the most needed, and carefully chosen, documents and materials; items that represented us in the event of our losing all the rest of our possessions. This was a different, and a very painful, process of selection. Only the essentials for existence were brought: mainly food and hygienic necessities. Children chose only their most precious toys, the remainder being left and possibly lost.

Displaced persons from the attacked and occupied parts of the country were very soon appearing in the capital, Zagreb. For the first time, I met people who had suddenly, and in an extremely painful way, lost not only the closest members of their families, but also all their material goods and possessions – houses, land, animals and objects. Generally, all they managed to save was their lives and perhaps little more than a bag of possessions.[1]

The curator of the town museum in Ilok lived through a similar experience. In the autumn of 1991, the whole town peacefully surrendered to the Yugoslav Army. Thousands of people left with no more than a bag, which was subjected to a humiliating inspection. The curator had hoped that he would be able to secretly evacuate the most valuable objects. When this proved impossible, he thought that he might at least manage to take some of his personal belongings, perhaps some books, or some of his own works. But in the end even this was not possible. Here is just part of a statement by Ivan, aged 40, who was banished from Vukovar:

> Imagine that I didn't take any of my things ... I regret [the loss of] the photographs we have had and many of those material things, I regret [the loss of] the clothes ... Only, what is left as memory, [are] those old jeans that I will keep as some exhibit ...[2]

These words evoked in my memory a provocative text by Peter van Mensch: 'Museum object – what and why?'[3] Here he reminded us that collecting is just one form of protecting our heritage, and that it is not always absolutely necessary to keep the originals in personal possession. But our displaced persons were grieving for their own objects, objects to which they were emotionally attached. There were no substitutes for their pictures and other mementoes: 'All that we had, all that we were, is now reduced to memories only.'[4] Their experiences confirmed my own view that those belonging to the 'European cultural circle' are not prepared to live a life devoid of collected materials.

Croatian soldiers, like their counterparts in history, brought back home different objects after military operations had ended: car plates, currency

---

1   These bags contained far less that those in Schlereth's exercise where students kept all the items they used within a period of 24 hours. See T.J. Schlereth, 'Collecting today for tomorrow', *Museum News* (March/April 1982), 29–37.

2   Institute of Ethnology and Folklore Research (IEFR), *Fear, Death and Resistance: An Ethnography of War: Croatia 1991–92* (Zagreb: IEFR, 1993), 180.

3   P. van Mensch, 'Museum object – what and why', in *Collecting Today for Tomorrow* (Lieden: ICOM International Committee for Museology, 1984), (ICOFOM Study Series 6).

4   IEFR, op. cit., 229.

used in the occupied areas, newspapers and pamphlets – war trophies, but also documents of the lives of some of their family members.

Museums, of course, also need objects. In spite of the redefinition of these institutions, and in spite of the use of new technologies and the concept of the virtual museums, the basic fund of museums will remain tangible objects. Even in the extreme dangers and uncertainties of wartime, curators in Croatian museums continued to collect. I had believed that protection and evacuation of collections, and perhaps protest exhibitions, were the only activities for museums in wartime.[5] Then the curator of the Croatian Natural History Museum in Zagreb told me about collecting taking place on the front lines of the battlefield. Instead of evacuation and protection, so symbolic of possible death and destruction, collecting had suddenly appeared as a symbol of the continuation of life.

This took place in the area of Velebit at the very beginning of the war. Velebit is the longest and the most beautiful mountain in Croatia, it stretches like a natural wall between the Adriatic coast and continental Croatia. Velebit abounds in plant and animal species, some of which are endemic, and over a hundred caves and pits. During the war, the southern part of the mountain was occupied – the front line held artillery and then minefields. It was here that my friend, with three colleagues, participated in the defence of that part of the country. At the same time they made collections of the indigenous plants and animals for the museum. These scientist-soldiers performed bird ringing and undertook several cave expeditions. The most important of these concerned the discovery of the so-called 1355 metre-deep Lukas Pit in 1993, named after the spelaeologist who was killed on the southern slopes of the mountain.

The spirit of the museum profession, then, accompanied the fighting. The process of collecting the natural heritage became a way to both protect the natural identity of the country and remain sane. The greatest problem was the delivery of the necessary equipment, such as butterfly nets or materials for preparation and preservation. Just like war hospitals, curators used domestic distillates, like brandy, instead of alcohol.

There are precedents for this wartime behaviour: Slovenian Egon Pretner made a collection of cave animals during the Second World War. Nevertheless, the experience of the curator of the Croatian Natural History

---

5   Long-term problems have resulted from this rapid evacuation of material.

Museum in Zagreb appears to me a unique proof of the strong need to collect.

Another example of this wartime resolve concerned the purchasing of museum objects by the Ethnography Museum in Zagreb. Purchase is not frequently utilised as a means of acquisition in Croatia; it seems even more remarkable, then, that it should take place in wartime. Whilst protecting its existing collections, the museum was also trying to purchase as many ethnographic objects as possible from displaced persons throughout Croatia. People had packed their most valuable possessions – these were often the richly decorated national costumes – into the bags they were allowed to take with them (Fig. 10.1). Destitution and the hardships of displacement drove them to sell even these last treasures. Fortunately, these were frequently offered to the Ethnography Museum.

Fig. 10.1 Male national costume from West Slawonia. One of many ethnographic objects purchased from displaced people.

The curator in charge told me her office looked like that of a social worker. She would listen to the sad stories of these unfortunate people and try to comfort them. But, on account of the museum's collecting policy and prior possession of similar objects, some offers had to be rejected. This stirred additional emotions; the suffering and horror of war was even present in the curator's office. This was another proof of the huge social significance of the museum.[6] It was particularly surprising to see the continuation of collecting in a museum where existing collections were themselves at risk. In a terrorist attack on Zagreb in May 1995, one cluster projectile exploded near the art nouveau building of the museum. Fortunately, the museum and the collections suffered no damage, but they might have been otherwise.

A final example comes from the Croatian History Museum, situated in the oldest part of Zagreb, the so-called Gradec. At the beginning of the war, in the autumn of 1991, the museum building was damaged in an air raid on the presidential palace. The museum building and its collections were at risk. Nevertheless, due to the attitude and efforts of the museum's director, the museum's staff recognised their obligation to document all contemporary historical events in the territory of Croatia. Interestingly enough, not for a moment did they stop to consider the lack of space and personnel necessary for so intensive a period of contemporary collecting. There was simply no time for such considerations. Having secured and partly evacuated the existing collections, staff dedicated their time and effort to arranging, throughout the world, exhibitions that documented the war events in Croatia, and to collecting new objects. The board of the museum met weekly to decide on the required tasks. Coincidentally, one of the curators was in London at the time, and she paid a visit to the Imperial War Museum. There she learned of the ways British colleagues had documented the Gulf War, and brought their experiences to Zagreb. Croatian curators established the same basic ground rules: to collect everything, register the new entries, but to leave the conceptualisation of the inventory for the future, when the perspective of history will be required.

The museum began by making a great collection of posters. The beginning of the war in Croatia was strongly marked by the posters and graffiti of the urban resistance. It was followed by the collection of publications, of thousands of war photographs and negatives, as well as of

---

6   The Rental Workshop for national costumes should also be mentioned here. More than thirty displaced women manufactured new costumes and restored old ones. As well as providing financial and psychological assistance, traditional knowledge was also protected.

video tapes. Objects documenting the development of the Croatian Army were also collected: uniforms, flags, emblems and medals. No effort was spared in gathering material from the enemy side also. After the Second World War, the majority of the surviving documentation came from the Allies; the museum wanted to avoid this.

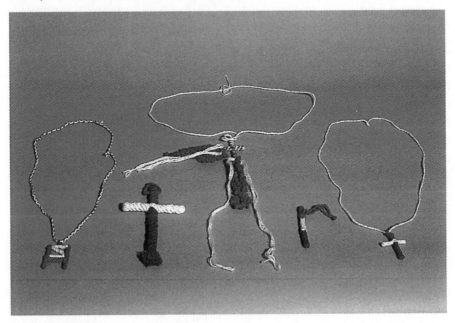

Fig. 10.2 Religious objects made by the Croatian soldiers in prisoner of war camps.

Lastly, the collection was to include a group of objects of immense emotional value. These were objects made by Croatian soldiers in prisoner-of-war camps: rosaries made of bread crumbs, crosses made of wool, playing cards and chess pieces (Fig. 10.2). It was not easy to collect these. Museum officials waited with families to meet prisoners of war as they returned. However strange and even morbid these activities may seem to ordinary people, members of the museum profession will understand the motives.

One gap in collecting which took place resulted from a failure to make a greater number of live recordings. It is also regretted that this museum is not ready to share or exchange this material with other museums in Zagreb which were less active during the war.

In war, people ceased to be object-oriented. Due to their tragic circumstances, they became oriented towards ideas; they collected memories. But memories could not satisfy them and again they started to collect, creating their material contexts. Museum professionals, surrounded by uncertainty and destruction, also turned their attentions to the acquisition of the new items. The closer a museum was to the front line (as in Osijek, Vinkovci, Karlovac or Dubrovnik) so its collecting activity diminished and even disappeared, and attention turned to the survival of museum collections. Museum collecting was more likely to continue in those areas that were more distant from the front line, especially in the museums and galleries of Zagreb. Some institutions collected, others did not. This is quite natural, since the policy of collecting is shaped and implemented by people. In those safer museums collecting and the creation of new collections was done by the people who were directed by a strong sense of the museum profession. It is to them, that I dedicate this chapter.

11 The politics of museum collecting in the 'old' and the 'new' South Africa

Graham Dominy

This chapter concerns the development of South African museums within the overall context of apartheid. The processes of transformation up to 1996 will be mentioned and two specific collections discussed in detail. These are the Campbell collections at the Killie Campbell African Library and Museum, University of Natal, Durban, and the Amandla[1] collection in the Natal Museum, Pietermaritzburg.[2]

South Africa's museum history dates back to the first officially proclaimed museum in Cape Town in 1825.[3] Its older museums are part of the attempted colonial intellectual conquest of Africa. They collected the scientific and cultural 'curiosities' of the subcontinent, from the artefacts and cultural products of the African population to wild animals. In contrast, works of art were collected from Europe to reinforce the cultural linkage between colonists and their home country. Until a very few years

---

1 *Amandla* is a Zulu and Xhosa word which roughly translates into 'power'. It was perhaps the most popular resistance slogan during the 1980s.

2 This chapter has developed from work undertaken on the collection of the material culture of apartheid and resistance in South Africa (Natal Museum's Amandla project, 1992–94) presented at the West African Museums Programme (WAMP) workshop, 'Museums and History', in Ouidah, Benin, in February 1995 and at the tenth ACASA (Arts Council of the African Studies Association) Triennial Symposium on African Art at New York University in April 1995.

3 See D. Webb, 'Winds of change', *Museums Journal* 94(4) (1994), 20–4; G. Dominy, 'From "Dead Zoos" to "Sources of Delight": new directions for old collections – changing exhibitions for new purposes', unpublished, presented to the Wits History Workshop, July 1992.

ago, African art was treated as ethnography and ghettoised in racially categorised collections in many museums.

During the decades after the Second World War, with the triumph of the racially extremist Afrikaner Nationalist Party in the white election of 1948, the policy of apartheid began to be strictly enforced and South Africa's darkest years began. Apartheid affected museums both directly and indirectly. While museums did not often legally prohibit African visitors, African staff could not be appointed to any posts other than the most menial. Furthermore, museums operated in the milieu of segregated schools, residential areas, facilities and an overall government strategy to devalue and deny changing African cultures and traditions, especially in the urban areas. Museums are now suffering the consequences of this policy – there are very few qualified African museum curators, and it will take several years to develop a museum profession which truly represents the South African people as a whole.

During the apartheid years, particularly from the 1960s to the 1980s, many cultural history museums were established essentially to celebrate the triumphs of white communities in South Africa, especially those associated with Afrikaner nationalist ideology and history.[4] Some ethnic museums were also established, by organs of the apartheid state, to emphasise the timeless, unique, separateness of tribal life (such as the Tsonga-Kraal Museum in the Hans Merensky Nature Reserve in the Northern Transvaal).

However, in this bleak period there were some positive developments. Although we can question the motives for collecting many traditional African artefacts, South African museums nevertheless saved important parts of the country's cultural heritage and kept it safe for the citizens of the new democracy to use, respect and enjoy as part of their patrimony. One of the most important of these collections, of both books and manuscripts, art and artefacts, was that assembled by the Campbell Family in Durban. Some museum professionals also began implicitly challenging apartheid ideology in the late 1970s and early 1980s. Archaeologists, for example, specialising in the Iron Age, played an important part in demolishing the apartheid myth that Africans migrated into South Africa from the north at the time

---

4   C.K. Brain and M.C. Erasmus, *The Making of the Museum Professions in Southern Africa* (Pretoria: Transvaal Museum and the South African Museums Association, 1986), 2. The authors of this work underplay the racial bias in the establishment of cultural history museums.

that whites were landing at the Cape, and that the land occupied by the whites was empty of human habitation.

Despite the atmosphere of repression prevalent in the late 1980s, some museums, largely those classified as 'general affairs', began developing programmes that would enable them to reach marginalised and oppressed communities. The Natal Museum appointed an African education officer who developed highly successful programmes with African schools in and around Pietermaritzburg, despite increasingly high levels of violence and the near civil war conditions which prevailed until April 1994. The Museum's Amandla project must be seen in this context of attempts to reposition and transform an old-fashioned and elitist institution where taxonomic research into the natural world had pride of place. Before this collecting programme, the cultural history collection reflected a Eurocentric, colonialist bias, with a strong concentration on the material culture of white settlers. The culture of the African majority was collected by the Anthropology and Archaeology Departments; the recent history of the African majority was not collected at all.

The Amandla project was one of a series of efforts to reposition existing institutions and develop new ones. The most prominent of these is the Mayibuye Centre for History and Culture at the University of the Western Cape which, somewhat ambitiously, 'focuses on all aspects of apartheid, resistance, social life and culture in South Africa'. In Durban, a long-held dream of the Campbell family of a museum of African cultures, is now becoming a reality with the development of the KwaMhule Museum in the old labour-control and 'Native Administration' offices. This project, which focuses on African urban life in Durban, is the product of a long process of wide consultation and community involvement, and bodes very well for the future. Even the National Cultural History Museum, formerly the flagship Afrikaner cultural museum and administered as a whites-only affair, has re-orientated its collecting, research, exhibition and outreach programmes with energy and enthusiasm.[5]

---

5   The catalyst for the transformation of this institution has been its acquisition of a semi-rural site containing an enormous meteorite crater as an eco-museum, the Tswaing Eco-Museum ('Die Soutpan' in Afrikaans). It is situated in an area of intensive and vast informal settlements and the Museum has made local community service, in the broad sense, one of its most important activities. A comprehensive process of consultation with community political, traditional and cultural leaders took place before a

The Campbell collections in Durban illustrate well the implications for collecting and collections under apartheid. The Campbells are a wealthy 'Old Natal' sugar-plantation family. In the 1920s their family seat, Muckleneuk, was built on Durban's snooty Berea ridge by the patriarch Sir Marshall Campbell. Designed by Sir Herbert Baker, architect of the Union Buildings in Pretoria, Muckleneuk is a magnificent Cape Dutch revival-style mansion. This building now houses the Campbell collections of the University of Natal. Marshall Campbell's daughter, Margaret Roach Campbell, known throughout her life as 'Killie', was the founder of one of the country's greatest collections. Killie Campbell never married, and devoted her life to the pursuit of South African history and African culture in the broader sense. She was more than an eccentric hoarder, she regarded it as her bounden duty to use her privileged position to collect rare cultural material for posterity and she particularly wanted her collection to be used by black and other students of African and Zulu history and culture.[6]

While Killie Campbell collected literature, manuscripts and illustrations of African life and Natal and Zulu history, her brother, William Alfred Campbell (known as 'Wac'), collected objects of the material culture of the African peoples. Working with well-known ethnographic artist Barbara Tyrell, Wac assembled a well-documented collection of so-called 'tribal' costume, art, items of domestic use, regalia and material used for ritual purposes. Together, Killie and Wac formed the material into the Mashu Museum of Ethnology ('Mashu' was Sir Marshall Campbell's Zulu nickname). Meanwhile, Wac's wife, Edith Armstrong, collected Cape and European furniture and art, which is also housed at Muckleneuk as part of the William Campbell Museum. Most of the collecting activity occurred from the late 1930s to the early 1960s. By the mid-1960s the research value of Killie's library had been discovered and was being exploited by scholars.

What makes the Campbell Collections differ from other collections made by wealthy eccentrics? Perhaps the major factor is the strong sense of duty that motivated the Campbells: they were not collecting for personal gratification, they were consciously collecting for posterity. Killie and Wac

---

development programme was established, and the museum and the communities have entered in resource- and profit-sharing activities so that local people feel they have a stake in the project. This is the theory, but thus far it seems to be working in practice.

6   J. Pim, *A History of the Killie Campbell African Library* (Pietermaritzburg: University of Natal, M.Bibl. Thesis, 1990), 11–12.

were particularly worried that the urbanised Africans were losing touch with their cultural traditions and becoming alienated in the city slums. Both encouraged Africans, and particularly Zulu people, to record their traditions from their elders and pass on any historical information they might have. Killie also sponsored an important historical essay competition during 1942 for African schoolchildren, the results of which are still kept in the Campbell Library.[7]

Wac, supported by Killie, was very keen to establish a museum of African life and entered into lengthy negotiations with the Durban City Council. Killie attempted to have a Chair of Bantu Studies endowed at the University of Natal and to donate her library to the university for the use of scholars. Even in the 1940s, before the National Party had come to power, the Durban City Council was ambivalent about establishing a Bantu museum, and Wac fought several long and hard battles with councillors and bureaucrats. A year after the Nationalists won the 1948 election, Killie and Wac offered their collections to the University of Natal for the establishment of a library and museum. One of the conditions was that the museum should be open to all races.[8] The university and the city council began squabbling over the availability of land for the proposed museum, and the scheme almost fell through completely. Partly to prevent the collapse of their plans, Wac donated Muckleneuk, the family home and home of the collections, to Durban City Council in 1955, a donation which was accepted by the city.

During the late 1950s, the political situation deteriorated still further with the Nationalist government focusing its energies on the suppression of dissent within the English-language universities and on the imposition of stricter racial segregation at these universities. In 1957 Killie Campbell wrote to the Minister of Education, protesting at the government's interference with the autonomy of the universities. She reported that the still semi-colonial government of Rhodesia had expressed an interest in her collections, but that as a South African who loved her country, she would rather the material remained in Durban, and concluded by asking the minister for an assurance that the money and the material she intended donating to the university would remain at their disposal and 'not be

---

7   Ibid., 17–18.
8   Ibid., 60–62.

conscripted by the government'.[9] The Minister of Education, Arts and Science replied in a placatory tone and urged her to continue with the proposed donation to the University of Natal. Significantly, he stated: 'I pledge my word of honour that there is no other intention than to serve the interests of our Non-European sections more effectively and that nothing is further from the Government's mind than to interfere with the autonomy of the existing European universities, including the University of Natal.'[10]

Killie[11] replied to the minister thanking him for his assurances and stating that as early as 1949 they had realised that there would be difficulties 'about Africans and Europeans seeing this Bantu Collection at Howard College',[12] and that they had therefore negotiated with the city council to obtain land in the city centre. The Campbells continued: 'Because of apartheid imposed now on Museums, it may be necessary to limit this Bantu Museum for Africans only, which would be a calamity as the interest shown by Europeans seeing this collection has astonished us.' Killie concluded: 'I am sorely worried about the future, and I would like to know if these arrangements could be in any way curtailed by Apartheid?'[13]

Two years later in 1959, the Nationalist Government passed the misnamed Extension of Universities Act, which enforced rigid segregation on the universities, eliminated their autonomy in the selection of students and established the so-called 'bush colleges' for black students in rural, tribal areas away from cities and centres of research and learning. While Africans were never formally barred from using the facilities of the Campbell collections as such, their exclusion from the University of Natal as students, and the strict controls imposed over their movements in the urban areas under apartheid, has meant that until very recently, the vast majority of users of the collections have been white academics.

Their fears over the future of the collections led the Campbells to split their bequest. The library and the two museum collections were donated to the University of Natal, but the property at Muckleneuk – both land and buildings – was donated to the city council. The property is leased back to the university by the city at a peppercorn rental, but as the expiry of the

---

9   Campbell to Minister of Education, 28 May 1957, Campbell Papers, KCM 6907 (File 36).
10   J.H. Viljoen to Killie Campbell, 7 June 1957, Campbell Papers, KCM 6907.
11   And possibly also Wac – the letter is not clearly worded.
12   The campus of the University of Natal in Durban.
13   [Killie and Wac] Campbell to Minister, 27 June 1957, Campbell Papers.

lease approaches, the university may be faced with demands for a more realistic rental at a time when it is under very severe financial pressure.

The Amandla project had its origins in a visit I made to the United States of America in 1989, with the object of ascertaining the extent to which American museums and battlefield interpretive programmes fostered reconciliation between old war enemies and between different classes, races and communities. A point was made of visiting an exhibition on the 'Jim Crow' era of segregation in the American South at the Valentine Museum in Richmond, Virginia. This exhibition contained slavery-related documentation and segregation-era signage and even Ku Klux Klan regalia, collected by Afro-Americans. The potential for similar programmes in South Africa was obvious, but there were problems. The first was that under the repression of the State of Emergency, much of the collecting would be of banned material from proscribed organisations. The second was that 'petty apartheid' had more or less vanished in the Natal midlands and the offensive racial signs were no longer readily available.

On 2 February 1990 the South African State of Emergency was lifted, the African National Congress (ANC) and other liberation movements were unbanned and there was a seismic change in the political scene. Nine days later Nelson Mandela walked free after 27 years' imprisonment and at a very mundane level, the Natal Museum was then free to set about the collection of the relics of the apartheid era. This freedom was, however, bounded by the constraints imposed by the turbulent political conditions in the Natal and KwaZulu region.

The political situation in Natal differed in many respects from that in other regions of South Africa, and this had a great influence on the project. In most other regions the homeland regimes had little or no popular support and the divisions between the apartheid state and the masses of people involved in the broad struggle were fairly clear-cut. In Natal, the African, predominantly Zulu-speaking, people were deeply divided. The strongest opposition to the apartheid state manifested itself in the urban areas of the province and was led by the African working classes, who supported the United Democratic Front (UDF) and later the ANC. But many of the rural areas were under the influence of conservative Zulu chiefs, the amakhosi, who were strong supporters of Chief Buthelezi, then Chief Minister of the KwaZulu homeland. Buthelezi had long played a double game: he refused to accept nominal independence for his homeland and thus set himself against the Botha regime, but he also opposed the UDF and the ANC, so he allowed the homeland and the Inkatha party structures,[14] as well as the amakhosi, to actively, and indeed violently, oppose the liberation movements. As has emerged over the past few years, the IFP (Inkatha Freedom Party) was also used by the notorious 'Third Force' of security operatives who attempted to undermine the ANC and the liberation struggle through acts of random violence.

The initial objectives in 1990 and 1991 were to collect signs, noticeboards, 'dompasses': all the symbols and documents that offered a visual identification of how the apartheid system, in all its manifestations and permutations, functioned. Our activities were widely publicised and a reasonable amount of apartheid signage was collected. This included signs from government offices which formally and legally designated separate entrances and facilities for various races. There were also signs from commercial concerns, such as the local City Tattersalls old 'Non-White Entrance'.[15] Signs indicating the status of officials in terms of their racially defined functions, for example, 'Clerk to the Bantu Affairs Commissioner', were also acquired.

Dating the signs enabled us to keep track of changing euphemisms. As apartheid unravelled, the system kept renaming people and departments while the oppressive structure remained in place under a new name. The collected signs are a partial reflection of the name changes. What was surprising was the rapidity with which these signs had disappeared and the extent to which amnesia about the apartheid era had taken hold in the very institutions predicated on the maintenance of the system. Many government offices denied that they ever had, or used, apartheid signs or racially classified services.

It also became clear that this was only part of the story, and that if the signage and material culture of the apartheid system was disappearing, then the more fragile and spontaneous cultural manifestations of the resistance struggle were likely to disappear even more quickly. Collecting began in a low-key, informal way, hampered by lack of funds. It was clear that the museum needed more funds to engage on the project in a meaningful way. It was also abundantly clear that the Natal Museum

---

14   After the unbanning of the ANC in 1990, the Inkatha Cultural and Liberation Movement was renamed the Inkatha Freedom Party (IFP) and changed its colours from black, green and gold (the colours of the ANC) to black, green, gold, white and red, the colours of the KwaZulu flag.

15   The City Tattersalls is the centrally situated betting shop.

needed to make a serious effort to reach out into the township communities around Pietermaritzburg; it was still perceived as a white-orientated, elitist institution. In 1991, however, the museum applied for funding to collect the story of resistance to the apartheid system in Natal.[16] The United States Social Sciences Research Council and the United States Council of Learned Societies established a competitive programme to initiate and assist cultural projects in Africa entitled the African Archives and Museums Project. Thirty awards were made across Africa, but only two were made in South Africa, one to the Natal Museum.

The objectives of the project were to collect the cultural and material evidence of the anti-apartheid struggle in Natal, with particular reference to the Greater Pietermaritzburg area, including:

1. Symbolic apparel: T-shirts, items of uniform and insignia, and so on.
2. Political ephemera: posters, banners, leaflets, pamphlets, and so on.
3. Private property of a political, historical or symbolic nature confiscated by the security police.
4. Photographic and visual evidence of the struggle.
5. Oral history interviews with participants in the struggle, thus assisting in the establishment of an historical context for the artefacts, photographs and ephemera collected.

The project was also to include full curation of the material and an exhibition which would reposition the museum within the communities of the 'New South Africa'.

The initial collecting programme for the 'Collecting the anti-apartheid struggle in Natal' project took place between August 1992 and March 1993.[17] The collecting of material evidence, including photographs, met with considerable success. Less success was achieved with the programme of oral history interviews. The special exhibition, entitled 'Amandla: The

---

16   G. Dominy, 'Collecting the struggle against apartheid in Natal', *Natalia* 22 (1992), 79.

17   See G. Dominy, 'Collecting the anti-apartheid struggle in Natal', an unpublished report to the United States Social Sciences Research Council and the American Council of Learned Societies for the *African Archives and Museums Project 1992-1993*' (17 August 1993). G. Dominy, '*Amandla!* The Natal Museum project to collect the culture of apartheid and the struggle against it', *Museums Journal*, 94(4) (1994), 26.

Struggle for Human Rights: Peace or Violence?', opened in 1993, on the anniversary of the Soweto rising of 1976.

A field research officer, Makhosi Khoza, paid numerous visits to the surrounding townships and established important contacts with community organisations, youth groups, trade unions and monitoring groups. She attended rallies, funerals, meetings and social events and obtained considerable support, particularly from trade unions, and consequently acquired a valuable collection of political ephemera.

Amongst the difficulties were those surrounding the acquisition of mourning dress, a common and tragically significant sight in the streets of the city; widows burnt their mourning clothing after the period of mourning. A well-known seamstress was therefore commissioned to make a set of mourning clothes for exhibition purposes. When this clothing was exhibited in the 'Amandla' exhibition, it attracted criticism from certain historians who found the concept ghoulish and demeaning. However, the cultural manifestations of widowhood during this time of violence were crucially important.

Problems were also experienced in collecting pre-1990 struggle material. Many informants stated that their private possessions and papers had been seized by the security forces during the State of Emergency and never returned. This issue is a national problem which is now being addressed by the Truth and Reconciliation Commission. Others lost all their possessions in the violence of the late 1980s and early 1990s when their homes were destroyed. Difficulties were experienced in obtaining a widely representative collection of material. The tension in the region also meant that people did not feel sufficiently secure to give oral testimony, thus sabotaging the oral history programme. Ironically, the collections of oral testimony in the Campbell collections were provided by informants who felt more free to speak under colonial rule or in the heyday of apartheid, than did those informants approached at the height of the transition process.

Certain political groups were more helpful than others. Political tension in the region made it impossible for one field research officer to collect from across the political spectrum. Inkatha and IFP material had to be obtained from the IFP Information Centre in Durban as the Pietermaritzburg IFP was actively hostile to the project. Once the 1994 election was over and relative calm returned to the region, the KwaZulu Cultural Museum in Ulundi collaborated with the Natal Museum and pro-IFP craftwork was acquired.

Apartheid did not inhibit the Campbells' collecting activities, but it prevented full public appreciation of their collections and forced an irrational arrangement to be made which is now threatening the long-term future of the collections. The demise of apartheid took place in an atmosphere of acute political tension, and this hampered the collecting activities of the Natal Museum at a time when there was formal freedom of speech and expression.

The Amandla project has served as a catalyst for the transformation of the Natal Museum as an institution. This is a slow process, but it has now firmly begun, and this is partly as a result of the change in attitudes within the institution brought about through the Amandla project. The project enabled us to reach into communities whose history we had not reflected and whose concerns we had not addressed. We built up a collection of artefacts, photographs and cultural material that reflects a crucial phase in our country's history.

The long-term plans for the Amandla collection are to exhibit it as part of an overall exhibition on human history, known as SOPISA, the 'Story of People in South-Eastern Africa'. This exhibition traces the development of human society in our region from the Stone Age to the rise of powerful African states such as the Zulu kingdom to the impact of colonialism and imperialism (this will require the reinterpretation of existing galleries), to apartheid and liberation.

The long-term future of the Campbell collections continues to be debated. Ironically, although the Campbell collections are a vital source for the understanding of the history of the black peoples of south-eastern Africa, the library and museum have acquired the reputation, justified or not, of being a stuffy colonial relic. The Killie Campbell African Library and Museum and the Natal Museum are in equal need of urgent and thorough transformation.

While the political climate is now favourable for the transformation of the two institutions and, for the first time ever, they can be truly open to all South Africans, there are acute financial constraints which threaten their long-term future. The most appropriate way forward is through regional co-operation, resource sharing and joint planning.

12 Folk devils in our midst? Collecting from 'deviant' groups

Nicola Clayton

The museum community has arguably been reticent about collecting material culture with difficult or controversial associations. Groups seen as deviant remain invisible through their non-representation. Discussion here focuses on two such groups: youth subcultures, and subcultures within the lesbian and gay community. It could, however, be extended to more extreme articulations of lifestyle such as the 'cultures' of tattoo and body piercing or 'leatherfolk'.[1] This chapter examines the challenge of collecting 'difficult' subject matter and suggests how contemporary collecting practices which do address such issues contribute towards documenting cultural richness and diversity, and derive positive results for museums themselves.

The relationships between these seemingly disparate groups are complex, but intrinsic. The 'gay skinhead' for example, has all the iconography of the familiar youth subcultural skinhead: the shaven head, Doctor Martens boots, drainpipe jeans, braces and bomber jacket. No visual distinction may seem apparent, yet both can have quite different ideological and political agendas. Similarly, the club scenes of 'house' and 'acid-house' were initially perceived primarily as gay music genres until international recognition diminished such references.[2] It is the labelling of their perceived cultural otherness as 'deviant', however, whether that be deviancy of a social or sexual nature, that historically and most significantly binds youth subcultures and those of the lesbian and gay community. The 'deviant other' label stems in part from academic

---

1   M. Thompson, ed., *Leather-Folk: Radical Sex, People, Politics, and Practice* (Boston: Alyson Publications, 1991).
2   S. Thornton, S., *Club Cultures: Music, Media and Subcultural Capital* (Cambridge: Polity Press, 1995), 73.

discourse, as subcultural theory grew out of sociological enquiry into deviancy and delinquency, and through precedents set by the government and media. British governments have, for example, consistently refused to recognise gay rights and the popular press often discusses such issues only through alarmist rhetoric. Constructed as the folk devils of twentieth-century popular culture, they are often placed as scapegoats for wider social problems.[3]

Connotations of deviancy which have been fabricated within the national consciousness have arguably served to inhibit museum involvement with such groups, resulting in the loss of valuable material culture. As the cultural identities of 'others' hitherto ignored by museums, such as women, ethnic groups, the working classes and people marginalised because of their disability, have begun to be recognised and celebrated to varying degrees in museological theory and practice, this acknowledgement is only slowly being extended to those whose identity is placed firmly within the realms of popular culture. Their absence from collecting practices can be attributed, therefore, not only to their status as 'deviant other', but also to the disregard which is afforded popular culture within museums in general which is only now being addressed.

Such groups have not generally been represented in museological literature nor in permanent museum displays and collections.[4] Lesbian and gay identities are rarely acknowledged in museums,[5] and often only appear within the more avant-garde realm of the art gallery. While youth subcultures have been increasingly recognised such as in the Victoria & Albert (V&A) Museum's 'Streetstyle: From Sidewalk to Catwalk 1940 to Tomorrow' or singularly as in Bradford's 'Sound and Fury; The Art and Imagery of Heavy Metal', such initiatives remain unusual and rarely contribute to the permanent collections.

---

3   See S. Cohen, *Folk Devils and Moral Panics: The Creation of the Mods and Rockers* (London: MacGibbon & Kee, 1972).

4   An exception is Amy de la Haye's article 'Travellers' boots, body-moulding, rubber fetish clothes: making histories of subcultures' in G. Kavanagh, ed., *Making Histories in Museums* (Leicester: Leicester University Press, 1996).

5   G. Bourne, *Invisibility: A Study of the Representation of Lesbian and Gay History and Culture in Social History Museums* (Leicester: University of Leicester, unpublished MA dissertation, 1994); S. Cole, 'What a queer collection – the problem of collecting lesbian and gay material in museums', Theory, Populism and Sub-Cultural Dress, V&A seminar, 11 November 1995.

The challenge of collecting

Attempting to represent any culture or community raises a number of problematic issues. An initial problem can be one of definition – reference to groups or communities may in reality prove impossible as they often do not exist as a single homogenous mass. Community is both a complex and contested term, and in reference to lesbian and gay identity it should be used with caution for arguably no such unity exists, the notion of a lesbian and gay community having been challenged as simply an imagined reality or media construction.[6] Visual collective identities may seem apparent, but one cannot necessarily assume uniformity; the ways in which a sense of identity and community are constructed are complex and influenced by variables such as geographical location, class, age, gender and race. How, then, can the museum gather and represent this diversity? The V&A overcame this problem by collecting outfits from individuals rather than collectives. Thus an outfit was taken to represent one person's interpretation of what an identity meant to them, rather than an amalgamated 'look'.[7]

Museums by their nature inevitably create stereotypical representations of their subjects, and stereotyped 'looks' are actually actively created by the communities themselves; gay 'clones', 'leather queens' and 'pretty boys' do exist, for example, as any leaf through the ads or personal section of the gay press will illustrate. However, it would be misguided to take such specific and loaded iconographies as visually representative of all male gay culture. Cultures and scenes are fluid, their boundaries merge and individuals can move between them with changing commitment. Polhemus's concept of the 'supermarket of style' used in the 'Streetstyle' exhibition, whilst an oversimplification, does begin to indicate the heterogeneity of existing contemporary subcultures, which operate in a complex dialogue of stylistic and cultural influence and appropriation.[8]

---

6   D. Bell, and G. Valentine (eds), *Mapping Desire: Geographies of Sexualities* (London: Routledge, 1995).

7   A. De la Haye, 'Trickle-down/bubble-up: the sourcing and dissemination of high fashion and streetstyle design 1947–94', Representing the Street: Subculture and Image, V&A study day, 25, November 1994.

8   T. Polhemus, *Streetstyle: From Sidewalk to Catwalk* (London: Thames and Hudson, 1994).

Given that the institutional structure of museums necessitates a process of labelling and categorisation, this fluidity of identified groups can thus have problematic implications for collecting practices. What does one use as criteria for defining any given group: style, music, mode of transport, sexual preference? How do we attempt to classify them? Is it sufficient to box individuals into neat categories, so that youth subcultures can be given a traditional and exclusive linear progression of teds, mods, rockers, skinheads, punks and so forth? Where should one place those individuals whose lifestyle and material culture should be of significance to the museum but who cannot be labelled? Similarly, how can one begin to recognise and record those for whom a high profile does not exist, those for whom legitimisation has not occurred through the normal channels of academic theory and the media because they are not visually exotic but rather mundane in character. Given the practical restrictions of museums and the ambiguities of collective identities, how can museums begin to record such cultures without simply creating parodies or tokenistic gestures?

A further obstacle lies in the anti-establishment stance of many of these groups, who are forced, or perhaps choose to go, underground. It was not until the Sexual Offences Act 1967, for example, that male homosexuality was substantially decriminalised in Britain. In such circumstances, collecting and documentation become difficult. Similarly, the codes and signifiers of so-called group allegiance can often be transitory in nature and one needs to be in the know in order to decipher their significance. Thus again there are questions such as how does one actually make contact, gain the trust of, and sustain a relationship with such groups? Given the perceived authoritarian and often conservative image of museums, how does one overcome their suspicions and persuade such groups to part with material culture? Will they want representation in such institutions at all? If, by their nature, such groups are positioned as deviant and subversive how then do museums capture this without sterilising and sanitising it? How will the legitimisation which inevitably comes with museum appropriation, affect the nature and perceptions of the cultures in question?

The terms of reference, such as deviant, youth subculture, counterculture, alternative, and homosexual, gay and queer are also problematic because they are often ill-defined, being both academically and internally contested. 'Deviant' is a socially constructed and ever-changing concept, for example, which is both problematic and an undeservedly pejorative term of reference for the groups in question, but one is compelled to use such a classification in the absence of anything more fitting. The term 'subculture' is also problematic, for in 'fragmented post-modernist society', can one assume there still exists a dominate culture or 'norm' of which such groups can be a subset? Such contentions must have obvious implications for collecting practices when actually attempting to define what one is to collect.

There also exist practical and legal constraints, such as Section 28 of the Local Government Act 1988 which outlaws the promotion of homosexuality by local authorities.[9] Similarly, the Criminal Justice and Public Order Act 1994 serves to criminalise certain groups and their activities, such as protest groups and the rave and dance scene.[10] There are also ethical issues. British reserve and an implied role for museums as moral guardians have ensured that an amount of self-censorship has been exercised. Issues concerning sex and drugs, for example, are considered taboo. However, other practical problems can emerge, such as establishing a dialogue with groups who may not have any central point of contact or orthodox means of communication. This was the experience of the V&A when attempting to collect material from the Donga tribe, who live a nomad lifestyle without telephones, postal addresses and so forth.[11] The difficulties encountered in collecting material from so-called 'deviant' groups are akin to those of collecting from marginalised others, but the similarities have rarely been acknowledged. Such collecting calls for both political and cultural sensitivity where issues of identity, community and ownership come into play.

A wealth of material culture

Contrary to prevailing misconceptions which assume that subcultures have no identifiable material culture of their own, an infinite amount exists to be collected. The visual and musical iconography, together with the perceived

---

9   J. Stacey, 'Promoting normality: Section 28 and the regulation of sexuality', in S. Franklin, C. Lury and J. Stacey (eds), *Off-Centre: Feminism and Cultural Studies* (London: Harper Collins Academic, 1991).

10   T. Marcus, 'Summer of chaos', *i-D*, 119 (1993), 78–85; T. Maylon et al., eds., 'United you're nicked: Criminal Justice & Public Order Bill Supplement', *New Statesman & Society*, 24(6) (1994).

11   De la Haye, 'Trickle-down', op. cit.

ethos of youth subcultures and the lesbian and gay community, have an all-pervasive and profound influence on our culture, whether this is illustrated in Memphis furniture or the interior furnishings of shops, such as Practical Styling being described as 'punk'[12] or film as 'camp'. Aspects which have originated from, or have been explored by subcultures are often subsequently taken up by the mainstream. For example, work for the Sex Pistols by Jamie Reid has had an enormous influence on graphic design and typographical styles used in advertising and the media.[13]

The relationship of 'deviant' groups to commerce and the mainstream is a complex one. Conceptions of an authentic subcultural existence tainted by capitalist exploitation should be challenged, for the cultures do play an active part in producing, marketing and retailing their own material culture in the form of clothing, furnishings and interior design, music-related ephemera such as records, CDs, promotional flyers, posters, fanzines and all manner of other material which is expressive of their identity and lifestyles. Here one may include politically associated material such as protest banners, placards, leaflets and so forth, of gay rights movements for example, or even more physical items such as the tree houses built by road protesters. Cohesive, self-sufficient alternative economies do exist such as that of the festival circuit, which supports:

> a network of crafts people, fire circuses, dancers, healers, astrologers, jugglers, cafes ... bars, jewellers, trapeze artists, children's entertainers, bands, clothes stalls, candle makers, tattooists, sound engineers, riggers, acid and hash dealers, lighting personnel, black-smiths, bookshops and piercers.[14]

Some groups have also become recognised as distinct market niches to be exploited by multinational companies such as those that support the fashions in skate-, surf- and snowboarding. Similarly, the gay market has become increasingly targeted in recent years by 'straight' companies.

The concept of the subcultural *bricoleur*[15] also provides another type of artefact – goods that have been produced for the mass market but which

---

12   P. Core, *The Original Eye: Arbiters of Twentieth-Century Taste* (London: Quartet Books, 1984), 182-3.

13   See C. McDermott, *Streetstyle: British Design in the 80s* (London: The Design Council, 1987) for broad introduction to the stylistic legacy of punk.

14   Marcus, op. cit.

15   D. Hebdige, *Subculture: The Meaning of Style* (London: Methuen and Co. Ltd, 1979).

are appropriated and their meanings changed. This might take the form of alteration to an object such as hair and make-up on dolls turned into a subcultural style or the customising of vehicles by New Age travellers. Similarly, it is the context in which an object is placed that can give it a new subcultural value – how secondhand clothes are worn, or objects such as the safety pin or the dummy and whistle becoming icons of punk and acid house subcultures. Cultural identification of a given group with an object can also make that object appropriate for collection by association. For example, material associated with Judy Garland can relate to Hollywood, but also to the gay scene, as she has been constructed as a gay icon. Similarly, the Body Shop's Peppermint Foot Lotion has been described as 'a mid-90s emblem typifying the agony and ecstasies of young gay love'.[16]

A body of material culture also exists which, while it is often based on the more visually elaborate cultures, is totally divorced from the original source's lifestyles or ideologies. Such material commonly takes the form of parodies of representation such as London tourist ephemera of punks on postcards, greetings cards and dolls. Similarly, symbols or icons can be appropriated such as the Smiley face, an icon of previous subcultures later associated with 1990s acid house, which has become a mainstream commodity. Divorced from its previous associations with drugs through the lapse of time, it became a safe and trendy icon.

It can be argued that there are more effective means of recording people's lifestyles, through video, film or photography rather than through objects,[17] yet objects remain a uniquely tangible primary source. They can symbolise one's place or pride in an identity, and 'the power of the real thing',[18] the 'authenticity' of objects, can serve to both emotionally move and educate us. They act as a memory for society, and thus their status as key elements in the preservation of cultural identities is undeniable. They can illustrate the human condition to reconstruct and influence the material space one inhabits, and as such they are integral to recording the existence of 'deviant' groups, their lifestyles and cultures of expression. The material ephemera which is produced also serves to reflect not only 'deviant' group culture, but the character and prejudices of the dominant mainstream to which they are constructed as in opposition. Museums must begin to

---

16   'Queer icons: peppermint foot lotion', *Pink Paper* 7(6) (1996), 39.

17   For example, the Channel 4 series, *Tribe Time,* 7 October–11 November 1995.

18   S. Pearce (ed), *Objects of Knowledge* (London: Athlone Press, 1990), 127.

acknowledge, when collecting, that artefacts can be polysemantic, and that the multiplicity of meanings attached to them must be reflected in the contextual material that is also recorded.

Implications of collecting

The implications of collecting material culture from the groups in question is far-reaching, for such collecting may pose a challenge to the very structure of museums, exposing inadequacies such as those inherent in existing discipline divisions. For example, is it appropriate to collect the Mod experience by splitting it between different departments – the scooter in the transport section, the parka and suit to costume, the records and record player to social history? In terms of collecting culture, this is obviously ridiculous, yet at present most British museums do not have the appropriate framework to cope with the practical implications that collecting lifestyles can entail. Initiatives such as that of Samdok which place emphasis on recording the social and cultural context of objects, in collaborative and thematic collecting projects, provide a useful model for collecting from 'deviant' cultures also.[19]

Collecting may also pose a challenge in terms of what museums see as their purview. Should collecting subcultural material be simply the responsibility of social history and costume departments? Why should the club flyer or record cover not be collected by the art department, or the technology department begin to recognise both the technological and cultural significance of such hardware as an 808 drum machine or light strobe which are so integral to the rave and techno scenes? Museums already collect from, or at least document, sites such as factories so why not night club interiors? Clubs such as Heaven or the Hacienda have played an enormous part in the creation and maintenance of scenes and cultures, yet the interior decoration, lighting systems and so forth which go to create an atmosphere are not collected.

The subversive or controversial nature of the material culture of so-called 'deviant' groups can be overestimated. However, because of the authority which museums are perceived to hold, collecting such material can actually afford the opportunity to alter the status of such material, desensitising and legitimising attitudes towards it. Such material can also provide a direct challenge to the existing complacency of many museums with regard to

---

19   See papers by A. Steen (Chapter 17) and B. Bursell (Chapter 18).

sensitive issues or groups, and demands for it to be collected call into question the museum's role in society as either passive onlooker or active participant in contemporary issues. By failing to recognise difficult groups and their material culture, one can argue that museums are thus guilty of maintaining prevailing misconceptions of such groups as deviant and insignificant. It is a question of setting a precedent, for even if controversial associations of material mean that it cannot be displayed at present, should it not be a matter of collecting the material now and waiting to display it when the climate is more favourable?

Collecting such material provides the means to address the bias of collections existing within many British museums, but it also necessitates a proactive stance, as such material is unlikely to come to the museum by traditional routes. As exhibitions such as 'Streetstyle' illustrate, collecting from such groups can be a positive and enlightening experience for all parties, and significantly impact on both visitor figures and visitor profile. This is especially appropriate if museums are to challenge the subordination of the culture of youth in general. It seems that at present it has been left to private collectors to save our more populist cultural heritage for posterity, but as public institutions, the responsibility for collecting for the future should surely also lie firmly with museums. Given the disposable nature of our society and the implications this has for collecting and documentation, should we be satisfied with leaving the record of contemporary cultural diversity in the hands of private collectors (however proficient their efforts may be)? Can museums continue to ignore the significance of material culture which plays such an integral part in many people's lives? Museums must begin to change to accommodate social realities other than that of the constructed dominant norm.

13 All legal and ethical? Museums and the international market in fossils

John Martin

There have been curators and students of palaeontology since the science's beginnings, and there have been professional collectors of, and dealers in, fossils for just as long. The relationship between these academic and commercial worlds has, therefore, been difficult for two hundred years. *Plus ça change.* Recent imports from developing countries of world-class 'firsts' in vertebrate palaeontology give us some new and truly important specimens to argue about. What should curators do in these circumstances? Do international and UK laws help? Does the law understand the real world of science?

Collecting palaeontological specimens has separated academics from collectors and dealers since the beginning of the nineteenth century. The story of the relationship of Mary Anning, the Dorset collector and dealer, with her academic gentleman customers between about 1812 and 1840 is so well known (and has so often been appropriated by groups wishing to draw a moral) that it has become part of palaeontological mythology.[1]

Whatever the sociology of Mary's business success (was she the first of a long line of collectors to be classified as 'working-class' and therefore to be treated differently from academic colleagues?), it is a fact that without her work vertebrate palaeontology would not have developed where and how it did. For many academics (including museum curators), it has always been easier and cheaper to buy fossils from professional collectors than to mount an expedition to collect for oneself. This is partly a matter of economics – scale and efficiency – and partly a matter of choice, with

---

1   See, for example, M.A. Taylor and H.S. Torrens, 'Fossils by the Sea', *Natural History*, 10/95 (1995), 67–71.

fieldwork seeming expensive, time-consuming, strenuous and dangerous, to say nothing of the weather often encountered in collecting localities. Relatively few curator-palaeontologists do collect, we instead rely on other methods of acquisition. We accept donations and, if our museum's collecting policy justifies it strongly enough, we buy.

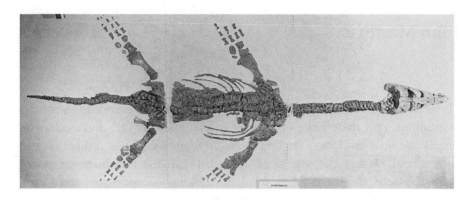

Fig. 13.1 The 'Kipper' (© Leicester City Museums).

The four methods of acquisition – collection, gift, exchange and purchase – are part of every museum's policy and practice. But when the choice is to buy, for example, a dinosaur fossil for display or research, all the old questions are asked again: Is the price too high? Can we trust these dealers? Should we encourage them to collect even if they don't gather stratigraphic data? Are we encouraging the destruction of the countryside? This feeling of mistrust is mutual, as curators who know or work with professional collector-dealers can confirm, and is probably at the heart of the problems we have with the ethics and law of purchasing fossils, both from UK sites and sites in the developing world.

The 'Kipper'

The 'Kipper' is the name given by local people in Barrow upon Soar, Leicestershire, to a fossil skeleton of the pliosaur *Rhomaleosaurus megacephalus* from the lower Liassic (Lower Jurassic) limestone which underlies their village (Fig. 13.1). The fossil was collected in about 1849, presumably by local quarrymen, and offered for sale by William Lee, a local farmer, lime burner, quarry owner and fossil dealer.[2] It is now part of the collections of Leicester Museum and Art Gallery, having been purchased by the Leicester Literary and Philosophical Society in 1851 (the money was raised by subscription) and donated by that society to the then newly formed Town Museum.[3] The 'Kipper', together with two fossil ichthyosaurs from the same quarry, cost the society £150. At current prices this equates to £30,000, and indeed this is what one would have to pay today for a fine, mounted, 7-metre pliosaur.[4]

The 'Kipper' was simply named *Plesiosaurus* in the museum's catalogue. In 1846 another specimen of the same animal had been collected from Somerset. This specimen became part of the Bristol Museum collection, and was designated the type specimen of a new species of *Plesiosaurus*. The Bristol specimen was destroyed by bombing in 1940. New research on the Barrow specimen has confirmed that it belongs to the same species as the lost fossil, and it has been designated the neotype specimen and named *Rhomaleosaurus megacephalus*.[5] In addition to being the international reference specimen for its taxon, other research has also revealed in the 'Kipper' many previously unknown features of the anatomy and physiology of pliosaurs.[6]

The 1851 purchase and donation thus added an internationally important vertebrate fossil to the museum's collections. It would not happen today,

---

2   J. Martin, E. Frey and J. Riess, 'Soft tissue preservation in ichthyosaurs and a stratigraphic review of the Lower Hettangian of Barrow-upon-Soar, Leicestershire', *Transactions of the Leicester Literary and Philosophical Society*, 80 (1986), 58–72.

3   M.A. Taylor and A.R.I. Cruickshank, 'The skull of *"Plesiosaurus megacephalus"* (Stutchbury 1846): the Barrow "Kipper"', *Transactions of the Leicester Literary and Philosophical Society*, 83 (1989), 20–4.

4   W.D.I. Rolfe, A.C. Milner and F.G. Hay, 'The Price of Fossils', in P.R. Crowther, and W.A. Wimbledon, eds., *The Use and Conservation of Palaeontological Sites* (London: Palaeontological Association, Special Papers in Palaeontology, 40, 1988).

5   A.R.I. Cruickshank, 'Cranial anatomy of the Lower Jurassic pliosaur *Rhomaleosaurus megacephalus* (Stutch.) (Reptilia, Plesiosauria)', *Phil. Trans. R. Soc. London*, Series B, 343 (1994), 247–60.

6   A.R.I. Cruickshank, M.A. Taylor and P. Small, 'Dorsal nostrils and hydrodynamically driven underwater olfaction in plesiosaurs', *Nature*, 352 (1991), 62–4.

however: it is the museum's policy to do nothing to encourage trade in natural history (including geological) and archaeological specimens. It is a matter of principle for zoologists and botanists – the conservation of living things – as well as within the law. It is also consistent with common practice in museums in the United Kingdom, and with the UK Museums Association's Draft Code of Conduct and Ethical Guidelines.[7] So what follows is not simply an issue of parochial interest.

Breaking the law?

Discussion here focuses on geological (specifically vertebrate palaeontological) specimens and their acquisition by museums. I concentrate on a relatively new area of difficulty for curators who are concerned about the ethics of acquisition: that of importing fossils from countries with export restrictions.

From this discussion it will be apparent that museums have almost certainly infringed the terms of the UNESCO Convention[8] and the more recent agreements and legal instruments: the UNIDROIT Convention[9] and European Regulations.[10] Whilst these documents concern cultural property, they also specifically include palaeontological specimens.

Are fossils 'cultural property', and if so, whose? Fossils are not like artefacts, which are arguably the products of the culture of a country whose present inhabitants can claim them as part of their history or heritage: such artefacts were made by the claimant people's forebears. In fact, this rationale is as much political as cultural; claims for restitution of cultural property are almost always politically motivated.

There is no such historic connection between fossils and people, except in the special case of specimens related to the history of science. Fossils are material evidence of life in the past which, once collected and studied, acquire scientific value; they exist because of rare accidents of death, burial,

---

7   Museums Association, *Draft Code of Conduct* (London: MA, 1996); Museums Association 1996. *Ethical Guidelines No. 1, Acquisition* (London: MA, 1996).

8   UNESCO, *Convention on the Means of Prohibiting and Preventing the Illicit Import, Export and Transfer of Ownership of Cultural Property* (Paris: UNESCO, 1970).

9   UNIDROIT (International Institute for the Unification of Private Law), *Convention of 24 June 1995 on Stolen or Illegally Exported Cultural Objects*.

10   EEC, *European Regulation 3911/92 of 9 December 1992 on the export of cultural goods, Council of the European Communities*.

preservation, mineralogy and so on in the geologically distant past. They relate to no geopolitical boundaries, nor to the cultural heritage of any group of people. They do, however, provide evidence for the genetic heritage of us all. So fossils are probably not 'cultural', and if they are ever anyone's property, once in the public domain they, and the information they carry, belong to the international scientific community, in trust for everyone. Any other interpretation implies that what is actually meant is financial value – at worst the 'it's ours, the price just went up and you will have to pay us if you want it' meaning of 'property'.

Fig. 13.2 Egg of therizinosaur dinosaur containing embryo, Cretaceous, Henan Province, PRC (© Leicester City Museums).

Of course, this is not a new argument. But all relevant laws and the conventions cited above are based on the premiss that fossils are cultural property, as though there were no argument about it. My contention is that property-based law about the import and export of fossils is not only inappropriate, but bad for people and bad for fossils.

The case of Chinese dinosaur eggs

Among the most exciting vertebrate fossil finds of recent years has been a series of dinosaur eggs from southern China (Fig. 13.2). What makes them so important is that some, perhaps 10 per cent, of these Cretaceous, 75 million-year-old eggs contain the skeletons of unhatched dinosaurs (six species at present estimate) at various stages of embryonic development. Some of these have soft tissues (skin, cartilage), egg yolk, the pupae and 'frass' of infesting insects and, possibly, dinosaur DNA still preserved. Naturally, these exquisite fossils are unique and of international importance for palaeontology. Their contents, and scientific value, have been realised as the result of expert preparation (removal of the sediment and minerals in which they have been buried) and analysis in England and North America. *National Geographic* recently featured these and other eggs, in an article which reportedly had a $1 million budget. Part of the costs involved travel to Henan Province, the area from which the fossil eggs come, for the *National Geographic* photographer and team, including an internationally respected dinosaur specialist.[11]

The team actually failed to reach the find locality, the Nanyang Valley, near Xinye. They now understand that a small payment should have been made to a local official (a useful way of expediting business in many developing countries) but that their hosts were too polite to mention this. The eggs – thousands of them – have been collected since 1957 by local people, dug out of soft sediment in modern river banks. The locals sell them for a few *renminbi*; this also is how things happen in developing countries, whatever we might prefer, or do, in the West. The eggs are a legitimate source of income for the local people. Without their collecting efforts the eggs would still be worthless pebbles in the ground. Indeed, who could disagree that the eggs are their property, to be sold, thrown away or left in the ground as they choose?

The eggs eventually find their way to Hong Kong or Beijing and thence to the West, where they are bought and sold by professional fossil dealers. However, Chinese law strictly controls the export, as 'cultural objects', of all vertebrate fossils and palaeoanthropological specimens.[12] The

11   Anon., in *National Geographic*, May (1996), 96–111.
12   PRC Standing Committee, *Cultural Relics Law of the People's Republic of China* (1982), Articles 27, 28; together with subsequent adapting Regulations (1985, adopted 1987) and *Prohibited Import and Export Goods Lists* (1989–1993).

government's agent in regulating these exports is the Institute for Vertebrate Palaeontology and Palaeoanthropology (IVPP) in Beijing; fossil vertebrates may only be exported temporarily, and only for research. So all the Chinese eggs sold in the West are, by this definition, illegal exports.[13] But is it cultural or scientific value which determines whether fossils stay in China or leave, or is it market value? Many of the fossil eggs sold in the USA now have a document issued by the Nature Beauty Company (apparently a trading arm of a Government-approved academic institution set up after Chinese eggs had begun to be sold on the open market in the West), which reassures potential purchasers that sale 'for research, not for business' via the Nature Beauty Company is legitimate;[14] this statement appears to relate to a 1989 change in the People's Republic of China Export Goods Lists.[15] In this complex system only the local youngsters get almost nothing for their trouble.

The problem in this story for those of us concerned about the advancement of science is that the last links in the chain of collection, research and publication, cannot be completed: firstly, because no reputable university or public museum acquires fossils which have been exported illegally (or 'doubtfully') from another country (in compliance with the spirit of UNESCO and UNIDROIT conventions) and, secondly, because no reputable palaeontological journal publishes papers whose subject is not in the public domain (in a museum or university). The eggs are therefore in a kind of limbo, their importance widely known but unpublishable. So should they have stayed in China?

With this question I stray into uncomfortable territory. Chinese scientists are as able as scientists anywhere – as is evident from the quality of work produced by expatriate Chinese palaeontologists. But there is a difficulty for science in China, associated perhaps with that country's system of

---

13   J.D. Murphy, 'Hong Kong, 1997, and the International Movement of Antiquities', *International Journal of Cultural Property*, 2 (1995), 4, 241–54; J.D. Murphy, *Plunder and Preservation: Cultural Property Law and Practice in the People's Republic of China* (Oxford & Hong Kong: Oxford University Press, 1995), 119, 160.

14   Anon. *Open Letter and Special Statement* (issued with fossil eggs for sale in USA) (Beijing: University of Science and Technology, 1992).

15   Anon., 'New provisions made by the Customs concerning the export of the fossils of ancient vertebrates and ancient peoples', *China Customs*, 7 (1990), 13.

allocating resources or with its politics, which seems to mitigate against accessible, quality scientific publication or the best standards of care for specimens. I am sorry if this reads as prejudiced, but it is, sadly, at least a partial, widely known, truth. If, as curators, our first concerns are for objects and science, our conclusion about Chinese dinosaur eggs may be that they are better off in the West, where they can be properly prepared, curated, studied and published, and thus shared world-wide. We might, at least, agree a way of extricating the eggs already here from their intellectual limbo.

Fossils from Brazil

A second example also concerns exceptionally preserved fossils of Cretaceous age. They come from the Santana Formation, which outcrops in Ceara Province in north-east Brazil. All geology curators will know the beautiful, complete fishes of the Santana Formation because most museums have examples in their collections: these fossils can be purchased at every 'fossil shop' in Europe. But again, local law prohibits the export of vertebrate fossils from Brazil and any museum holding such specimens is almost certainly contravening the terms of the UNIDROIT convention.

Some Santana fossils are, like the Chinese eggs, of international importance. The quality of preservation, and the richness of the fauna they represent, puts Ceara in the top handful of fossil localities in the world. Recent finds have included fishes with gills and muscles – remarkable for fossils 75 million years old – as well as several completely new kinds of dinosaurs and pterosaurs with wing and other membranes still in place.

Like the Chinese case, this is an uncomfortable story of what we might call corruption, but which to Brazilian people is 'just life'. Quarries are worked by the local people – peasants and their children – specifically for fossils. There is an international market for these objects, after all. The locals are largely controlled by a chain of middlemen (in another line of business they would be called pimps) whose power is enhanced by the rifles they carry. Fossil specimens produced by this system can be exported 'legally', provided a provincial official can be persuaded to sign a docket listing them as rock samples, whose export is not restricted by Brazilian law. Eventually, the by now 'legitimate' fossils reach professional dealers in Europe and North America, where most are sold to collectors; some go into museums. As a result of this system, a fossil turtle for which a local farmer was paid $10 was eventually acquired in Europe, after everyone had taken their cut and some preparation had been done, for $16,000. Even if they chose to ignore the legality issue, few if any European scientists or museums have $16,000 to spend on a 35-centimetre fossil, however important, so most important specimens leaving Brazil this way are effectively lost as far as the scientific community is concerned. They are generally acquired by wealthy private collectors.

Some US and European scientists visit Brazil themselves. By doing so, and by becoming friends with the local people and treating them with respect, it is possible to acquire important fossils direct. The fossil turtle mentioned above might cost $100 – paid direct to the farmer who excavated it from his own land – plus the scientists' travel costs. The 'rock samples' document is still required, but this approach is in every other way better, for local people, for fossils and for science. But it is still in contravention of the spirit of local law, and of those cultural property conventions whose existence is ultimately the main or only reason for the black market and the huge price mark-up; why carry a rifle, bribe officials and take a big cut if there is no law to be avoided?

Fossils as property

One issue on which I remain ambivalent is that of property. As a palaeontologist I believe that fossils are the property of nobody and no one nation – only of an undefined scientific community which makes them available, through research and publication, to everyone, and that museums are entrusted with such objects, but do not own them. On the other hand, I am personally persuaded that (for example) Chinese peasants and Brazilian farmers have a right to be recompensed for their work in excavating fossils from their own fields, in which case I must be prepared to pay them for what is, in financial terms, their property. However, I do not believe that fossils are the property of local officials or governments, and thus the subject of bribe payments or taxes.

I am prepared to pay for legitimately added value, in particular for the time taken on expert preparation of important fossils. I take a realistic view of the relative costs of paying professional collectors, dealers and preparators for fossils compared with the cost of going to Brazil myself in the hope of finding the 'perfect' fossil. As scientists, we cannot expect to obtain fossils from distant continents for nothing, so we should be prepared to pay the legitimate costs of one method or the other.

British law is unclear, one could say cynically so, about the import and export of fossils. Successive governments have, in the name of market freedom, declined to sign UNESCO and UNIDROIT conventions;[16] so it remains legally possible to import a fossil which has been illegally exported from Brazil or China. British law on exports, on the other hand (but possibly for the same reason), places no restriction on movements of fossils; this was tested in the case of 'Lizzie', a fossil Carboniferous reptile from Scotland.[17] European Community law requires a licence for export of fossils and collections of fossils valued at over £39,600 ($64,600), but I do not know of any test of this inconsistency in the courts. The law relating to art and antiquities is not inconsistent in this way, principally because the criteria for control are monetary value and 'culture'. Palaeontologist-curators in our museums do valuable science and make a real contribution to learning, but are put at a disadvantage compared with curators in other subject areas by the property-based nature of the laws and conventions for imports and exports.

Curators and scientists who are also concerned about ordinary people's lives should be quite clear in their own minds: our professional mission is to do always (within the law) what is best for specimens and science. But if the law (and its sometimes corrupt implementation) is at odds with this, and results in the exploitation of peasants and farmers in developing countries, we should collaborate to do something about it. The law is ready for change, and we should take the opportunity to change it for the benefit of internationally important fossil specimens.

---

16   At the time of writing, a change in this policy seems likely.

17   W.D.I. Rolfe, 'Export controls for valuable fossils – the trials and tribulations of "Lizzie"', *Earth Science Conservation*, 27 (1990), 20–1; *Export of Works of Art 1989–90*, Thirty-sixth Report ... (London: HMSO, 1990).

14 What is in a 'national' museum? The challenges of collecting policies at the National Museums of Scotland

Michael Taylor

A museum is made a museum by its collections, so that its collecting policy, past and present, helps define its very role and identity. Yet that policy itself depends on how the museum sees its mission. The explicit aim of the National Museums of Scotland (NMS) is to bring 'the world to Scotland, Scotland to the world', and this is indeed closely reflected by its collecting policy.[1] Bringing the world to its public by acquiring, for instance, German pterosaurs or Chinese porcelain, is of course a standard aim for any large multidisciplinary museum. But to bring Scotland to the world, the NMS has to collect Scottish objects, from killer whales and coalfield fossils to Celtic quaichs and beam engines. Yet what is Scotland that it can be displayed in a museum?[2] A potential political and cultural morass, this question was barely discussed in the museum literature till planning began for the new Museum of Scotland, and even today little has been said on collecting policy.[3]

---

1   For example, National Museums of Scotland, *National Museums of Scotland Acquisition and Disposal Policy* (Edinburgh: National Museums of Scotland, 1996).

2   The views expressed here are my own and should not be taken as an official statement of the policies of the trustees of the National Museums of Scotland.

3   But see T. Ambrose, ed., *Presenting Scotland's Story* (Edinburgh: Scottish Museums Council and HMSO, 1989); R. Anderson, 'Scotland's history in the National Museums of Scotland', in Ambrose, op. cit., 64–73; R. Anderson, 'Museums in the making: the origin and development of the national

Scotland is a separate nation within the United Kingdom. The Scots typically share a strong and usually benign view of themselves as comprising a nation, with a concern for self-determination and a pride in a shared culture, lacking the extreme connotations of nationalism seen elsewhere. This reflects the historic facts. Unlike Ireland and Wales, whose undoubted national identities are too complex to be properly discussed here, Scotland was never conquered by England. Scotland and England remained independent states till 1707, when they were merged into a new United Kingdom under the Treaty of Union (having shared a monarch since 1603). The treaty secured the continuance of Scotland's separate government, especially the separate legal system, established church, and administration. So it is entirely meaningful to talk of a Scottish national identity.

The NMS is the national museum of Scotland. It was set up under the National Heritage (Scotland) Act 1985 by merging the Royal Scottish Museum (a government museum derived from a university museum) and the National Museum of Antiquities of Scotland (another government museum developed from a private society collection).[4] The NMS is run by a board of trustees, and has charitable status, but it has statutory responsibilities, and is strongly influenced by UK Central Government policy, as it depends for some 85 per cent of its income on the Secretary of State for Scotland, who also appoints all its trustees. The museum thus answers ultimately to the Secretary of State who is the cabinet minister responsible for Scotland, and thus to the government of the UK, independently of the other national museums in England, Wales and

---

collections', in J. Calder, ed., *The Wealth of a Nation in the National Museums of Scotland* (Edinburgh/Glasgow: National Museums of Scotland/Richard Drew Publishing, 1989), 1–17; H. Cheape, 'Collecting on a national scale', *Museums Journal*, 90(12) (1990), 34–7; D.V. Clarke, 'Me tartan and chained to the past', *Museums Journal*, 96(3) (1996), 26–7; D.V. Clarke, 'Presenting a national perspective of prehistory and early history in the Museum of Scotland', in J.A. Atkinson, I. Banks and J. O'Sullivan (eds), *Nationalism and Archaeology* (Glasgow: Scottish Archaeological Forum/Cruithne Press, 1996), 67–76; A. Fenton, 'Essential evidence: the material culture of Scotland', in Calder, op. cit., 19–42; M. Jones, 'From haggis to home rule', *Museums Journal*, 95(2) (1995), 26–7.

4   Anderson, op. cit., Calder, op. cit.

Northern Ireland. In 2000, the new Scottish Parliament assumed responsibility for the NMS.

The boundaries of Scottishness

The 1985 Act's only explicit recognition of the NMS's 'Scottishness' is to specify that 'in carrying out [the usual museum] functions the Board shall have due regard to the Scottish aspect'. As well as its large size and level of specialist expertise, the Scotland-wide collecting remit identifies the NMS as a truly national museum; other museums in Scotland are more limited geographically (local authorities) or in subject area (for example, industrial archaeology).

Scottish objects are those which grew or were made in Scotland, or were imported and used there. But how should 'Scotland' be defined? As Banks points out, nationality can be defined by geographical territory or by ethnic affiliation.[5] The territorial meaning, normal in contemporary Scots politics, is the one I adopt. Scotland's administrative boundaries have been well defined for centuries. It is plainly simple for geologists and biologists to concentrate their collecting within modern Scotland and its adjacent seas. Yet these can cut across natural boundaries; for example, the Tertiary volcanic rocks of western Scotland extend to Northern Ireland. However, this is a relatively minor issue; one simply extends one's collecting just across the border unless of course another museum is collecting there anyway. The possible inappropriateness of modern administrative boundaries is far more of a problem for interpretation, especially in human history, as Clarke reminds us: the modern concept of Scotland is only valid for the last thousand years or so; to speak of, let alone 'collect', Roman Scotland when the Romans had no such concept confines ancient history in a modern straitjacket.[6] Nevertheless the NMS would doubtless give priority to Roman remains from modern Scotland over those from, say, Asia Minor.

The alternative ethnic meaning of 'nation' touches on highly sensitive ground and needs to be used with care – think of Central European history.[7] Yet it can also be useful when one is dealing with cultural matters. For instance, a collecting policy for Scottish history demands consideration

---

5   I. Banks, 'Archaeology, nationalism and ethnicity' in Atkinson et al., op. cit., 1–3 and other papers in this publication.

6   Clarke in Atkinson et al., op. cit.

7   See Atkinson et al., op. cit.

of the world-wide Scots diaspora, such as the Canadian descendants of emigrants who have preserved their Gaelic culture and language. Other cultural exports worth considering include transfers of technology abroad, such as Boulton and Watt beam engines made in Birmingham, and Suntory whisky distilled in Japan.

Non-Scottish items become relevant to a Scottish collecting policy in different ways. Some are adopted from abroad and assimilated culturally: national symbols such as the royal lion, the unicorn, and St Andrew's cross – even haggis and bagpipes – are all imports if one looks sufficiently far back, as is even the word 'Scot': the Scotti were Dark Age Irish immigrants. But such assimilation is true for most cultures.

Some of the NMS's 'Scottish' acquisitions are only Scottish by personal ownership. For instance, Napoleon's tea service was acquired because of its 'very strong Scottish connections', in other words its purchase by the 10th Duke of Hamilton.[8] Yet consider the full variety of imported objects held by Scots: perhaps an Inuit harpoon kept for 150 years in the family of a Hudson's Bay trader from Orkney, or the dinner service a relative of mine bought in the Far East when serving in the Royal Navy. To my mind these are even more truly Scots than the tea service, for they are direct evidence of overseas trade and military service, major strands of Scots history. Likewise one should add the scientific specimens collected by expatriate Scots, such as David Livingstone's geological specimens from Africa.

The problem of defining Scottishness is even more difficult for modern objects. The specialisation and concentration of production in certain areas, and the worldwide homogenisation of modern industrial society, make it increasingly difficult to speak of Scotland's material culture except in the sense of things actually made and used in Scotland. The NMS's Museum of Flight at East Fortune includes aircraft which served on Scots bases although built elsewhere, such as the Spitfire. It also focuses on aircraft built in Scotland, such as the Jetstream business aircraft. Yet this differs only in relative detail from aircraft built with similar technology elsewhere in the world. There is no longer the local distinctiveness which, for instance, nineteenth-century sailing ships had. We see the same with the 'tartan and heather' side of Scotland's image. By Victorian times, traditional Highland deerstalking was already swamped by imported Anglo-Scottish genteel

---

8   Anderson, in Calder, op. cit.

ritual. Native Highland ponies were replaced long ago, first by Solihull-built Land-Rovers and now by Japanese 4WD vehicles.

In similar fashion, Glaswegian popular culture between the wars was heavily influenced by Hollywood films. Not surprisingly, the NMS staff are divided on how to collect twentieth-century 'Scottish' material. The new 'Art and Industry' gallery sidesteps the problem by adopting a 'world to Scotland' approach, but it will have to be tackled in the twentieth-century galleries of the new Museum of Scotland.

The rights of a nation

National museums sometimes have to deal with objects with powerful political or ideological connotations. Perhaps surprisingly this has never been a major problem for the NMS. This probably partly reflects the lack of modern historical displays pending the building of the Museum of Scotland: there has been nothing controversial to get excited about. But perhaps more importantly Scotland has been a stable entity for so long that there is universal consensus on the very concepts of a Scottish nation, and therefore a Scottish national museum, something which is not necessarily true of, say, Ulster. However, in 1996 the NMS made a bid to house the Stone of Scone on its repatriation to Scotland. This is supposedly the stone on which Scots kings stood to be acclaimed, until it was stolen by Edward I of England in 1296. In the event, this high symbol of Scots national sovereignty was placed in Edinburgh Castle, alongside the Honours of Scotland (the crown regalia). Had it been placed in the museum, some might have taken this as an implication that Scots sovereignty belonged in the past. However, there is a counter-example: the Crown of St Stephen, the symbol of Hungarian nationhood, is housed in the national museum at Budapest.

It is self-evident, in my view, that Scottish museums have a moral right over non-Scottish museums when it comes to acquiring the heritage of Scotland. In turn it is the NMS's stated policy 'to avoid conflict with collecting policies of other museums'.[9] This is consistent with the Museums Association's guidelines on the 'ethics and practicalities of acquisition': a museum should 'take account of the acquisition policies of other registered museums collecting in the same or related subjects or geographical areas' and that certain items 'cannot be acquired ethically ... [including] items

---

9   NMS, op. cit., 3.

better owned by another museum or public institution for reasons of care, access, use, or context ... [and] items better held for moral reasons by individuals, groups, societies or peoples'.[10]

Crowther[11] identifies four key interest groups associated with acquisition: the museum's management and governing body (concerned with policy and resource implications); professional staff (concerned with policy and professional matters); the general public (the object's attractiveness and value); and the research community (research potential). The first three interests support the retention of Scots objects in Scotland as a rational use of resources and staff expertise, hopefully supported by public interest.

The fourth, academic, group, however, has entirely different interests, and this can result in conflict. But this can work both ways. When the NMS was offered an important fossil amphibian from north-eastern England, it notified the local Tyne and Wear County Museums Service, which acquired it. If Tyne and Wear had not done so, the NMS would have checked with the Natural History Museum in London (the implied, though not explicitly designated, national museum for England). It would have been a fine addition to the NMS collections and some might suggest we were wrong to defer. However, we saved resources for other, more urgent, specimens. Similarly, when the Staatliches Museum für Naturkunde in Stuttgart acquired 'Lizzie', the type specimen of *Westlothiana lizziae*, a fossil then considered the oldest known reptile (from East Kirkton, west of Edinburgh), they kindly stood aside and let the NMS match the price to retain it in the country.[12]

However, the 'moral right' argument, in practice, only applies to the rarest and even unique objects. We have to be selective: we cannot retain all the highest-quality Scottish material. The NMS did not try to purchase all the East Kirkton fossils. Some, including type specimens (by definition

---

10   Museums Association Ethics Committee, 'Acquisition. Guidance on the ethics and practicalities of acquisition', *Ethical Guidelines*, 1 (1996), 1–4.

11   P.R. Crowther, 'Questions of acquisition: conflict and compromise in a regional museum', in C.L. Rose, S.L. Williams and J. Gisbert (eds), *Current Issues, Initiatives, and Future Directions for the Preservation and Conservation of Natural History Collections* (Madrid: Consejería de Educación y Cultura, Comunidad de Madrid, and Dirección General de Bellas Artes y Archivos, Ministerio de Cultura, 1993), 167–78.

12   W.D.I. Rolfe, 'Export controls for valuable fossils – the trials and tribulations of "Lizzie"', *Earth Science Conservation*, 27 (1990), 20–1.

unique), are now in collections in Cambridge and London as well as Glasgow. This raises the question of what is the 'best' material from a given site (or artist or maker). For natural sciences such as palaeontology, the 'best' is the scientifically most important specimens (type specimens, published specimens, and so on). But the issue is complex, and there should be a selection of other specimens showing the range of fossils and their preservation. Any particularly clear or attractive display specimens would also be important, regardless of scientific value.[13] Of course, this is the converse of our own need for quality foreign material. The museum acquired a beautiful Bavarian fossil pterosaur in 1994, mainly for display but also for research; it is not a major loss to Bavaria, which already has large collections.

Objects of a nation

In practice, it is difficult to achieve entirely harmonious co-operation with museums outside Scotland, even for major objects of the Scots heritage. Archaeology is a partial exception because of the *bona vacantia* provisions for treasure trove in Scotland. These cover all archaeological finds, not just precious metals, and direct worthwhile finds to Scottish museums.[14] This is a great improvement on the 1890s, when the British Museum was at one point in simultaneous dispute with the Edinburgh and Dublin museums over its acquisition of Scottish and (illegally) Irish material, leading to a

---

13   See S.J. Knell, 'What's important?', in J.R. Nudds and C.W. Pettitt (eds), *The Value and Valuation of Natural Science Collections*, Proceedings of the International Conference, Manchester, 1995, (London: Geological Society, 1997), 11–16; A.J. Jeram, 'Criteria for establishing the scientific value of natural science collections', ibid., 61–7; S. Timberlake, 'A scientific/ historical/educational heritage for whom: the value of geological collections in a small museum', ibid., 127–35; and other papers in this volume.

14   A. Sheridan, 'The Scottish "Treasure Trove" system: a suitable case for emulation?', in G.T. Denford (ed), *Museum Archaeology – What's New?* (Society of Museum Archaeologists, *The Museum Archaeologist*, 21, 1995), 4–11; A. Sheridan, 'Portable antiquities legislation in Scotland: what is it, and how does it work?', in K.W. Tubb, ed., *Antiquities Trade or Betrayed. Legal, ethical and conservation issues* (London: Archetype and United Kingdom Institute for Conservation Archaeology Section), 193–204.

parliamentary inquiry.[15] However, although the British Museum does not (and cannot) now collect Scottish archaeological objects, it still collects Scottish antiquities. Moreover, there are no provisions to protect the Scottish heritage in other fields. Export controls apply to the UK as a whole and do not recognise Scotland independently, and are completely absent in some areas, such as geology, hence the crisis over 'Lizzie' described above.[16]

In those circumstances we therefore have to rely on persuasion, incentives and moral pressure to discourage the export of Scottish objects, and, as might be expected, we are only partly successful. When 'competing' museums outside Scotland have their eyes on the same objects as the NMS, the result can depend on the vagaries of their internal institutional decisions (for instance, if they have formulated and published a collecting policy) and on curators' personal attitudes – a hazardous situation which Rolfe calls negligent.[17] The results are uneven. In some fields, such as minerals, which, of course, tend to be collected as groups of duplicate specimens rather than as unique objects, co-operation is excellent; in others, not so good. Yet there is little that the NMS staff can do in cases where the other institution has not even published its own collecting policy.

---

15 *Report of a Committee appointed by the Lords Commissioners of Her Majesty's Treasury to inquire into the circumstances under which certain Celtic ornaments found in Ireland were recently offered for sale to the British Museum, and to consider the relations between the British Museum and the Museums of Edinburgh and Dublin with regard to the acquisition and retention of objects of Antiquarian and Historical interest; with evidence, appendices and Index. Ordered, by the House of Commons, to be Printed, 1 May 1899* (London: HMSO); Cheape, op. cit.; K. Neill, 'The Broighter hoard, or how Carson caught the boat', *Archaeology Ireland*, 7(2) (1993), 24–26.

16 Rolfe, op. cit.; M.A. Taylor, 'Exporting your heritage?', *Geology Today*, 7 (1991): 32–36; M.A. Taylor and J.D.C. Harte, 'Palaeontological site conservation and the law in Britain', in P.R. Crowther and W.A. Wimbledon (eds), *The Use and Conservation of Palaeontological Sites* (London: Palaeontological Association, Special Papers in Palaeontology, 40, 1988), 21–39; M.A. Taylor and J.D.C. Harte, 'Fossils, minerals and the law', *Geology Today*, 7 (1991), 189–93.

17 W.D.I. Rolfe, 'Acquisition policy in palaeontology', in M.G. Bassett (ed), *Curation of Palaeontological Collections*, (London: Palaeontological Association, Special Papers in Palaeontology, 22, 1979), 27–35.

Other problems can arise. Some institutions simply do not see fit to cede priority to the NMS.[18] Or maybe a change of policy elsewhere forces the NMS to react. A good example of this, leading to positive co-operation, concerned the collection of specimens associated with a government-funded investigation of whale strandings in English and Welsh waters by the Natural History Museum in London which decided not to collect this material. The NMS stepped in to acquire over 700 individuals, thus saving an important complete research collection for cetacean studies.

In the absence of legal protection the NMS has to do what it can to forestall the permanent export of important objects. In the field of vertebrate palaeontology, we ask researchers to consider donation at the start of their project (so that, technically, they retain the material on loan thereafter). This enables us to support fieldwork and processing with funds or in kind (and can be useful in ensuring that long-term conservation is taken into account). With amateur collectors, we sometimes pay a fee covering the estimated costs of collecting and processing but excluding any element of purchase; this simplifies the legal situation, especially when landowners or conservation agencies are involved; the fossil then becomes a direct gift to the NMS from the landowner.

I have developed an impression that the idea of keeping key Scots objects in Scotland is uncomfortable – even unacceptable – to academics in universities as well as the more research-oriented staff of large museums elsewhere. Roy Clements remarked: 'I object strongly to the nationalistic notion of *British* fossils; they are part of a global heritage and it is quite irrelevant which country they end up in, so long as they remain accessible for study and are properly cared for.'[19] This is a fair statement of the academic point of view. Yet it ignores wider public issues which museums must take into account. Ian Rolfe rejected it in the same discussion, noting that the best material should never be removed from its source area as it would be best appreciated there by locals and visitors.[20] The NMS's public campaign to purchase 'Lizzie' was driven by the perception that it was unacceptable to let such heritage leave Scotland.

Is it justifiable to allow academic researchers to export even the most important objects, insofar as these objects only become important by being

---

18   Cheape, op. cit.
19   Taylor and Harte in Crowther and Wimbledon, op. cit., 39.
20   Ibid., 39–40.

studied and published? It might be argued that the objects ought to go to a specialist centre where they could sit amongst comparative collections in the charge of those with an appropriate specialist interest. There are, however, risks in this: research collections only remain a dynamic resource whilst serviced by an appropriate researcher, but research interests shift and collections end up orphaned – ripe for disposal. The current UK practice of transferring such geological collections to designated university museums is valuable, but perhaps repatriation to a major Scottish institution would be even better. If the material is outside Scotland but secure and well cared for, the element of urgency disappears. Nevertheless, I remain unconvinced about the merits of having research collections of Scottish material scattered all over the world as historical markers for the research interests of now-departed researchers. The same aims can be achieved by keeping the specimens in the collections of Scottish museums. In the long term, the NMS and other Scottish museums are quite simply the only institutions which have a predictable commitment to Scottish material.

Diversity and localism

The last few decades' strong upsurge of political and cultural nationalism has been accompanied by the development of very strong localist, at times almost separatist, tendencies within Scotland.[21] This is not surprising, for Scotland's 'tartan and heather' image is profoundly misleading.[22] In fact, Scotland is culturally and linguistically diverse, almost three nations in one: the Lowland Scots 'south' (including the north-eastern coastlands), the Gaelic west and north-west, and the Scandinavian Northern Isles.

This growth of localism coincided with the enormous improvement of local museums through increased support by local government, the Scottish Museums Council and other agencies. Fewer than 40 per cent of local authorities had professionally staffed museum services in 1982, compared with more than 90 per cent in 1996.[23] One result is that over 60

21 For example, see Sheridan, op. cit.; V. Turner, 'Belovèd Thule: Shetland at the centre', in Atkinson et al., op. cit., 89–94.

22 J.A. Atkinson, 'National identity and material culture: decoding the Highland myth', in Atkinson et al., op. cit., 59–66; Clarke, 'Me tartan ...', op. cit.

23 T. Ambrose, 'The Scottish Museums Council: a model of museum support', *Museum International*, 191 (1996), 43–6.

per cent of archaeological material directed to museums under treasure trove now goes to local museums.[24] This raised another issue: the degree to which Scotland's heritage should be centralised, if at all.

Suggestions for the local retention, and even return, of objects usually rely on the cultural argument: local heritage should stay local. However, geography is also important. Edinburgh is in the south, and not that accessible for many Scots. Also, tourism is critically important to many local economies, which need undercover attractions such as museums to compensate for the variable Scots weather.

History also plays its part. The undoubted centralisation of objects in Edinburgh, and even London, is partly due to museums having developed unevenly within Scotland.[25] There was no local museum to house the Viking chessmen found on the Isle of Lewis, and so they are now in the NMS and the British Museum. They were temporarily lent to the newly opened Museum nan Eilean (Museum of the Isles) in Stornoway in 1995. By contrast, many important Permo-Triassic fossil reptiles from Morayshire remain in the Elgin Museum, which was open when these fossils were being collected in the nineteenth century.[26] Although the situation has improved, provision is still patchy due to local government legislation which forbade Regions to operate museums (until their recent abolition) and the inability of some museums to take on the full range of material.[27]

For the national museum, working with local museums is further complicated by the media, which tend to seize on any apparent conflict. The loan of the Lewis Chessmen, for example, was accompanied by a local media campaign for their retention in the Western Isles. In these circumstances, the museum must have a reasoned case. In the case of a fossil footprint trackway from the shore near Elgin collected with the co-operation of the local museum, the NMS could justify its acquisition in terms of its resources and the threats to the trackway if left uncollected. The media were entirely supportive. The case of the Dupplin Cross near Perth, which celebrates the union of the Scots and the Picts in the ninth century,

---

24   Sheridan in Tubb, op. cit.
25   See, for example, Cheape, op. cit.; K. Sangster, 'George Gordon and Elgin Museum', in I. Keillar and J.S. Smith (eds), *George Gordon: Man of Science* (Aberdeen: Centre of Scottish Studies, University of Aberdeen, 1995), 105–,16; Sheridan, in Denford, op. cit.
26   Keillar and Smith, ibid.
27   For examples in archaeology, see Sheridan, op. cit.

was more controversial. It is suffering erosion, and with general agreement that it should be put under cover, both the local church and the NMS's new Museum of Scotland in Edinburgh were offered as appropriate repositories.[28] The case went to public inquiry; the Reporter rejected the proposal for local display because of 'rather cramped display arrangements' as well as inadequate consideration of costs and funding, but still preferred the local option if these problems could be remedied within a reasonable period.[29]

The question of which museum should acquire a particular object can be further complicated by potential conflicts of interest. Due to the relatively small number of Scottish museum professionals, they sometimes find themselves fulfilling more than one role. Most obviously, the NMS administers the grant-in-aid fund to assist other Scottish museums in purchasing objects, using the NMS staff to advise on proposals. Plainly it must avoid conflicts of interest when it intends to acquire the same object. A related problem arose over the treasure trove system and its routine administration by the NMS staff on behalf of the Crown Agent, the Queen's and Lord Treasurer's Remembrancer. A few years ago, an important set of finds, including a lead and cannel coal necklace, from a Bronze Age cemetery at Wast Water, Peeblesshire, came up for allocation and was bid for by the NMS and by Tweeddale Museums. At that time the Treasure Trove Advisory Panel, which advises the Remembrancer, was chaired by the director of the NMS. The disadvantage of this arrangement was that the NMS was seen as combining the roles of administrator, competitor and referee. So, when the panel advised allocation to the NMS, suggestions of bias in favour of the NMS were made, but by then the director had resigned in favour of a more obviously independent chair. In the end, the reconstituted panel again assigned the necklace to the NMS on the grounds of its national significance and its need for regular monitoring by specialist conservators.

Collaboration and the future

A possible answer to the dilemma of the best place for an object is to distinguish between the short term (display) and the long term (acquisition). One possibility for the national museum is to loan an object to

---

28 *Perthshire Advertiser*, 15 December 1995.

29 *The Scotsman*, 8 May 1996; *Perthshire Advertiser*, 10 May 1996.

a local museum. The NMS's statutory duties for such outreach have never been defined beyond the basic requirement of 'collaboration with other institutions' enunciated by the 1985 Act, and, more recently, the trustees' confirmation of its desirability. Displaying the NMS material in local museums equally meets its remit; but should the museum actually acquire material with this objective in mind?

Collaboration seemed to be the answer when a German collector found Scotland's first dinosaur bone on Skye. It was donated by the landowner, Sir Iain Noble, on condition that, when a suitable museum is opened on Skye, it should be displayed there. The bone is scientifically important and so should be under the care of specialist palaeontological curators, impossible on Skye. It needed to be formally registered in a public collection to be reported in the scientific literature. Immediate accession into the NMS collections, with the eventual intention of displaying it on Skye, resolved these needs and enabled the NMS staff to organise its rapid study and publication. Such co-operation is essential if rare Skye fossils are to be preserved for the benefit of the local community, especially at a time of increased illegal collecting.

The NMS has recently developed a stronger, even proactive, loans policy, collaborating with local museums and assisting them where resources permit. The partial closure of the National Museum of Antiquities of Scotland, in preparation for the opening of the Museum of Scotland in 1998, enabled the NMS to offer museums all over the country their local treasures for temporary display.

A new means of giving Scots greater (if partial) access to their heritage is being pioneered by the Scottish Cultural Resources Access Network (SCRAN), a project organised by a consortium including the NMS. Amongst other things this places at least a selection of the Scottish history collections online.[30] It will be interesting to see how this influences the national versus local debate.

Scotland has a historically stable and well-defined national identity defined on the basis of territory as much as on the more problematical basis of ethnic identity. The NMS's role of collecting Scottish objects is therefore made relatively easy compared to museums in countries whose very national and ethnic identities are disputed. Objects can be Scottish by

---

30 But not, for the moment, the natural science collections; see H. Falconer, 'Get netted', *Museums Journal*, 96(5) (1996), 25–7.

origin, by ownership, or by use by Scots, either at home or abroad, although the homogenisation of global culture makes it difficult to decide just how and when a modern object is Scottish. In practice, a more important problem for the NMS is promoting co-operation with other museums, both those outside Scotland (to minimise the loss of Scottish heritage to 'foreign' museums) and local museums within Scotland, which want to retain their own local heritage. This co-operation is necessary to minimise the risk of conflicts, which are often exacerbated by media reporting. The problems are worst if co-operation cannot be achieved on a rational basis (for instance, a consideration of staff skills and technical facilities) and if the object is unique. Increased co-operation on acquisition policies will help resolve some concerns. However, these problems are essentially political, and will often be solved, if indeed they can be solved, by compromises reflecting political rather than professional factors.[31]

---

31   Whilst this paper reflects my own views, I am grateful to many colleagues within and outside NMS for information and comment on earlier drafts.

15 Who is steering the ship? Museums and archaeological fieldwork

Janet Owen

The majority of museums concentrate the resources they have allocated to archaeology on the collection of archives from systematic field archaeology projects. Casual finds made by people walking the dog, working in the garden, ploughing the land, and so on are these days only collected to fill gaps in a collection's type series of artefacts. However, in recent years many museums in the UK have become disenfranchised from the organisation and implementation of systematic field archaeology projects. There are notable exceptions to this trend where integrated services are still provided, such as Norfolk and Exeter, for example, but these are now the exception rather than the rule.

The late 1960s and early 1970s marked a major watershed in the management of archaeology in England and Wales. Prior to this, archaeological fieldwork was largely carried out by museum staff, universities and amateur archaeology groups. The stimuli for individual fieldwork varied, but incorporated a mixture of research (identifying and answering particular questions raised by previous work) and rescue (fieldwork aimed at recovering material from sites threatened by development). Rescue began to take off in the late 1960s and early 1970s in response to increased land development, and a heightening of public awareness of archaeological sites and their rate of destruction. This burgeoning support also produced a loosening of public purse strings to help finance archaeological endeavour. The archaeology community, particularly through the work of RESCUE,[1] fought hard to integrate archaeological concerns into the planning process. Several museums

---

1   The British Archaeological Trust.

managed to persuade local authorities to inform them of proposed developments in advance of work being undertaken.[2] But it soon became clear that existing provision (museums, amateurs and universities) could not cope with this increased workload. County archaeologists were employed by a number of county museum services to assist in this work. A number of new archaeology units were also established, including those in Winchester, Lincoln, York and Exeter. Some of these were placed within the existing museum framework, but many were set up independently. There were a number of vocal supporters of the RESCUE movement who were uncertain that museums were up to the task of taking on this late twentieth-century role:

> Museums have notoriously limited budgets; far from engaging in rescue excavation or field projects, many of them have enough difficulty in conserving and displaying their existing collections.[3]

Though museums had always had their critics, the early 1970s possibly marks the beginning of the real disenfranchisement of museums from the archaeological process.

It is interesting to note that the ambitions for the newly founded archaeology units were not exceptionally far-reaching: 'It is difficult to imagine the independent consultancies becoming a major force within British archaeology.'[4] A glance at the framework for managing archaeology in England and Wales today, however, demonstrates that these independent consultancies have become a major force. Throughout the late 1970s and 1980s the role of archaeology units grew, primarily carrying out rescue fieldwork funded by public money. But in 1990 the Department of Environment issued the document *Planning and Policy Guidance 16* (PPG16),[5] which brought archaeology officially into the planning process. In particular, PPG16 introduced the 'polluter pays' concept, and the developer, not the state, is now required to pay for any archaeological work necessary in advance of development. In tandem with the introduction of PPG16, competitive tendering was also introduced – developers now have

---

2   K. Barton, 'Rescuing museums', in P.A. Rahtz (ed), *Rescue Archaeology* (London: Penguin, 1974).

3   C. Thomas, 'Archaeology in Britain 1973', in Rahtz, op.cit., 7.

4   C. Musson, 'Rescue digging all the time', in Rahtz, op.cit., 89.

5   Department of Environment, *Planning and Policy Guidance 16: Archaeology and Planning* (London: DoE/HMSO, 1990).

the right to choose their own archaeological contractor to execute any archaeological intervention considered necessary.

Consequently fieldwork is now carried out by increasingly independent and commercially orientated archaeology units. It is now planning archaeologists, many attached to local government planning departments, which most often decide which sites are of archaeological significance and should, therefore, be the subject of fieldwork. Museums are increasingly sidelined by archaeologists and museum managers into the role of interpreters with a duty to provide access to material collected by others, disenfranchised from decisions about what is recorded and preserved.

From a collecting perspective, this is clearly unsatisfactory for a number of reasons. Firstly, museum archaeology collections represent the primary information database for archaeology. This existing body of knowledge and information should be helping to guide present and future research priorities. It is vital, if the long-term preservation of archaeological archives in museums is to be justified, that they are used in this way. As planning and field archaeologists become distanced administratively from museums, so the influence of museums and their collections on future fieldwork weakens. Many museums now find their collections are rarely considered when the archaeological potential of a site is being evaluated. Perhaps what is more worrying is that now most archaeological work is undertaken as a reaction to commercial development, it is the developers who are really setting museums' collecting agendas!

Secondly, the currently fragmented management structure suggests that the long-term curation requirements of the archive are something of an afterthought in the fieldwork process. Perhaps this is most clearly seen in the remit of PPG16, which ensures that the developer is financially responsible for the fieldwork, finds analysis and publication aspects of a project, but which fails to identify any means by which the long-term curation costs of the archive are to be met. It is also quite possible, under current arrangements, for a museum not to be aware of fieldwork being carried out in its collecting area until the field archaeologist telephones, or writes a letter, to inform the museum that the archive is ready for deposition. The field archaeologist will have prepared the archive as he or she sees fit, and the museum will have little say in its nature and content until it is in its possession.

A final reason for concern is that this piecemeal approach to the creation of archaeological archives may impair our understanding of the information content of the archives. In the absence of a clear overview of the research potential of the overall archive, it would be difficult, for example, to identify future research strategies for a region, or to interpret a region's archaeology for display.

The museum community must therefore ensure that museums and the archaeological material they contain have an active role in the shaping of future collections. The rest of this paper will summarise developments that need to take place in order to encourage integration, and will identify progress currently being made. All these initiatives are based upon performance targets identified by the Museums and Galleries Commission (MGC) and are standards which any museum responsible for curating archaeological material in the UK should be striving to attain.[6]

The first of these is for museums to ensure that their archaeological collections contribute to the identification of research priorities at a national, regional and local level. Although most archaeological fieldwork carried out in England and Wales is now in response to planning proposals, it is still influenced by research priorities determined by the archaeological profession. The very act of selecting sites, for which fieldwork prior to development is necessary, involves assessing the potential of the site against these research priorities. Museums need to develop research strategies for their archaeological collections in line with overall museum objectives, perhaps as part of a collection management policy, and should ensure that identified research priorities are integrated into any regional, and possibly national, archaeological strategy which may be developed.

In this way, museum priorities can be assimilated into local plans. The Stoke-on-Trent *City Plan 2001*, for example, explicitly states that little is known about the development of Stoke prior to the eighteenth century and suggests that this is an area of priority for preservation and recording. The plan also states that the written policies in this document regarding the protection of archaeological remains form part of a wider strategy to protect and promote the city's archaeological resources, and that this wider strategy is carried out by the Stoke City Council's Department of Museums, Arts and Heritage.[7]

---

6   Museums and Galleries Commission, *Standards in the Museum Care of Archaeological Collections* (London: MGC, 1992).

7   City of Stoke-on-Trent, *City Plan 2001* (City of Stoke-on-Trent, 1991).

Regional and local research strategies should have much broader relevance than their application in the planning process. They could be used to structure amateur and university-led fieldwork in a region, with museums perhaps acting as a focus for this work. They could also provide the framework for research carried out on existing collections in museums, and for the development of public services: exhibition themes and publications, for example.

The MGC also recommend that archaeological museums pass information about their collections to the Sites and Monuments Record (SMR) at regular intervals. An SMR is the index of all known archaeological sites in an area, and is perceived as the key source of information about an area's archaeology. It is vital therefore that a close relationship exists between SMRs and museums. Adequately detailed information about the content of archives in museums must be recorded in SMRs in order for them to contribute to the shaping of future collections. In Norfolk and Leicestershire, for example, such a relationship has been established. However, a recent unpublished survey carried out by Kenneth Qualmann of Winchester City Museums suggests that this is not always the case.[8]

The MGC also suggest that museums must encourage the wider archaeological community to think carefully about which material justifies retention in the long term, and which should be considered for dispersal. In 1993, the UK's Society of Museum Archaeologists published guidelines regarding the selection, retention and dispersal of archaeological material.[9] This document was drawn up in consultation with other branches of the archaeological profession, and encourages all museums (in collaboration with relevant archaeological organisations within an area) to devise local guidelines for the selection, retention and dispersal of archaeological material. A number of museums are in the process of doing so. However, the traditional approach of 'quantity before quality' is still very much the norm, with many museums collecting all that is deposited with them by field units. Perhaps, as Wingfield suggests, museums need to focus on

---

8   K. Qualmann, Archaeological Archives and SMRs, (Leicester: University of
     Leicester, unpublished thesis, 1996); G. Denford, (ed), *Representing*
     Archaeology in Museums, Museum Archaeologist, 22 (London: Society of
     Museum Archaeologists/Museum of London Conference Proceedings, 1997).
9   Society of Museum Archaeologists, *Selection, Retention and Dispersal of*
     Archaeological Collections. Guidelines for Use in England, Wales and Northern
     Ireland (SMA, 1993).

quality, and the archaeology community as a whole needs to consider the 'wider issues of for whom we collect this material, and why'.[10]

Finally, the museum community must raise the awareness of the wider archaeological profession to issues of long-term curation, and to the importance of museum involvement throughout the creation of the archaeological archive. Several museums have issued conditions for the transfer of archaeological material into their care. These conditions stipulate minimum standards in a number of areas, including the expected degree of museum involvement in the process of creating the archive, the format of the archive, and the condition of the archive on deposition.[11] It is still early days, and difficult to determine how effective this approach, and related developments, are in encouraging the active participation of museums in an archive's creation. However, initial reaction suggests that at the very least the archaeology profession as a whole is becoming more aware of the issue of long-term curation.[12] Perhaps most significantly, the Museums and Galleries Commission and English Heritage are currently promoting a joint project to explore the problem of funding the curation of archaeological archives in the long term.

Museums, then, must have an active role in the collection of archaeological material: it is a fundamental principle of archaeology that new knowledge should build on a framework of existing knowledge, even if it is only to refute that existing knowledge. However, museums are having to reconsider how that active role can be achieved and sustained in contemporary archaeological practice.

---

10   C. Wingfield, 'Some thoughts on Hedley Swain's observations ...', *Museum Archaeologists News*, 23 (1996), 8.

11   The Society of Museum Archaeologists published guidance in 1995 for any museum archaeologist preparing such documents, see J. Owen, ed., *Towards an Accessible Archaeological Archive. The Transfer of Archaeological Archives to Museums: Guidelines for Use in England, Northern Ireland, Scotland and Wales* (SMA, 1995).

12   The Institute of Field Archaeologists' 1996 and 1997 conference programmes, for example, both included a session on the relationship between field archaeologists and museums.

16 Collecting: reclaiming the art, systematising the technique

Linda Young

Among the host of transformations museums have lately undergone is the shift in focus that has replaced the old centrality of collections with a new priority for education and public programmes. The timely justice of this step has been generally acknowledged by curators, but it must be said that alongside the movement in resources has come a slide in influence and status. (The slack hasn't all been gathered up by museum educators; rather, it has moved to managers.) Museums are more complex organisations today, with more senior managers, more differentiated staffing and more pressure to produce spectacular public goods. Hence, collecting is often driven by exhibition needs rather than the proactive programmes that are sometimes advocated, or the traditional kind of reactive acquisition of things as they come up. I propose two positive ideas on the nature and practice of collecting, with which to counter this slip in faith. Firstly, we should reclaim the art and skill of connoisseurship from the elitist connections it has held since the nineteenth century – it should be claimed as the unique and special skill of curators. Secondly, we need to make our collecting decisions more systematic and more explicit.[1] It is hoped that these steps will revive the honourable traditions of the curator, the specialist collector and the connoisseur.

Connoisseurship

In the more ancient forms of museums and collecting, the judgement of an artefact's significance was the province of the connoisseur, literally 'one who knows'. When the word was adopted into the English language in the early eighteenth century, it signified a combination of knowledge,

---

1   These ideas were first developed in an article in *Museum Management and Curatorship* 13 (1994), 191–9.

understanding, sensibility and discrimination applied to the study of art and antiquities. 'Thus to See, Thus Nicely to Distinguish things nearly resembling one another, Whether Visible, or Immaterial, is the Business of a *Connoisseur'*, wrote Jonathon Richardson in 1719.[2] Today it would be doubtful to claim to be able to discern the ethereal aspects of most objects! However, curators know the sensation of mentally running through an array of objects, comparing whatever is to hand and thus forming an opinion not only of expertise, but of experience – and if this is what Richardson meant, then we continue to practise 'the business of a connoisseur'. The focus of the idea of careful study as the basis of connoisseurship narrowed in the late nineteenth century to techniques for the attribution and authentication of artworks as practised by dealers and antiquarians. The mature statement of systematic attributional method was the work of Giovanni Morelli, who argued that informed observation of the internal evidence of an artwork is sufficient to identify its author and other aspects of his career, teachers, and so forth, regardless of secondary documentation. The Morellian code of comparing paintings by their minute details, such as ears and lips, to reveal the identity of an artist was based on the expectation that craftsmen develop conventional nuances for the ordinary, repetitive elements of painting. Hence, having identified the mean standard Giotto ear, other painted ears could be compared with it to spot the same artist's hand at work. The need to identify artists is an expression of the great nineteenth-century flowering of art historical scholarship, associated with the blossoming market for Renaissance and pre-Renaissance artworks. Bernard Berenson, the impresario of this market, soon afterwards codified the Morellian method into a hierarchy of identificatory details (ears, hands, drapery and background landscape at the top; cranium, chin, colour and chiaroscuro at the bottom), augmented by an eye for quality.[3] This environment of the art market still touches the concept of connoisseurship. In fact, it is perfectly respectable in art museums – perhaps the only museum type where curators are still heroic

2   J. Richardson, *A Discourse on the Dignity, Certainty, Pleasure and Advantage of the Science of a Connoisseur* (London, 1719), quoted by C. Gibson-Wood, *Studies in the Theory of Connoisseurship from Vasari to Morelli* (New York: Garland, 1988), 119.

3   B. Berenson, 'The rudiments of connoisseurship', in *The Rudiments of Connoisseurship: The Study and Criticism of Italian Art* (New York: Schocken Books, 1962 [first published 1902]), 144.

personages. To other kinds of curator such as anthropologists and historians, however, the title 'connoisseur' these days is coloured with elitist, aestheticist and antiquarian values, with which few would care to identify.[4]

This is a shame, for apart from the anonymous, generic 'researcher', the knowledge and skills of artefact investigation are not defined by any other description. We have devalued, perhaps even lost, the term, and without it we lack a handle to honour the art and mystery of the curatorial craft. The term survives among some United States scholars of material culture to describe the process of artefact analysis culminating in a cultural contextualisation which seeks to interpret the object to the modern world.[5] The techniques suggested in this literature formulate the practice that curators engage in when they research and assess artefacts for acquisition, exhibition and publication. I propose that we should reclaim the skills of connoisseurship to mean not the finicky 'nose-jobs' of Morellian method, but the base of knowledge and experience that enables curators to identify and assess the importance of artefacts, as well as the theoretical models that have been developed or applied to material culture research.

It is important to assert the nature of such skill and discipline, for without a name, they are invisible. It is assumed by management that curators possess the skill and know the parameters of the discipline; that is what curators are appointed for. Despite the excellent programmes of museum studies which now equip the minds of most entrants to curatorship, the deep knowledge that informs connoisseurship depends on experience, which requires time in the specialised environment of the museum (or sometimes the dealer's shop), for anthropological and historical artefacts are not so common that they can be studied in many other places. To this degree, what curators do is certainly a 'mystery'. While professional status may be dependent to some extent on the possession of exclusive

---

4   The nadir of this inflection is expressed in the magazine *Connoisseur*, until the mid-1980s a scholarly journal of the decorative arts, thereafter a showcase for glitzy antiques and luxury goods, representing all a curator's worst fears about the trivialising of objects.

5   For example, T. J. Schlereth, ed., *Material Culture Studies in America* (Nashville: AASLH, 1982); R.B. St George, ed., *Material Life in America, 1600–1860* (Boston: Northeastern University Press, 1988); B.G. Carson, *Ambitious Appetites: Dining, Behaviour and Patterns of Consumption in Federal Washington* (Washington, DC: AIA Press, 1990).

knowledge, it is not strategic these days to hide it; on the contrary, amidst the threats of downsizing and restructuring, a high profile is a professional necessity. Women have long known the consequences of undertaking invisible work – it is unvalued work, and the people who do it do not get much recognition either. In light of the slide in curatorial and collecting status within museums, the public face of our craft would benefit from attaching to it a title which describes its unique tasks. We must reclaim connoisseurship from its current connotations, and achieve this simply by using the term.

Systematising collecting

My second proposal for lifting the reputation of curators as professional collectors moves beyond nomenclature to a tactic of practice: the systematising of collecting according to explicit criteria which enable a more-or-less standard assessment of the significance of acquisitions. There are two steps in this process: firstly, the establishment of sets of criteria relevant to each museum's purposes; and secondly, the practice of writing a formal statement of the cultural significance of each acquisition. The technique is a crossover from the management of heritage places in Australia, where it is enunciated in the Burra Charter (Charter for the Conservation of Places of Cultural Significance) of Australia ICOMOS (the Australian National Committee of the International Council on Sites and Monuments), the major professional association of people involved with built heritage. The Burra Charter has become the industry standard in Australia, and many of its methods have potential for applications in other fields of heritage practice, such as museums.[6]

This is not to suggest that museums are without systematic approaches to collecting. At least three strategies embody methodical approaches: collecting policies, acquisitions reports, and curatorial expertise or connoisseurship. However, none of these is consciously structured towards the particular goal of the assessment of cultural significance. Consequently, the decision about the threshold of significance that determines what objects will be preserved in museums is neither a standard practice nor the subject of much analysis by the community of curators. Most museums

---

6   Likewise, museum practice has techniques that could be usefully applied to built heritage management; some are suggested in a forthcoming paper in *International Journal of Heritage Studies*.

these days have collecting policies developed by staff and endorsed by boards of management, stating the ambit of the museum's interest, together with caveats about condition and ownership. Typically, the policy indicates collecting in certain fields of time, place, culture, material, scientific discipline and so forth, all of which define significance more generically than specifically. For example, the range of ceramic tablewares from Britain in the nineteenth century, or samples of New Guinea spears to compare with those from other Pacific islands. In large museums where acquisitions are purchased, expenditure above a certain amount is usually justified by curatorial report and recommendation; de facto, an acquisition report may fulfil the function of a statement of significance. But it is an inconsistent method, and determined by whether the object in question has a market value – which many objects of undoubted significance do not.

More often, acquisitions are the product of the judgements of connoisseurship (whether or not consciously claimed as such). This is the most traditional strategy of assessment, whereby the curator applies his or her knowledge to determine which objects are relevant and meaningful to the purposes of the museum collection: a rare example of an engine which will enlarge the spectrum of engines already held, a representative example of the piano to document its use in the context of colonial Australia, or a fine example of wedding jewellery to illustrate the global range of this rite of passage. But within these limits, I observe that most curators make their collecting decisions in fairly informal ways, based on personal knowledge and experience. If I remember my own collecting decisions, I ran over the issue in my mind, perhaps checked the catalogue or store to compare the thing in question with what was already in the museum, and perhaps also considered if or how the new object might fit into an exhibit. This was collecting based on knowledge and expertise – on connoisseurship, indeed, but looking into the mechanics of the decision, it is so centred on the individual's experience and interests that it has to be called idiosyncratic.

By comparison, it is useful to compare the systematic processes which have developed over the past ten years to resolve this kind of question in the field of heritage place registration – a form of symbolic collecting (rather less onerous than real object collecting). Items such as buildings, ruins and archaeological sites are assessed for inclusion on state and national lists on the basis of their cultural significance. The method was first articulated by Australia ICOMOS, and is detailed in its Burra Charter and associated 'Guidelines'.[7] The Burra Charter is a statement of principles and processes for the conservation of heritage places, today widely recognised and prescribed as the Australian industry standard. The idea of cultural significance was referred to in Article 1 of the Venice Charter,[8] but becomes the foundation of the Burra Charter process. Its special utility lies in requiring a methodical document assessing all the claims and values of the place in question – the stage known as the 'conservation analysis' – leading to a clear expression of the importance to society of the place – a product called the 'statement of cultural significance'.

The statement of cultural significance justifies why it is worth giving attention, time and perhaps money towards listing and otherwise conserving a site, and for the same purpose, the same process could as well be applied to collecting an object. A statement of cultural significance is also useful in public projects, first as a means of opening up the matter to public discussion, and secondly as a means of arguing for and subsequently accounting for the public money spent. The statement of cultural significance also serves to identify the commitment of future conservation treatments and interventions which will be required to maintain – and not to compromise or otherwise damage – the cultural significance of the place or thing in question, including an appropriate management strategy (a conservation management plan).

Australia ICOMOS offers not only a process by which to structure the assessment of significance, but also four broad classes of value in which to locate it: aesthetic, historic, scientific and social. These represent a mixture of traditional ideas about what is important enough to be preserved, together with some contemporary thinking.[9] The tendency to prioritise the

---

7   Australia ICOMOS, Charter for the Conservation of Places of Cultural Significance (The Burra Charter), 1979, 1988 and presently under revision. The most accessible form is P. Marquis Kyle and M. Walker, *The Illustrated Burra Charter* (Canberra: Australian Heritage Commission, 1992); its use is discussed in M. Pearson and S. Sullivan, *Looking After Heritage Places* (Melbourne: University of Melbourne Press, 1995). Venice, Burra, and other heritage charters are presented in ICOMOS Canada, *Preserving Our Heritage: Catalogue of Charters and Other Guides*, 1990.

8   Second International Congress of Architects and Technicians of Historic Monuments, Venice, 1966

9   Compare D. Lowenthal, 'Benefits and burdens of the past', *The Past is a Foreign Country* (Cambridge: Cambridge University Press, 1985), 36–52; P.

importance of beauty as a criterion of significance derives from nineteenth-century romantic interest in spectacular natural and built places, especially in reaction to the perceived ugliness of the industrial environment. The preservation of old buildings in Australia, as elsewhere, began as an aesthetic movement largely fuelled by architects, and the early formal identifications of heritage value were predominantly described in this language. In modern times, the aesthetic criterion has not been examined critically, and this doubt is expressed in professional practice, where it is used sparingly. The concept of historic value has primal roots in the human regard for associations between places and great people or events. It remains a powerful idea in contemporary consciousness, whether expressed by amateurs or professionals.[10] In practice today, historic value is widely seen to underlie almost all the other criteria. On the other hand, the category of scientific value is intended to express a special physical or biological character, either unique or representative; the Burra Charter also lists an aspect of scientific value to refer to the importance of places such as unexcavated archaeological sites, which may contribute substantial information in the future. The concept of social value acknowledges the importance of certain places to contemporary groups of people, for reasons of cultural feeling such as spirituality or nationalism.[11]

Assessment criteria

The intention of the Burra Charter framework of four categories of value is to standardise individual judgements, in order to give them a common ground which can make assessments of significance comparable. In practice, the categories are so general as to be capable of elastic shrinking or stretching according to the needs or knowledge of the heritage specialist undertaking each task of assessment, and the criteria have therefore been refined and expanded by various cultural heritage specialists and agencies. Jim Kerr, one of the original drafters of the Burra Charter, has developed

---

Spearitt, 'Money, taste and industrial heritage', *Packaging the Past? Public Histories* (Melbourne: University of Melbourne Press, 1991), 33.

10 G Davison, 'The use and abuse of Australian history', in S. Janson and S. Macintyre, (eds), *Making the Bicentenary* (Melbourne: University of Melbourne Press, 1988).

11 C. Johnston, *What is Social Value? A Discussion Paper* (Canberra: Australian Heritage Commission, 1992).

criteria based on a place's ability to demonstrate cultural expressions such as philosophy, custom, taste, design and usage, and to give evidence of aspects of the past of which no other evidence remains.[12] Taking a more detailed approach, based on a review of several years of experience, the Australian Heritage Commission now lists eight criteria for inclusion of items on the register of the National Estate:

1. Importance in the course or pattern of Australia's natural or cultural history
2. Possession of uncommon, rare or endangered aspects of Australia's natural or cultural history
3. Potential to yield information which will contribute to an understanding of Australia's natural or cultural history
4. Importance in demonstrating the principal characteristics of 1. a class of Australia's natural or cultural places; or 2. a class of Australia's natural or cultural environments
5. Importance in exhibiting particular aesthetic characteristics valued by a community or cultural group
6. Importance in demonstrating a high degree of creative or technical achievement at a particular period
7. Strong or special associations with a particular community or cultural group for social, cultural or spiritual reasons
8. Special association with the life or works of a person, or groups of persons, of importance in Australia's natural or cultural history.[13]

These criteria are expanded in guidelines in the form of explanatory notes, a statement of the scope of each criterion, inclusion and exclusion guidelines, and a handful of examples. They could as easily refer to heritage objects as to places, being thoughtful, considered statements, and it is difficult to think of a heritage object type which would not be recognised according to them. This kind of methodical approach systematises what many curators already do without much conscious deliberation, and its special virtue therefore lies not so much in originality as in the rewards of the systematic application of standard operations.

---

12   J. Semple Kerr, 'Part 3: Significance', *The Conservation Plan* (Sydney: National Trust, 1982).

13   Australian Heritage Commission, 'Criteria', *Annual Report 1990–91*, (Canberra, 1991), 18–20.

The applicability of the method to museum collecting is suggested in several experiences: the Nordiska Museet's Samdok report of 1977, the 1991 collection development policy of the Powerhouse Museum, Sydney, and the 1996 collections development policy of the National Museum of Australia.

Six criteria were suggested for acquisitions under the Samdok project:

1. Frequency: the commonest objects
2. Step-ladder: emphasis on long term change in objects
3. Representation: objects which represent ideas and value judgements
4. Appeal: objects associated with a particular person or event of importance
5. Domain: objects associated with individual (as opposed to social) environments
6. Form: objects of aesthetic attraction.[14]

The collection development policy of the Powerhouse Museum lists eight criteria for acquisitions.[15] Four of these are management constraints, assessing the viability of the acquisition in terms of conservation condition, degree of provenance, potential for exhibition use and co-ordination with other collecting institutions. The remaining four require analysis of significance within the whole sphere of material culture, the presence and adaptation of material culture in Australia, and (uniquely specific to this museum) innovations in material culture.

Significance constitutes the most complex of the six criteria recently developed by the National Museum of Australia.[16] Significance is defined as relating: 'to themes, issues or persons of national scope or importance'; 'to subjects nominated by the Collections Framework for collecting activity', and making 'a lasting contribution to understanding and

---

14   G. Cedrenius (untitled paper in sub-topic no. 2), 'Criteria for the selection of museum objects and the current constraints that limit the selection', *Collecting Today for Tomorrow*, Papers of the 6th Symposium, (Leiden: ICOM International Committee for Museology, 1984) (reprinted in *ICOFOM Study Series*, 1 (1995), 45). Despite the title of the sub-topic, no other papers addressed the issue of criteria.

15   Museum of Applied Arts and Sciences (Powerhouse Museum), *Collection Development Policy* (Sydney: Powerhouse Museum,1991), 3–4.

16   National Museum of Australia, *Collections Development Policy* (Sydney: NMA, 1996), 5.

interpreting Australian history and culture'. The other criteria are provenance, originality, research value, display value and conservation qualities.

How do these systems work? Recent communications with the Samdok secretariat indicate that in the last twenty years of practice, the criteria proposed by Cedrenius never took off. Since the brief of the project's various thematic 'pools' is to document and sometimes collect the totality of its subjects, it has been felt that most of the criteria were fairly adequately covered anyway. Further, the aspects of material culture that were felt under-represented, such as symbolic functions, did not appear among the criteria to begin with.[17]

However, it is clear that a rigorous watch is kept on collecting at the Powerhouse and the National Museum of Australia, not only for good collection management but for reasons of accountability. The acquisitions committee at the Powerhouse reports that proposals considered borderline or otherwise dubious are often resolved by reference to the collecting criteria, and that staff feel that having made such decisions, they can justify them responsibly thanks to the criteria. The National Museum of Australia is following the Powerhouse path in this respect, with the extra incentive of weeding collections acquired in less thoughtful days.

The assessment of significance will always contain a subjective element, but the experiences cited above show that criteria-based collecting decisions are useful because they make decisions more comparable, thanks to a common baseline and a common conceptual language for thinking about why an object is worth collecting. Clearly, a museum interested in the process would tailor its criteria to suit its purpose: not all museums have to represent the entire natural and cultural history of a place. But the general schema can easily be adapted to specialist ends.

Having been sidelined from the definitive business of museums, collecting has become the subject of unprecedented academic study, especially in the historical and political dimensions. Politically inspired criticism, mainly feminist, has documented the absence or misinterpretation of major social groups in the museum record of material

---

17 E. Stavenow-Hidemark, *Home Thoughts from Abroad: An Evaluation of the Samdok Homes Pool* (Stockholm: Nordiska Museet/Samdok, 1985), 21. See also A. Steen (Chapter 17) and B. Bursell (Chapter 18), and 'Contemporary museum research in Sweden' (thematic issues), *Samdok Bulletin*, 19(3) (1995).

culture. Post-modern approaches to the study of institutions have reconstructed the authority of professionals as a form of power, and explanatory accounts as repressive master narratives. These critiques suggest that museum collecting needs to become much more transparent, more explicit and more accountable. Without dispatching the skills of the connoisseur – indeed, by asserting them in a systematic manner – curators may re-establish their relevance to museums which have moved on without them.

17 Samdok: tools to make the world visible

Anna Steen

The distinctive characteristic of cultural history museums is that they relate the human experience.[1] They have been perceived as the memory of society, having the power and responsibility to decide what should be remembered, and taking on the role of narrator and communicating stories of national identity, democracy, progress and enlightenment. This requires museums to create new knowledge: knowledge which enables users to identify with their museum, their history and their own time.

To meet this challenge, museums must collect contemporary culture, despite the seemingly overwhelming problems this brings. It is too easy to maintain that the contemporary world is so chaotic, so impossible to fully comprehend, that one cannot make decisions regarding what is important or significant. Overflowing museum stores and limited funds provide further disincentives. But not to rise to this challenge is to convert the museum into a mausoleum, a monument to a past age, completely out of touch with its own time.

If museums refrain from deciding what should be remembered from the present, they will fail in their mission. They will be underestimating their own competence and the museum's capacity to create new knowledge, and denying future historians an invaluable resource. To put it more strongly, they will be betraying their profession. And, indeed, simply choosing not to collect is itself a method of selection, and one with considerable consequences. The alternative is to leave the choice to others. Are museums really prepared to do this?

---

1   T. Bennett, *The Birth of the Museum* (London: Routledge, 1995), 19ff; G. Vestheim, *Museum i eit tidsskifte. Fortidsarv som underhaldning?* (Oslo: Det Norske Samlaget, 1994), 93ff.

What museums need are tools to make contemporary reality more comprehensible; tools for perception and organisation. These tools should enable us to choose which areas to study, what objects should be acquired, and who should be interviewed. In 1977, cultural history museums in Sweden formed Samdok with the aim to research and record contemporary life. Samdok has become a kind of 'tool kit' which enables these issues to be resolved (Fig. 17.1).

Fig. 17.1 The Magnusson family kitchen on display at the Nordiska Museet in 1991. The museum collected a complete kitchen and all the objects belonging to it, as well as information about the crucial role of the kitchen in the everyday life of a Swedish family (Photo: Birgit Brånvall, Nordiska Museet).

The word 'Samdok' is derived from *sam* meaning contemporaneity, co-operation and co-ordination, and *dok* meaning documentation. This term is now used widely outside Scandinavia to mean 'contemporary documentation', a process involving contemporary life and the collecting of associated objects, written materials and photographs. 'Documentation' here refers to the collection and interpretation of verbal, visual and material sources. Samdok uses a methodology of ethnological or anthropological, fieldwork as, indeed, do all cultural history museums in Sweden.[2]

Samdok

The origins of Samdok can be traced to the centenary celebrations of the Nordiska Museet in 1973. A review of this museum's collections showed the main focus to lie in the period 1750–1870; the twentieth century was scarcely represented at all. Thematically, agriculture and pre-industrial craft activities, such as urban trades, were predominant. Lower social groups and industrial activity were either under-represented or not present in what was in effect the national memory bank of the Swedish people. The result of this evaluation was a recommendation that museums should record and collect material from the present rather than searching for early examples or simply recording what was dying out. Contemporary collecting and documentation was to become a continuous and planned museum activity rather than a rescue operation. In order to manage the challenge of collecting what is generally mass-produced material, all Swedish museums were to co-ordinate their work and share the responsibility.

After much discussion, the Samdok secretariat came into being in 1977. The first issue of the *Samdok Bulletin* was published, the database known as the Samdok Register was established, and the first pools, as working groups are called, began work. The Samdok council heads the whole operation, chaired by the director of the Nordiska Museet, and consisting of representatives from the county (or regional), local district and city, and central (national) museums as well as Svenska Museiföreningen (the Swedish Association of Museums). The Samdok secretariat is based in the Nordiska Museet, but is a resource for all the member museums. The secretariat forms the executive body of the council, publishes the *Samdok Bulletin*, and acts as the hub of the network. It also looks after the Samdok Register, arranges in-service training, plans the meetings of the pools and distributes information about contemporary documentation.

---

2   E. Silvén-Garnert, 'Contemporary field research in Swedish cultural history museums. New aspects on material culture', *Actes du Séminaire l'Objet Contemporain* (Quebec: Musée de la Civilisation, 1994), 71–87.

At present Samdok's work is based on researching the modern context of human existence. This involves the analysis of living conditions from cultural, material and temporal viewpoints. Samdok was originally conceptualised as 'collecting today for tomorrow', but is now more concerned with using research to analyse and elucidate our own time.[3]

The pools

The pools are at the heart of Samdok. They have the job of deciding what constitutes the memory of society and turning this into a reality. At the superficial level, the Samdok pools appear similar and give the impression of neatness and efficiency, and perhaps of dull regularity. In reality, however, there is much diversity, both in terms of age and character. This diversity may appear to add complexity, but it does much to strengthen the effectiveness of the whole organisation. The individual make-up and mode of operation of each group reflects their area of interest, the differing needs of component museums, and varying theoretical and methodological starting points.[4]

There are 12 pools and one working group. The division into pools was made in the late 1970s and early 1980s, when the ethnologists' extensive interest in working life gave Samdok a strong bias towards trade and industry (Fig. 17.2). The Home Pool was nevertheless the first to begin work in 1978. The latest, the Group for Cultural Encounters, was formed in 1993 and, like the Home Pool, it is not oriented towards trade and industry. The Public Administration Pool is the largest with 21 members, while the Home Pool has just six. Each pool includes different types of museum (local, national, and so on) in varying combinations. Today Samdok has 82 member museums, distributed throughout the country. In 1997 the organisation of the pools was restructured; the strong emphasis on trade and industry or, more generally, 'work', was removed. In Sweden some 25% of the population (schoolchildren, pensioners, the unemployed, the sick) are outside the labour market.

A telephone survey carried out by the Field Research and Acquisitions Department at the Nordiska Museet in the summer of 1995 showed that member museums conduct many more research projects than Samdok or the pools get to know about. One of the reasons for this was that there were

---

3   Ibid., 74.
4   A. Andrén, 'Samdok's base: the pools', *Samdok Bulletin*, 19(3) (1995), 18.

no pools for many of the areas which museums felt they needed to document: for example, life in local communities, special groups of objects and people's life histories. The reorganised pools cover all contemporary research projects carried out in the cultural history museums of Sweden. Pool divisions now reflect more closely museum needs with regard to discipline, current research and changes in society subsequent to the first division into pools in the 1970s.

Fig. 17.2 The members of the Metals Pool on their way to a joint fieldwork session at the Rönnskärsverken, the Boliden smelting plant in Skellefteå in the province of Västerbotten, during their autumn meeting in 1991 (Photo: Johan Jonsson, National Maritime Museum, Sweden).

Membership and activities

Membership of Samdok is voluntary. Museums choose to join particular pools based on their collections, the economic structure of the county, and/or their special field of interest. Each museum finances its own participation, as well as its own research projects, and has a permanent representative – usually a curator with an orientation towards ethnology, fieldwork and contemporary research – in each of those pools. These representatives participate in the work of the pools over periods of many years.

The pools are democratic assemblies, with no one museum having a greater say. In consultation with fellow pool members, each museum decides which projects to conduct, in line with the pool's programme. Programmes were written in 1991–92 and have consolidated the internal workings of the pools and clarified tasks which are shared or in some ways similar.

Pools meet once or twice a year for one to three days, for discussion, seminars with invited researchers, fieldwork and/or study visits. Long-term participation in a pool produces a broad knowledge of these various spheres of responsibility. Each has become a centre of expertise for such aspects of Swedish life as its engineering industry, its principles of modern commerce, the nuances of the service concept, and so on. The pools are also centres for expertise in contemporary ethnological fieldwork – the distinguishing mark of Swedish cultural history. It is precisely this continuity of active pool involvement which characterises Samdok and gives it its high quality in terms of work and organisation.

Half of the pools carry out joint fieldwork enabling practical co-ordination and co-operation. Methodological and theoretical insights and difficulties are covered in a forum where participants have shared experiences, and where newcomers have an opportunity to learn from more seasoned workers. This permeates each participant's work at their home museum.[5]

This method of working brings together people of different backgrounds, but who carry out roughly the same tasks, and thus have the opportunity to discuss their results. It also prevents constant re-invention of established principles. There are generally two or three curators per county in Sweden (with 24 counties altogether) who actively undertake ethnological fieldwork, so it is clearly difficult to develop and maintain a high standard of work without the collaboration of colleagues in Samdok.[6]

The compilation of joint materials also allows the discussion of questions of ethics in fieldwork situations, the confidentiality of archive material and

---

5   A. Andrén, 'Resande i korta dokumentationer', *Samdok Bulletin*, 18(4) (1994), 12–13.

6   Ibid., 13.

the integrity of informants. One also learns the importance of good planning and time management.

Like the pools, documentation programmes differ, but also share certain features. Some present detailed accounts of what they have done, while others reflect on the task of the pool in a broader social perspective. Some penetrate crucial concepts and issues, while others start with an activity. These programmes enable us to realise how many different ways there are of tackling the same task, and emphasise that there is more than one way of researching contemporary life.[7]

Samdok's policy declaration visualises Swedish cultural history museums as a joint resource. Yet it achieves this not through centralised directives, but through democracy, diversity, continuity and dialogue.

If these museums do form a joint resource, then we should now be able to talk of joint results of this work. The main result, of course, is in the form of research projects carried out from 1977 to the present day. These have resulted in new collections of primary material as well as publications and exhibitions. The Samdok Register now holds some 900 entries which cover a wide range of completed research projects. There is, for example, research on how mobile telephones are used, fruit growers in the province of Skåne, individual families and their homes, the modern miner, hospital patients, and the state visit of Queen Elizabeth II to Sweden.

Another joint result is a change in attitude. Cultural history museums today regard contemporary documentation as their duty – a natural part of their activities and training. The network formed by Samdok also opens the way for continual discussions on method, theory and practice – at pool meetings, at the annual method courses and in the *Samdok Bulletin*. The long-term commitment of its participants has resulted in a constantly evolving cycle of study which has derived wide benefits for museums.[8]

The aim has been not simply to collect, but also to analyse, interpret and understand what has been collected, so that this can be communicated to visitors and future researchers. Analysing the significance of our own time for the history writing of the future is one of our main functions. To achieve this museums must continue to collect, they must understand what objects mean and symbolise, and create new knowledge. It is not necessarily just a question of knowing about production techniques, materials, producers of

---

7   Andrén, op. cit., 1995, 18.

8   Silvén-Garnert, op. cit., 76–7.

objects and their users. Now we also have to include the communicative significance of objects, people's likes and dislikes, and the way they have gladdened or saddened their users – aspects which we can capture through contemporary ethnological fieldwork.[9]

When Artur Hazelius, founder of the Nordiska Museet and its sister foundation, Skansen, started his collecting activities in 1873, he was more or less the only person interested in the everyday life of ordinary people. His only 'rivals' were those authors of novels who wrote in the new realistic style, in Sweden best represented by August Strindberg, and in Norway by Henrik Ibsen. The museums of today face significantly tougher competition from others also working in the documentary field, so that we now have to reckon with film directors, journalists in a range of media, rock singers, and so on. People in general, too, write about themselves and their lives to a much greater extent now than they did a hundred years ago. Or, as a colleague put it: 'The world is full of people who think they have something interesting to tell us.' But much of this information is typically only accessible in two-dimensional or electronic form. In effect, none of it is tangible.

Museums are, perhaps, no longer the sole holders of power in deciding what is worth remembering and what should be forgotten. Others are also involved. But they are the only institutions in society whose job it is to make memory of the tangible. They have the power and the knowledge to interpret material culture as it appears to us in its original form. We are the only agents who have charge of maintaining that part of cultural heritage to be found in the same dimension as ourselves – where we need no electronic aids to see, feel, witness or understand. We are, in other words, alone in having access to cultural heritage unplugged!

---

9   Ibid., 81.

18 Professionalising collecting

Barbro Bursell

Research into contemporary Sweden has, for more than two decades, been an important duty for Swedish museums.[1] Work carried out under the auspices of Samdok has met with considerable success, but now needs strengthening if the organisation is not to fall into decline. It is suggested here that this might be achieved by improving the quality of the work undertaken so that it is more conscious, focused and responsible.

Investigating commissions in Sweden in recent years have shown that politicians and museum committees often display great ignorance concerning the work of museums, not least in their collecting, research and recording functions. They know neither how or why museums collect, and consequently question the very need.

One recently published museum report did not even discuss collecting, but instead designated it as an aspect of conservation work.[2] The report's focus was on work with the public and conservation problems associated with existing collections. It went on to suggest that if museums were to continue to collect as previously, they would simply add to the conservation mountain. It was therefore better to reduce collecting, and in this respect Samdok came in for praise, having collected fewer objects in recent years than formerly.

Despite perceptions outside the country, object collecting remains the least comprehensive activity in Swedish museums. When compared with other fundamental duties (education, display and care of the collections), recording, collecting and research get little attention from museum directors and committees, and in consequence are allocated few resources.

---

1   See A. Steen, Chapter 17, for a discussion of the establishment and organisation of Samdok. See also 'Contemporary Museum Research in Sweden', Samdoksekretariatet, Nordiska museet, *Samdok Bulletin*, 3 (1995) (English edition).

2   *Museiutredningens betänkande Minne och bildning. Museernas uppdrag och organisation* (Stockholm: State Government Official Reports, 1994), 51.

Statistics for 1991 show that for 24 regional cultural museums, an average of one person per annum in each museum worked on collecting, researching and recording contemporary life. Comparable figures for collection care and work with the public are five and seven.[3]

These figures show that collecting today is given low priority. It is therefore also very vulnerable. Those of us engaged in this field are uneasy. Only half of the investigations carried out in recent years by the Samdok museums have resulted in object acquisition. Only 367 items were accessioned within the network during the period 1992–96. It is now difficult to carry through research projects as staff get transferred to other, usually more high-profile, public duties.

Museums around the world are considering how to rationalise collecting in order to reduce the rate of acquisition, but is this appropriate? The twentieth century has transformed human existence, and yet it is poorly researched and documented by museums. This is certainly so in Sweden, where the emphasis in the collections often remains on pre-industrial farming society.

Rather than accept decline, museums must argue for resources to record and collect from contemporary society. They must put together an agenda which demonstrates that collecting is the key to the future of museums. Without ongoing collecting activity, museums will lose their memory function; they will cease to be living institutions, but rather fossilised monuments to a vanished age.

It is not simply the loss of an archive which will be mourned, but also the loss of skills in terms of museums' abilities to record life. Such knowledge and skills need to be nurtured and developed.

What can museums do to ensure that collecting is given higher priority? There are two major obstacles to be overcome. The first concerns resources. Space and maintenance costs will continue to rise as collecting continues. However, other organisations have had no difficulty in attracting such resources: Kungliga Biblioteket[4] and the Riksarkivet[5] have both recently acquired new stores. If the printed word and documents from our own time are to be stored and maintained, as demanded by legislation, then space is found. There is no expectation that the size of books or documents

---

3   *Länsmuseernas verksamhetsnivå 1991* (Länsmuseernas samarbetsråd, 1992).
4   The National Library of Sweden.
5   The Swedish National Archives.

should dictate whether or not they should be kept for posterity. Why should the same not be true for museums? And when will the law recognise that society must take charge not only of the printed word, archives, ancient monuments, ancient forest, and churches, but also of some of those objects we produce and use, and with which we surround ourselves.

The second obstacle is of a more qualitative nature. Those in power will not allocate resources if they continue to perceive collecting as a misguided and ill-thought-out activity. This might be overcome by improving the quality of the collecting work, increasing consciousness of why and how collecting is undertaken. This requires greater focus and responsibility, and an ability to articulate our purpose in professional ways.

Collecting policies lie at the heart of this, both in laying down guidelines and raising awareness, and also by generating internal debate and thought concerning the collecting process. This requires an analysis of existing collections in terms of object categories, period, and social and geographical representation. It also demands historical revision of the institution's past collecting activity. From this, guidelines can be developed on future collecting (and, by implication, 'non-collecting'). Forums, such as the museological seminars staged at Nordiska Museet, also allow collecting issues to be discussed and a wider consensus found.

Collecting in the field

Making collecting an integral part of fieldwork may be yet another way of developing more professionalised collecting. Two approaches to collecting might be adopted. The first is object-focused. Categories of objects (children's clothes, kitchen furniture and so on) are selected and a decision taken on which types, materials and models would form a representative twentieth-century collection. The second method focuses on people. Which objects do these people have around them and what do they mean to them? The first approach takes a production perspective; the second a perspective of consumption. Each method has different information objectives: one is product-oriented cultural history; the other is directed towards cultural anthropology (Fig. 18.1).[6]

---

6   B. Bursell and S. Eklund Nyström, 'Different ways of collecting things', *Samdok Bulletin*, 3 (1995), 15–17. U. Brück, 'Kommersialism och prylvärld.

Fig. 18.1 Collecting as an integrated part of field research. Objects and meanings are gathered. This 1952 Volvo PV 444 was collected in 1996 as part of the Motor Car project. As well as symbolizing postwar Swedish society, it was also a personal possession of this man for 40 years (Photo: Peter Segemark, Nordiska Museet).

The collecting techniques associated with each approach also differ. The first might be satisfied by gap-filling donations offered to the museum. The second demands that the collector take a more proactive role and seek out a subject and determine which symbolically loaded objects to acquire for the museum. This latter is the approach adopted by Swedish cultural history museums in their contemporary research. The approach not only generates high-quality collections, but also educates the collector in the meaning of objects.

Hur får vår materiella tillvaro sin utformning – och hur kan den studeras?', *Ting, kultur och mening* (Stockholm: Nordiska museets förlag, 1995).

Fig. 18.2 Collecting through field research means objects acquire rich contexts. Documentation of contemporary Swedish wedding traditions involved collecting the bridal couple's whole outfit down to the underwear. Here a curator helps the bride get ready for church on the wedding day (Photo: Birgit Brånvall, Nordiska Museet).

Field collecting provides a resource where the object and its meaning are integrated and contribute to answering wider questions of the research project.[7] For example, an ongoing project at the Nordiska Museet is studying how the motorcar and automobility have changed Swedish society in the twentieth century. This investigation has involved interviewing large numbers of people about their memories and experiences to do with cars. Objects have also been collected from informants: everything from embroidered car cushions to caravans and holiday films.[8] In another investigation, the museum has studied the way a

---

7   E. Silvén-Garnert, 'A network of Swedish museums', *Samdok Bulletin*, 3 (1995), 3–5.

8   A. Rosengren, 'The car as an object and the cultural meaning of automobility', *Samdok Bulletin*, 3 (1995), 6–8.

number of families, both Swedes and immigrants, celebrate different high days and holidays over a period of a year. Apart from interviewing, photographing and describing their traditions, the presents (in this case exact copies/duplicates of the real ones) which figured in our informants' celebrations of Christmas, birthdays, and so on, have also been collected (Fig. 18.2).[9]

Building in collecting as an integral part of fieldwork means that objects acquire a rich context. They have an interesting history to tell in future displays and exhibitions. They represent not just form and colour, but also meaning: a simple stocking becomes a precious Christmas present; a caravan a symbol of the good life. Most importantly, this active search for significant objects forces the curator to decide which object or objects are central to the investigation and therefore also important to the museum's collection. The Swedish historian of ideas, Sverker Sörlin, suggests that the future value of museum collections lies precisely in the particular issues controlling why they were collected in the first place.[10]

Pruning at source

Work in the field can result in extensive collections. Some years ago the Nordiska Museet acquired a complete kitchen, consisting of some 1000 objects belonging to a single family.[11] Usually, collecting is more discriminating. In a large-scale investigation of a modern engineering workshop, the curator concerned chose only a handful of items with which to illustrate the issues.[12] Pruning at source – that is, rejecting material – is of key importance. The Nordiska Museet reckons to refuse about 75 per cent of the objects offered as donations. This is not difficult if the museum has a clear collecting policy.

One way of developing collecting work may also be via displays and exhibitions. When the purpose of collecting is direct use in an exhibition, there is much more consciousness of what objects are needed in order to present different themes in visual form. The Motor Car Project, for

---

9   K. Lövgren, 'Ceci n'est pas une pipe', *Samdok Bulletinen*, 2 (1994), 16–17.

10   S. Sörlin, 'Samla eller dö – om museisamlingars värde', *Samdok Bulletinen*, 2 (1996), 6–8.

11   Steen (Chapter 17).

12   E. Fägerborg, 'Rapporter från arbetslivet. En utvärdering av Samdokundersökningarna', *Samdok Bulletin*, 2 (1992), 9–22.

example, was long ago recognised as likely to generate an exhibition and, consequently, objects have been an integral part of the research. This raises questions in terms of what should be selected: props or broader acquisitions? Objects which provide for research or which provide an experience?

Participating in the whole process, from research and collecting through to exhibition and publication, not only generates satisfaction but also ensures quality. It also eliminates the conflict between collecting and outreach which can so easily arise.

As museums develop their knowledge and consciousness of object collecting, they improve its quality and focus. In doing so, they might escape the suspicions of others that collecting today only means problems tomorrow. To be effective collectors, we must also be able to articulate our special knowledge of the process of collection building. If politicians and the wider public fail to understand why and how museums collect, then the task will continue to be perceived as unimportant.

In Sweden, the Samdok network has become a model for contemporary collecting and forms a platform for discussion of method. The *Samdok Bulletinen* keeps track of planned and ongoing projects, while annual courses and handbooks give the opportunity to discuss fieldwork and the development of object collecting methodologies.[13] This latter function within the organisation was not envisaged twenty years ago when Samdok was started, but is today one of its most important contributions to museum work.

---

13   The handbooks deal with museum research, recording and collecting; the role of material culture in contemporary research and recording; interviews; and turning field research into publications. Each book has a summary in English, they are Nordiska Museet/Samdok, *Verbalt. Visuellt. Materiellt* (*Verbal, Visual, Material*), on field research and acquisition in museum work (1991); *Tumme med tingen* (*Mind Over Matter*), on the role of material objects in contemporary documentation, (1992); *Muntliga möten* (*Meeting Minds*), on interviews in museum contemporary documentation (1993); *Text i tryck* (*Text in Print*), from fieldwork material to publication (1995). All are published by Nordiska Museets Förlag, Stockholm.

19 Developing a collecting strategy for smaller museums

María García, Carmen Chinea and José Fariña

The Organismo Autónomo de Museos y Centros (OAMC) manages six museums located in Tenerife. These museums aim to rescue and preserve the Canarian heritage, which would otherwise be scattered through national and larger museums all over the world – lost in stores amongst thousands of other objects. OAMC'S greatest difficulty in achieving this is derived from the lack of a written policy setting out criteria for collecting. Incoming objects are accepted according to directors' or conservators' judgement and taste, economic opportunities or pressures from the politicians who control the OAMC board. The result for preventive conservation, and for co-ordination, and indeed co-operation, among the museums' staff, is problematic.[1] Consequently, despite significant annual expenditure, provision for collection care and conservation remains inadequate.

The organisation detected that the efficiency of collecting, and collection care, could be improved by the adoption of a strategy which graded incoming objects according to their worth and condition.[2] Data was gathered from curators in order to gauge individual criteria used in evaluating objects during accessioning and deaccessioning, and preventive and remedial conservation. The survey showed that there were nearly as many collecting criteria as there were curators. This was particularly so in the Natural History Museum, due to its highly specialised methods of preservation and documentation. Collecting criteria bore no relationship to

1   B. Lord and G.D. Lord, *The Manual of Museum Planning* (London: HMSO, 1991).

2   S. Michalski, 'A systematic approach to preservation: description and integration with other museum activities', in A. Roy and P. Smith (eds), *Preventive Conservation: Practice, Theory and Research*. Preprints to the Ottawa Congress (London: International Institute for Conservation, 1994).

current or expected annual budgets, and there was little co-operation among curators. In addition, it showed that most curators had little knowledge of preventive conservation despite having responsibility for the inspection, packing and storage of incoming objects, and for the prevention of biodeterioration.

A strategy was designed with reference to conservation surveys undertaken by museums in the United Kingdom, Canada and the United States.[3] However, the amount of time required to undertake these surveys, together with their cost and the need for trained staff, meant they did not entirely meet the organisation's needs. OAMC has a limited and diverse staff, and this, together with the mixed nature of the collections, means that curators often do not have the expertise to evaluate all the objects in their care. Similarly, the poorly-equipped conservation laboratory, with its one conservator, which supports four museums, could not meet collection assessment expectations.

The strategy, therefore, had to be simple. It had to be undertaken by staff with little experience of object evaluation and with minimal supervision from curators and the conservator. The proposed method is given in Table 19.1.[4] This divides the evaluation process into four major areas, with each of these having a further three to nine subcategories scored according to their importance.

Using this scheme every incoming object is given a code number consisting of four digits (one from each of the four sections), which not only gives a summary of its value and conservation needs but also allows for its categorisation into one of six groups:

1. High-value objects with sensitive conservation requirements
2. High-value objects with standard conservation requirements
3. Average-value objects with sensitive conservation requirements

---

3   K. Walker and L. Bacon, 'A condition survey of specimens in the Horniman Museum: a progress report', in *Recent Advances in the Conservation and Analysis of Artefacts* (London: Summer School Press, 1987); S. Keene, 'Audits of care: a framework for collections condition surveys', in M. Norman and V. Todd (eds), *Storage* (London: UKIC, 1991); H. Kingsley and R. Payton, 'Condition surveying a large varied stored collection', in Roy and Smith, op. cit.

4   C. Costain, 'Framework for preservation of museum collections', *CCI Newsletter*, 14 (1994), 1–4.

4. Average-value objects with standard conservation requirements
5. Low-value objects in good conservation condition
6. Low-value objects in fair or poor conservation condition.

Acquisition of objects which fall into group 5 is a matter for discussion; objects falling into group 6 are rejected.

Table 19.1. Collecting assessment

Geographical origin
    1. Tenerife
    2. Canary Islands
    3. Rest of the world

Age
    1. Dated. Within museums' scope
    2. Uncertain. Within museums' scope
    3. Not within the museums' scope

Collection-related function
    1. New in the collection
    2. Completes sections of the collection
    3. Extensively documented
    4. Further analysis might bring forward relevant information
    5. Gives maximum information on the culture/environment it comes from at first glance
    6. Society requesting. Special concern on their conservation and display has been shown by Canarian people
    7. There are other items
    8. Scanty or not documented
    9. Reproductions

Conservation condition
    1. Good, only standard storage and display
    2. Fair, future treatment might be required
    3. Poor, immediate treatment
    4. Very bad, urgent treatment

The assessment chart is accompanied by guidelines and illustrations which aim to assist in the detection of conservation problems. These incorporate those problems currently found in the Canary Islands, grouped by their seriousness into 'fair', 'poor' and 'very poor'. The conservator will only be called when an object needs immediate treatment or doubts about its condition arise. This categorisation should allow for more efficient management of resources. The code might also be used to indicate the possible uses of the objects.

OAMC is also taking its discussion of these issues out into the community; preserving heritage should concern everybody. An educational programme has been designed to show the public how the collecting strategy works and how OAMC manages collecting problems. The public remained unaware of the bulk of the OAMC collections, and this led to attitudes of distrust, and disregard for museum curatorial activities. These feelings are exacerbated by the curators' resistance to opening stores and workshops to visitors or allowing them to handle original specimens.

The programme aimed to increase public interest in museums, their staff and Canarian heritage, to demonstrate that the Islands' heritage belongs to all Canarians and that all islanders share responsibilities for its care, conservation, study and display. This was achieved by giving the public access behind the scenes and allowing them firsthand scrutiny of museum work and its associated difficulties. Catalogues and guides were also published which incorporated information on preventive conservation and curation, and workshops organised for various groups where these issues could be further explored.

The OAMC strategy seeks to set criteria for accepting a new object into the collection and classifying it according to its value and conservation condition. Although it was initially intended for use by Canarian museums, some modifications are being discussed so that it can be used by other small- to medium-sized museums. Having the collections categorised according to the same system will allow a more efficient and rapid exchange of information and experience among museums.

Since an object's value and its conservation condition might vary substantially over time, the categories must be sufficiently flexible to allow for subsequent reclassification. Moreover, social and cultural processes affect the curator's approach to an object, so objectivity when categorising a collection is difficult to achieve.

20 Towards a national collection strategy: reviewing existing holdings

Jean-Marc Gagnon and Gerald Fitzgerald

In times of economic constraint, collection-holding institutions world-wide face similar challenges. Among critical issues of concern is the need to marry a decrease in resources and the growing numbers of orphaned collections with continual requests for new acquisitions. The result is a pressing need to improve the quality and efficiency of collection management, and particularly collecting. An initial and essential step to the elaboration of any national or international strategy on issues such as collection development is the examination of present collections: that is, where they are and what they contain. To achieve this in Canada, information on natural sciences collections was compiled from specific survey reports and collection indexes.[1]

---

1   These were: R.H. Arnette, Jr., G.A. Samuelson and G.M. Nishida, *The Insects and Spider Collections of the World* (Florida: Sandhill Crane Press, 1993), 36–52; Biological Survey of Canada, 'Collections of Canadian insects and certain related groups', *Bulletin of the Entomological Society of Canada* (suppl.), 10(1) (1978), 1–21; B. Boivin, *Survey of Canadian Herbaria* (Université Laval, Provancheria No. 10, 1980); Canadian Museum of Nature, *Inventory of Natural History Collections* (Ottawa: Collection Division, Canadian Museum of Nature, 1992–94); P.K. Holmgren, N.H. Holmgren and L.C. Barnett, *Index Herbariorum, Part I: The Herbaria of the World* (New York: New York Botanical Garden, 1990), 60–77; N. Lemay, *Inventaire des collections de sciences naturelles au Québec*, Volume 1 (Québec: Gouvernement du Canada, Rapport soumis au Ministre des Communications, 1990); Canadian Society of Zoology, *Natural history collections database of the Canadian Society of Zoology* (Ottawa: Canadian Heritage Information Network (CHIN), 1993).

Eleven different types of collections (plants, molluscs, and so on) were distinguished and only those that were reported in the available literature are included in this review (Table 20.1). Unfortunately, not all published information was up to date, details of the specific geographic coverage of each collection were not available and earth sciences collections (minerals, rocks and gems and fossils) were not included.

Table 20.1 Types of natural history collection considered in the present study, number of collections surveyed and total holdings reported

Taxonomic group	Number of collections	Number of lots/specimens
Plants	178	7,203,375
Molluscs	41	256,274
Annelids	16	189,420
Crustaceans	31	349,835
Insects	110	22,204,609
Parasites	10	63,483
Other Invertebrates	43	469,663
Birds	52	432,010
Mammals	51	322,209
Fish, Amphibians and Reptiles	51	931,482
Unspecified Vertebrates	34	52,756
TOTAL	616	32,475,116

In all, 616 collections were reported from 260 institutions, giving a total of approximately 32.5 million lots or specimens (Table 20.2). With the recent rapid growth of the National Insect Collection in Ottawa this number can be increased by at least another 5 million specimens. Of the 260 institutions, 100 have holdings of more than 10,000 lots or specimens and represent 98.9% of all holdings in Canada. Of the larger institutions, only 22 had holdings of more than 200,000 lots or specimens, but these accounted for about 85% of all holdings in Canada.

There are substantial differences in holdings between provinces, with the majority of collection holdings found in the National Capital Region, Ontario, Québec and British Columbia (Fig. 20.1). A few institutions with a national mandate and correspondingly large collections that represent almost 43% of all natural history collection holdings in Canada are located in the National Capital Region (NCR), which is centred around Ottawa. The content of the federal collections in the NCR are such that, in many respects, they complement the collections held in other parts of the country. This broad-brush view of collections, however, disguises the particular nuances of individual centres. For example, the New Brunswick holdings reveal considerable fish collections derived from fisheries and marine biology stations in St Andrews.

Table 20.2 Natural history collection holdings reported in Canada

Geographic region	Number of institutions	Number of collections	Total number of lots	Percentage of national total
British Columbia	26	72	1,958,703	6.03
Alberta	30	70	1,736,798	5 35
Saskatchewan	12	25	413,283	1.27
Manitoba	14	26	1,266,875	3.90
Ontario (excluding NCR)	50	99	5,136,318	15.82
National Capital Region (NCR)	6	28	13,962,593	42.91
Québec (excluding NCR)	83	204	6,629,416	20.41
New Brunswick	10	32	528,643	1.63
Nova Scotia	13	32	599,428	1.85
Prince Edward Island	3	3	10,830	0.03
Newfoundland	8	17	229,279	0.71
Territories	5	8	2,950	0.01
CANADA	260	616	32,475,116	100

Results of the recent Canada Country Study of Biodiversity (Table 20.3) indicate that groups such as vascular plants, birds and mammals have been well described. The 7.2 million plants, 430,000 birds and 320,000 mammals presently in collections throughout Canada suggests that collection-holding institutions can be more selective in their future collecting in these areas. Emphasis in collection development should be directed at less well-represented groups such as viruses, bacteria, algae and invertebrates (Table 20.3). This, of course, does not preclude the need to continue research on the well-represented biological groups. In this case, however, a careful examination of available material from collections throughout the country and possibly abroad would prevent duplication of effort and ensure strategic development of collections for well-represented groups. Although there is a lesser necessity to carry on selective collecting for ill-represented biological groups, priority should still be given to addressing issues that are socially and economically critical.

In the context of a national strategy, it is essential that the major collection-holding institutions in Canada work in concert on the development of natural history collections by:

1. Defining collection development priorities, with emphasis on specific ill-represented collection types or biological groups.
2. Elaborating a strategy which would take into account various ways of generating revenues.
3. Establishing and maintaining collaboration and exchange of specimens, information, and expertise on collection care and management.
4. Facilitating the computerisation of databases and standardisation of data to address important societal issues such as the biodiversity crisis and global warming.

Table 20.3 Estimated numbers of described and living species in Canada[2]

Group	Est. no. of species reported	Est. species total	Percentage described
Vertebrata (excl. Pisces)	662	662	100
Plantae	4,120	4,256	97
Algae	5,300	7,280	72
Fungi & Lichens	11,310	16,465	69
Pisces	1,021	1,521	67
Invertebrata (excl. Insecta)	17,362	28,327	61
Insecta, etc.	29,985	54,653	55
Protozoa	1,000	2,000	50
Bacteria	2,000	22,000	<0.1
Virus	200	150,200	<0.01

2   Modified from T. Mosquin, P.G. Whiting and D.E. McAllister, *Canada's Biodiversity: the variety of life, its status, economic benefits, conservation costs and unmet needs. The Canada Country Study of Biodiversity* (Ottawa: Canadian Museum of Nature, 1995)

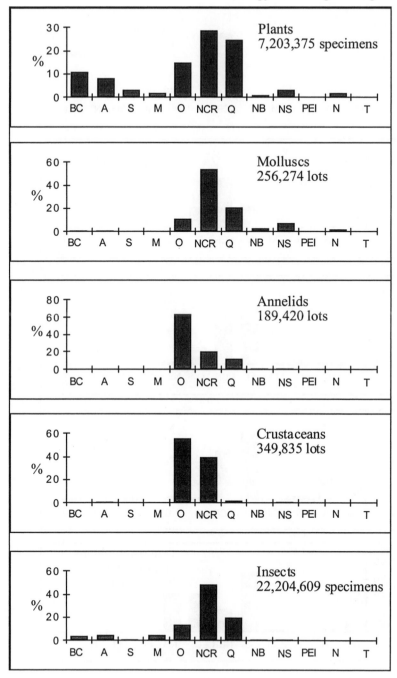

Figure 20.1 Distribution of lots/specimens by province/territory.

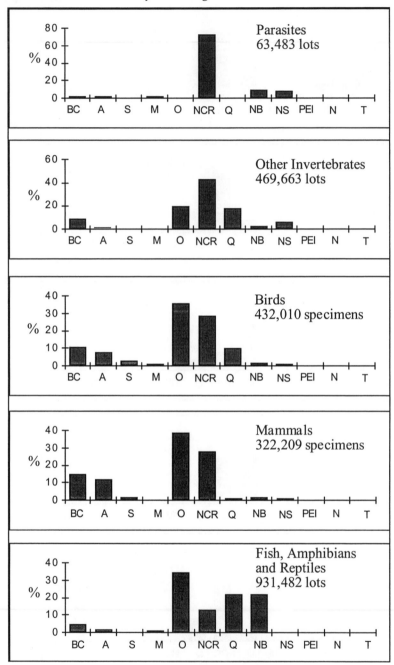

Figure 20.1 Distribution of lots/specimens (continued).

In practical terms, it means that under a national strategy, one or few specific institutions could assume, in co-ordination with the other participating institutions, the future development of collections for certain biological groups or for certain geographic regions. When appropriate and suitable, this approach could provide the opportunity to centralise certain collections (in part or in totality) to facilitate access and increase efficiency of use.

Important steps in the process of developing a national strategy include examining all issues relating to the co-ordination of collections development and establishing protocols to facilitate sharing of collection-based information amongst participants and outside users. The greatest challenges facing any organisation that seeks to establish such a national or even international strategy are particularly those which surround ownership of data and specimens. The elaboration of a national or international collection strategy has to proceed carefully to ensure that all concerns are being addressed. These include issues such as the real costs of developing, maintaining and making collections available, and an appropriate financial return on investment. A national collection strategy will not be acceptable to many until these issues are fairly resolved.

21 Ranking collections

Martin Wickham

A rational approach to ranking items in museum collections is a professional virtue to which we should aspire. The alternative is to be open to the accusation of being irrational by those we serve and by those who fund us.[1]

At the heart of a museum's collecting must be a means to discern value. Based on the varied collections of armoured vehicles at the Tank Museum, Bovington, UK, this paper describes an attempt to establish a rational, simple and yet practical numerate method of ascribing individual objects with relative values. A problem at the heart of all collecting is the subjectivity of decisions regarding value, and while this cannot be entirely eradicated its effects might be minimised by tempering individual opinion, so far as is reasonable, perhaps by using consensus input from a group of scorers. The results of this activity must also have transparency so as to facilitate review.

The Tank Museum collection was considered to be sufficiently comprehensive to enable a proper assessment for this project. It comprises around three hundred vehicles (from 27 countries), mainly AFVs (Armoured Fighting Vehicles), but complemented by 'soft-skinned' vehicles, Classroom Instruction Models, turrets without vehicles (and vice versa), some trailers and towed guns. This diverse collection includes prototype and production models, relating to both Armoured Corps and others such as engineers, signals and so on. The project also offered opportunities to consider how this approach might be developed into a national register.

Towards a grading system

To enhance objectivity, it was decided that the ranking system should be quantitative rather than qualitative. The identification of relevant criteria

---

1   T. Besterman, 'The ethics of disposal', *Museums Journal*, 101(12) (2001), 31–3.

and the allocation of numeric scores to each criterion would, at a superficial level, provide a quantified input, unless the scores were derived from value judgements.

Before an effective system could be established, the criteria giving importance to armoured vehicles within a museum collection had to be identified, and their relative importance evaluated. Linking the criteria through a simple mathematical model would facilitate production of an overall score for each vehicle. All this sounds simple, but the connoisseurship inherent in museum work favours subjective judgement. However, it did not matter too much if the grading system was slightly subjective, as this might ensure that it conforms in some degree to the curator's instinctive ranking. Consensus also reduces concerns over subjectivity, and provides a means to validate the grading system. Any anomalous results would give rise to closer inspection and iterative improvement and, indeed, this was key to the development process. The project involved extensive discussions among the Tank Museum staff, its Collections Committee, and staff at several other museums.

The initial work was based on a small sample of the collection to which was added a hypothetical vehicle (the 'Leonardo Tank'), which, had it existed, would have been the most important vehicle in the collection. Early results were judged against this vehicle and criteria were introduced, amended or rejected as the need became apparent. The model was tuned to steadily reduce the number of results regarded as anomalous. A small working party was set up to operate as a focus group, provide input and assess the results. The Imperial War Museum was also asked to comment on various aspects, using an early version of the software.

A number of existing quantitative methods for object evaluation were also explored in order to determine the characteristics of the model to be used at Bovington. Condition surveys, for example, such as that used by Birmingham Museum and Art Gallery, follow a method where a numeric score is allocated to various predetermined criteria. In a rather different way the National Airframe Register applies a simple points system which permits an airframe to be allocated as 'Benchmark', 'Significant' or 'Noteworthy'. It was derived from the Railway Heritage Register, and like the model developed here it clearly demonstrates the need to determine eligibility criteria so as to locate the boundaries within which the grading system will effectively work. The National Register of Historic Vessels applies a five-point scoring system for 15 categories, which is applied by committee against predetermined criteria but is resource-intensive. The AFV system sought to devise a simpler and more efficient system.[2]

The initial list of criteria providing importance to an AFV collection was compiled from a basic understanding of the subject. Colleagues were invited to comment on and extend the list, and thus most of the relevant criteria were identified with little difficulty. To ensure that significant parameters had not been omitted, a search was then conducted, both of similar projects and of disparate types of collection. A review of material culture methodology also identified several sets of properties for assessing the importance of an object. Elliott identified material, construction, function, provenance and value, which Pearce modified to embody history, environment, significance and interpretation, while Batchelor preferred idea, material, manufacture, marketing, art and use. Natural science collections also offered several leads, with Nudds and Pettitt providing many approaches, and Jeram giving one view of scientific importance that proved useful.[3]

Mikesh describes American aircraft museum practice which identifies three importance categories (representing association with a historical event, technical significance or type significance), and four condition categories. This model is too simplistic to provide the fine resolution necessary to grade a collection effectively. The category definitions are relatively complex, so that an object might fall between two categories, with a tendency to create sub-categories (cf. A-, B+ etc). Collins discusses historic importance, and identifies parameters such as age, uniqueness of the original design, rarity, and technology. In addition, association with

---

2   K. Ellis, *National Aviation Heritage Register – Airframes held in Museums and Collections in the UK*, second edition, (British Aviation Preservation Council, 2001). M. Cope, 'The Railway Heritage Register – Carriage Survey Project', *Museum Documentation Association (MDA) Information*, 5(2) (May 2001), 25–32.

3   R. Elliott, 'Towards a material history methodology' (1982) in S.M. Pearce (ed), *Interpreting Objects and Collections* (London: Routledge, 1994), 112; S.M. Pearce, 'Thinking about things' (1986) in Pearce, op.cit., 125 – 132; R. Batchelor, 'Not looking at kettles' (1986) in Pearce, op.cit., 139 – 143; J.R. Nudds, and C.W. Pettitt (eds), *The Value and Valuation of Natural Science Collections* (London: The Geological Society, 1997); A.J. Jeram, 'Criteria for establishing the scientific value of natural science collections', in Nudds and Pettit, ibid., 61–7.

persons, places or events, and spiritual, cultural or political significance and exceptional aesthetic qualities were all identified. These criteria were drawn from industrial collections, but included aspects of obvious relevance to AFVs such as the inclusion of condition, the extent of original material remaining, and whether the object remains in operational order.[4]

From such sources, a list of criteria was identified, from which several categories were discarded after due consideration. In all, 20 were selected to form the basis of the grading system. There was no restriction to a convenient round number; these simply comprised the full list of significant variables that could be scored in a pragmatic manner. It was believed that this set of characteristics adequately defined the worth of an object to a collection in terms of its acquisition and retention or, indeed, in the resources to be expended on its survival or display.

Scoring and weighting

Each vehicle in the collection would be scored for each attribute. For simplicity, a decision was taken to score each variable between zero and ten marks. An impression of finer resolution could be achieved by scoring each variable as a percentage, but few variables could be scored objectively to this degree, and overall accuracy would not be improved. A clear definition of top score and zero score was determined for each parameter (see Table 21.1). The person scoring must have these definitions immediately accessible; without such guidance, inconsistencies would emerge.

Each criterion was examined for the possibility of providing specific definitions for each intermediate mark, to avoid any interpolation. This was achieved for five of the criteria (age, size, rarity, costs, and health and safety), which significantly reduced subjectivity for 25% of the variables. The corollary is that 75% of the criteria are marked subjectively in what purports to be an objective assessment. However, these value judgements relate to specific criteria, which are given more detailed definition than is permitted here.

4   R. Mikesh, *Restoring Museum Aircraft*. (Shrewsbury: Airlife Publishing Ltd, 1997), 22 – 33; C. Collins. The Integrity of Transport Collections (unpublished MA dissertation, University of Leicester, 1993).

Table 21.1 Top score and zero score for each parameter in the grading system.

Characteristic	Zero score	Top (10) score
Age	Post-1988	Pre-1661
Background History	Unknown	Associated with particular act of conspicuous bravery, for example
Completeness	Manifestly incomplete	Complete with stowage and tools/publications/supporting provenance etc.
Condition: External	Not fit for display	Full credit to the display
Condition: Internal	Not fit for display	Full credit to the display
Condition: Operational	Could never be operational	Fully operational (weapons excepted)
Cost commitment	Requires only routine maintenance and cleaning	All sub-systems require specialist conservation
Damage	Extensive 'post-service' damage	No damage excepting battle damage or service history
Educational Value	Difficult to give educational interpretation	Ideal for educational purposes
Health & Safety Considerations	Not safe for public display in medium or short term	No health and safety hazards
Historical Significance (of Type)	Negligible historical significance	Significantly changed the course of history
In-House Labour Requirements	Requires complete conservation/restoration	Requires only routine maintenance/cleaning
Originality (Authenticity)	Substantially modified	Time capsule of a known date/totally authentic
Ownership	Loaned in, with extensive strings	Exceedingly beneficial-terms, long term loan
Particular Significance	No *particular* relevance to museum	Very close fit with museum's collection policy, & locality or regimental connections
Rarity	Readily available secondhand	Unique, or sole survivor
Size	As large as a main battle tank	No larger than a small car
Stability of Condition	Unstable, needs urgent/extensive attention	Stable, and likely to remain so
Technological Features	No unusual technology	Breakthrough technology
Wow Factor	So what?	cf. Elgin Marbles

Clearly some of the parameters are more important than others, so a sum of the category scores does not produce a satisfactory total. Weighting factors were introduced to reflect the relative importance of each category. Constraining the weighting factors to add up to a total of 100 allows easier visualisation but is not essential. It assists the iteration process, since before a factor can be increased, it is necessary to consider which factors should be correspondingly reduced. Thus the weighting factor, shows the percentage of the total that could be derived from each category.[5] As an illustration of this process, consider a category with a weighting factor of 5, (meaning that 5% of the total marks could be derived from that category). Thus if a vehicle was awarded top marks (ten marks out of 10) for the category, it could still only achieve a normalised score of 5. In other words, each mark would contribute just 0.5% to the total. The normalised scores for each variable were then added to give the overall 'Attribute Score'. The model allows the weightings to be varied, in order that the results are a 'best fit' with judging criteria. Too many anomalies suggested the need for adjusting the weighting factors. (Ultimately, a power of veto remains, so that a curatorial opinion could be accommodated.)

Attributes and disadvantages

In identifying the criteria deemed of importance in an AFV collection, it was quickly apparent that several of these were disadvantages rather than attributes. For example, the bulk of a tank tests the resources of museums that might like one in their collection. An object in an unstable condition, and needing expensive conservation treatment tends to be regarded as less important than a similar object in excellent condition. Whilst there are cogent arguments that the importance of an object is not inherently dependent upon its condition, it would be inappropriate to disregard these 'negative' criteria. Inevitably, they would feature prominently in any decisions regarding acquisition or rationalisation. Therefore, positive attributes *and* disadvantages were both scored in the same manner, and then weighted separately, to give each object both an Attribute Score and a Disadvantage Score. Finally, these scores were combined into a Final Score by applying a further weighting factor. This was on the basis that positive Attributes were fundamentally more important than Disadvantages. Since

5   M. Cassar, *Cost/Benefit Appraisals for Collection Care: A Practical Guide* (London: Museums and Galleries Commission, 1998), 7.

a Disadvantage Score of 100% meant that the object had no disadvantages, it was the shortfall from this ideal which affected the final result. After some iteration, it was considered that a disadvantage shortfall of five marks would reduce the final score by one mark.

There were several reasons for calculating the final score in this way. It allowed easy and separate analyses of the attributes and disadvantages, using a simple reiterative process to optimise the final weighting factor. Because the model is not claimed to be perfect, further optimisation is facilitated. Though devised for AFV collections, an objective was to assess the application to other types of collection; a simple identification of positive and negative criteria assists such adaptability. Scoring was simplified, and the marking logic afforded good transparency. In due course the relative importance of individual criteria is expected to change; the methodology allows such changes to be effected easily.

As the model developed, it became apparent that a criterion called the Wow Factor was one of the more important parameters. Clearly, this was not helping the objective of creating a consistent and objective method of ranking a collection, simply because the Wow Factor is so indeterminate. Further analysis suggested that, for many vehicles, it was possible to say what it was that triggered the Wow Factor, and this was regarded as the single most important attribute of that vehicle. This opened the possibility of slanting the weighting system to suit every individual vehicle, at the same time constraining the Wow Factor to reasonable levels.

It is often straightforward to select the most important criterion of a particular object, reflecting a typical judgement of a tank as being especially important because of its association with an act of conspicuous bravery or success, notwithstanding that it lacked (or displayed) several other qualities. Its particular claim to a place in the collection, that it took part in an historic encounter, is a redeeming feature which perhaps offsets the fact that it is neither rare nor in fine condition, whilst it may lack both educational value and technological characteristics. By enhancing the weighting for 'Background History', its importance in the collection would be better judged. Another vehicle may be regarded as 'perfectly ordinary', that is, in exactly the condition that many ex-crewmen would immediately recognise and, for precisely that reason, deserving of a place in the collection. By enhancing its weighting for originality/authenticity, its importance is more accurately reflected against the remainder of the collection. It is analogous to 'playing the joker' in card games or team games, whereby the strength of a particular case is enhanced above its normal station. By this means, the generic view (for example, that rarity is more important than completeness, or that technological features are less important than age) can be tempered to suit individual exceptions. The generic view as just exemplified begs justification, which is notoriously difficult; it is, in effect, comparing apples with oranges.

It follows that enhancing the weighting of one criterion requires a corresponding reduction in another. The Wow Factor attempts to quantify the *je ne sais quoi*, whilst the Most Important Attribute focuses the *pour quoi* on one particular variable. Therefore, the reduction was made to the Wow Factor. If no single criterion can be identified, the Wow Factor retains its high weighting. Only the attributes were considered for this tailoring exercise; it was considered unnecessarily complex to perform a similar exercise on the disadvantages.

To reduce subjectivity, it was considered important to have several people involved in the scoring. This would not eliminate subjectivity *per se*, but should reduce its effects considerably. The almost endless stream of polls used by television and radio programmes to determine the greatest actor, monarch, Briton, sportsman and so forth demonstrates that large numbers of scorers will not necessarily reduce subjectivity. The AFV grading model requires scoring by a carefully chosen few, who between them could be expected to provide as objective an input as reasonable. It was felt that four would be an optimum number, all of whom should have an in-depth knowledge of the collection, but each should have a different area of expertise within the subject. Table 21.2 illustrates the scoring methodology.

Limitations and applicability

The most obvious limitation that has manifested itself is that of time. Using a score sheet for an individual vehicle, it is likely to require several minutes to score the 20 criteria. Some measurements may need to be taken (actual width, length and gun overhang) and some background information may need to be consulted (such as battle weight) as well as the vehicle's object history file, condition reports and other documentation. The procedure can be conducted at a brisk pace provided all this information is to hand, and that the scorer is familiar with the scoring process, the collection in general and the vehicle in particular. However, the criteria have to be considered quite carefully if scoring is to be accurate and consistent. Though they each have definitions of zero score and full marks, three-quarters of the criteria require interpolation to achieve an individual score. Only age and size scores are based on simple facts requiring minimal interpretation or understanding.

Table 21.2. An example of scoring where 'Rarity' gives the score for 'Most Important Attribute'.

Attribute	Score	Weighting factor	Normalised score
Year Made	10	8	8
Particular Significance	9	6	5.4
Rarity	8	12	9.6
Historic Significance (of Type)	7	14	9.8
Completeness	6	5	3
Originality (Authentic)	5	6	3
Background History	4	8	3.2
Technological Features	3	8	2.4
Educational Value	2	6	1.2
Condition: External	1	6	0.6
Condition: Internal	0	3	0
Condition: Running Order	1	5	0.5
Wow Factor	2	6	1.2
Most Important Attribute	8	7	5.6
Total (attribute score)		**100**	**53.5**
Disadvantage			
Ownership	3	15	4.5
Size	4	15	6
Damage	5	10	5
Stable Condition?	6	20	12
In-House Labour Required	7	15	10.5
Cost	8	15	12
Health and Safety	9	10	9
Total (disadvantage)		**100**	**59.0**
Disadvantage Shortfall		100 – 59 =	41
Benefit Penalty		20% of Shortfall =	8.2
Final score		53.5 – 8.2 =	**45.3**

To be authoritative, the results must properly reflect the consensus view of four or five people. However, there are few people who know the collection sufficiently to be able to give an informed opinion. Of these, only a proportion can spare adequate time to the task, and then they may be in the wrong location and unable to access the information. Those well versed in the historical aspects might not be familiar with the condition of each vehicle, and vice versa. Inevitably, therefore, there is a tendency for the model to be a joint effort, but not a consensus of informed opinion, since different people score different aspects.

The process considers each vehicle in isolation, and grades it in order of importance within a collection. Its scope does not extend to ensuring that the collection is well rounded, or comprehensive. If the model is used to support a rationalisation process, it would be very inappropriate to regard all objects scoring less than a certain score as being fit for disposal. A gardener will consider the overall appearance and health of a plant when selecting which parts to prune; there is a direct analogy with a museum collection. The model attempts provide objective evidence to guide rationalisation or acquisition decisions, it does not initiate the proposals.

There is no apparent reason why the model might not be adapted to suit any other type of vehicle or transport collection. It should be noted that the model does not include every item in the Tank Museum's collection; only its vehicle collection. The small artefacts collection could also be ranked using an adaptation of the model, but the model is not intended to rank medal with tank. In the same way, the model could be suitable for an agricultural collection, once it had been separated into a few major categories (for example, hand tools). With large collections, however, the time taken to score each individual object might be regarded as time not used to best advantage. With around 300 vehicles in the Tank Museum's collection, and 20 variables being scored, the model demands at least 6000 separate scores to be entered, ideally undertaken by four independent assessors. Of course, other types of collection may be adequately defined by fewer criteria. It is the combination of such parameters that is likely to determine the applicability of the model to different types of collections; the underlying model is not particular to the Tank Museum.

For the model to be of use to other collections, and other types of collection, it can be assumed that many of these would already be collated onto a computerised database, though possibly not onto a spreadsheet. Thus an early decision would be which computer application to use, and whether to import the information on to a new programme or to manipulate the existing database. Because it would be necessary to consider both the criteria and their relative importance weightings, the process is in effect started from scratch. A suggested framework for development is:

1. Identify most of the assessment criteria. This will include those aspects regarded as enhancing the object's value within the collection, as well as those criteria which are disadvantageous. A brainstorming session involving a few of the interested parties should be able to isolate most of the variables within a single session.
2. For each variable, consider the datum which will warrant a zero score, and that which will earn top mark.
3. Select a sample (perhaps 10% of the collection up to a maximum of 30 objects) for use in a trial. This should include several of the more contrasting items, as well as a subset of very similar articles, and a reasonable proportion of 'typical' objects. The trial should then show whether the model could cope with the extremes, whilst having the resolution to grade quite similar objects.
4. Consider which criteria can have intermediate marks based on specified criteria
5. Score a larger sample of the collection
6. Refine the criteria and their weightings in the light of these results, until a reasonable order of ranking is achieved
7. Review the initial results with other interested parties to ensure a reasonable consensus has been obtained. Criteria can be added, modified or rejected to improve the model, though this will of course introduce some re-scoring of the existing sample.
8. Score the remainder of the collection.
9. Run the model for the full collection and review the full results.
10. Fine-tune the score system as required. Note that the model is unlikely to eliminate all anomalies. Those that remain should be sufficient to provoke interesting curatorial discussion. If there are too many anomalies, then the model requires further modification.
11. Expect to adjust the weightings, and perhaps the criteria, in the fullness of time. Unless the criteria are independent of time, the collection would need to be re-scored at intervals.

One of the most valuable aspects of the exercise was that it demanded close attention to identifying the attributes that added importance to any object in the collection, and confronting and weighing up the inherent disadvantages. At the end of the day, even if the grading model produced highly anomalous results (which it did not), the curatorial benefits of analysing the collection in such a way would probably have been worthwhile. Ironically, even if the data input was totally objective the results could not be totally objective since they were reviewed subjectively. After all, if those vehicles generally regarded as being important within the collection did not finish near the top of the list, the parameters were adjusted until they did. This was done in one of three ways:

1. By modifying the marks awarded for various criteria
2. The introduction of different scoring categories
3. Adjustment of the relative weightings factors.

Such tuning was iterative, and to reduce subjectivity, the results were considered, at several stages, by a panel, with each member having a different bias regarding the various elements being scored. As the iterations progressed, only fine-tuning was required, until a consensus view was achieved that the results properly ranked the collection in order of importance with only a modest number of anomalies. Because each of the grading criteria can be ranked independently, the model has produced a powerful assessment tool. For example, objects of high educational value or with intrinsic background history can be listed easily, and so produce a picking list to assist boosting particular aspects of a display.

The results are a rationalisation, currently regarded as being of great importance to collection management doctrine.[6] Since subjectivity has been controlled rather than eliminated, the process is reasonably objective. More importantly, it provides transparency. Almost daily, we hear of relative merits being ranked on the whim of a judging panel, and the public at large then tend to regard such decisions with a certain disdain, disbelief or even contempt, as witnessed by the Oscar, Booker or Turner prizes. Nevertheless, there would seem to be an almost insatiable demand for lists in order of merit (for example, schools' and hospitals' performance). Though this model was not devised primarily for public consumption, the

---

6   D. Viner, 'Rational Thinking', *Museums Journal*, 101(12) (2001), 26–9.

results may well become public. By banding the list into, say, four categories, unnecessary arguments regarding relative merits would be greatly reduced. It was devised primarily as a working tool for museum staff to compare 'apples with oranges' as objectively as possible.

The model could be adapted easily to suit a national AFV register. It would require some revision to the criteria weightings, notably 'Particular Significance' and 'Ownership'. These criteria would have a very low (possibly zero) weighting, since on a national basis they are almost meaningless. Almost, but not quite, since they indicate whether the national asset is housed in the most appropriate places. It is expected that the criteria and weightings would be generally agreed among the participating bodies, then published, and remain firm to provide transparency to the process. Eligibility for the national register would need some consideration; for example, unarmoured variants of AFVs might usefully be included. It was suggested that because of the high number of vehicles in private hands, the national register should be restricted to museum vehicles only. This would greatly reduce the difficulties of tracking changes of ownership and the identification of vehicles built out of several others. However, 'No nation's museums can deploy the resources to be the sole repository of its heritage: the greater part will continue to be preserved in private hands.'[7] Given that a major part of the AFV heritage remains in private hands, it may be incumbent on a national register to be inclusive. The grading scheme could cope with a list of almost any size, though consistent scoring requires a comprehensive knowledge base, possibly lacking if many different teams (or even individuals) score a few vehicles each. The National Register of Historic Vessels uses a central team to ensure consistency, though this imposes significant costs and AFVs greatly outnumber historic ships.[8] Regional moderators, assisted by individual curators or owners, may prove a cost-effective option, in accordance with latest doctrine.[9]

---

7   D. Penn, and G. Wilson, 'Concerns relating to the world heritage of arms, museums and firearms collections and arising from proposals intended to control the illicit trade in small arms and light weapons' (Brussels: International Committee of Museums of Arms and Military History, 2001).

8   National Register of Historic Vessels (London: National Maritime Museum, 2001) (www.nmm.ac.uk/nrhv).

9   Re:source, *Renaissance in the Regions* (London: Re:source, 2001).

22 Deaccessioning as a collections management tool

Patricia Ainslie

In 1993, Glenbow Museum in Calgary, Canada, adopted six strategies to enhance its effectiveness, reduce expenditure, increase revenue and renew the museum's commitment to public service. One of the six strategies was to deaccession selected international collections. After the first two decades of world-wide collecting, Glenbow has increasingly focused its mandate, with a primary emphasis on the history and settlement of north-western North America. The current strategy involves focusing more closely on this core mandate. Glenbow will deaccession and sell selected items from its non-core international collections in order to create a Collections Restricted Fund. This fund will be protected against inflation and kept intact for the future building of the collections. The income from this fund will be dedicated to the care and maintenance of the core collections.

Early in June 1992, Glenbow's senior management team reviewed a five-year budget forecast, to determine the implications of reduced revenues from the public and private sector. The shocking news was that at the current rate of expenditure we would be bankrupt in five years, with an accumulated deficit of 7.7 million dollars. This situation created a need for immediate action. It was in this context that deaccessioning, one of the six strategies, was seen as a way to augment income to care for the collections, while at the same time refining and focusing our collections. We felt that deaccessioning was a prudent, responsible and realistic approach, given our current situation and the nature of our collections.

Glenbow is the largest museum in western Canada, with a diverse collection of approximately 1.3 million objects and three floors of exhibition space totalling over 93,000 square feet. It also has the largest library of western Canadiana and the largest non-government archives in Canada. Glenbow's primary mandate is to document and preserve the history and development of the north-west quadrant of North America, and secondly, to provide a national and international context for these core collections.

Glenbow's history and past methods of acquisition make it unique in Canada. Eric L. Harvie, Glenbow's founder, was a philanthropist with eclectic tastes and wide-ranging interests. He built two major collections: the first of over 120,000 objects (plus books, archives and photographs) which was given to the people of Alberta in 1966, and the second of over 37,000 objects (plus books, archives, and photographs), which was given to the province of Alberta in 1979. Glenbow holds both of these collections in trust. Over the years, other donations and purchases have been added.

Harvie collected with the passion and enthusiasm of a collector in the true Victorian sense of the word, and not with the professional eye of a curator. He told his staff to go out and 'Collect like a bunch of drunken sailors.' And they did! As the collections grew, new warehouses were found to house them. One of Harvie's more intriguing enterprises was the acquisition of entire private collections or major holdings from museums. In 1964, over 600 objects were purchased from the Royal United Services Museum in London. These now form the core of Glenbow's military history collection. The Schuller Museum of Art and Chivalry in New Hampshire was acquired in 1973 and included medieval arms and armour, Japanese armour and saddles, and European sixteenth-, seventeenth- and eighteenth-century furniture. To augment the native American collections, Harvie bought the Roe Indian Museum in Pipestone, Minnesota, the Sioux Indian Museum in Sioux Falls, South Dakota, and the Fort Cherokee Indian Museum in Oklahoma. For the Canadiana collection, Harvie acquired the Frontier Ghost Town, with over 6000 items, mostly from old mining towns in British Columbia. As a result of these large-scale purchases, the quality of the collections is uneven. Certain collections have outstanding range and depth, while others lack cohesion, focus, and relevance to Glenbow's mandate.

In May 1978, Glenbow developed a policy for deaccessioning. Deaccessioning became an active part of professional collections management at Glenbow through the 1980s. Collections care involves maintenance and ongoing expense; the museum could no longer justify keeping material which was not germane to its purpose.

In the 1980s, objects were deaccessioned primarily because they were reproductions, not of museum quality, were inferior duplicates or lacked provenance. Most of this deaccessioned material was sold at auction in

Calgary, and the proceeds were put into acquisition funds. In the period up to 1992, the museum deaccessioned approximately 30,000 objects.

Though the museum remains committed to keeping selected international collections, the current plan will allow it to refine those collections which are not central to its mandate. It is with this current deaccessioning strategy that the museum departs from tradition. Plans included the deaccessioning of collections of high value and of museum quality, and the diversion of the income from the funds generated into collection care and maintenance.

The central principle in this deaccessioning strategy was that Glenbow's curatorial staff would make the selection based on their knowledge of the collection and their field. The process for all deaccessioning involves selection of material by the curator responsible for the collection, approval by the director of collections and by the executive director, recommendation for approval by the collections management committee of the board, and approval by the board of governors. There are clear policies, procedures, and a system of checks and balances to guide Glenbow's deaccessioning.

Only two examples of Canadian museum deaccessioning have previously been publicly documented. The Western Development Museum provides a good model of careful planning in the mid-1980s. Objects deaccessioned were given to other non-profit museums in Saskatchewan, and the remaining material was sold at public auction. Monies realised were used for acquisition, cataloguing, conservation and restoration. There was no negative response to this deaccessioning. On the other hand, the deaccessioning of over 700 objects at the New Brunswick Museum led to public outcry and a government enquiry.

Planning and consultation

Our project team consisted of the registrar and a curator from each collection. Initially, there was resistance by staff to the project for moral and ethical reasons, the proposed loss of some international collections, and the broader use of funds from deaccessioning. To allow a thorough airing of these issues, the museum planned a meeting in September 1992, with our team, other Glenbow staff and directors, and members of Glenbow's board. The team developed the questions for what was a lengthy meeting with substantial debate.

The result of the discussion was consensus on the way to proceed. It was agreed that public institutions in Canada would be given a reasonable opportunity to purchase objects, at a fair market price. The museum would address any of the possible ethical issues; it was decided to keep objects which were too sensitive.

There was agreement that decisions should focus on the needs of individual collections, and not be in response to a blanket deaccessioning policy. Private donations were excluded altogether, and most of the 3000 items subsequently selected were from Harvie's major public gift to the people of Alberta in 1966.

During October and November 1992, each member of the team contacted professional colleagues across Canada to discuss the deaccessioning project and to seek their advice. We talked to some major donors and the founder's son, who were supportive of the strategy, though the latter wanted to approve each step in the process. Discussions were held with the museum's partners, the City of Calgary and the provincial government, as well as with the Canadian Museums Association (CMA) and the Canadian Cultural Property Export Review Board. The CMA felt that Glenbow should be precise about the use of any income generated, but did not restrict the use of funds to acquisitions only.

The six strategies were presented to the Canadian Museum Directors Group and the Canadian Art Museum Directors Organisation (CAMDO). These organisations felt Glenbow was in a unique position due to the size, value and overall diversity of the collections, but were cautionary, with some members openly opposed. Following up on CAMDO concerns, the museum subsequently had discussions and correspondence with the chairman of the Ethics Committee of the Association of American Art Museum Directors.

Further justification for the deaccessioning came with the American Association of Museums' decision in June 1993 to adopt important changes to their code of ethics, which ended six years of debate. This declared that proceeds from the sale of deaccessioned materials must be used for 'acquisitions or the direct care of collections.'

Legal opinion also supported these moves, deaccessioning being deemed necessary for Glenbow to carry out its business mandate and because we were acting reasonably, in good faith, and in the best interests of the people of Alberta. An accountant was also contacted concerning the Canadian Institute of Chartered Accountants' proposal to capitalise museum and art gallery collections. He was quite firm that the collection is not a financial asset, and it cannot be depreciated over time as occurs with other assets.

The balance sheet shows the liquid position of an organisation with assets and liabilities. The collection is not a trading asset, and therefore it does not appear on the balance sheet.

Making the decision

During the autumn of 1992, the curators did intensive work reviewing all of the international collections, determining criteria to either keep or deaccession collections. A policy decision was made to deaccession our entire natural history collection of books and art. Glenbow is a human history museum, and these natural history collections were an anomaly. This material was seldom exhibited in the over thirty years it was at Glenbow, and there was almost no public or scholarly interest in it. We therefore felt this collection was appropriate for deaccessioning.

An important West African collection of about 5000 objects, with depth and breadth in various cultural groups, has been put on permanent exhibition. There are significant academic links between the University of Calgary and West Africa in the fields of archaeology and anthropology, as well as important links through the oil industry. For these reasons, this collection was to be kept. Our collections from other parts of the continent were less representative and less useful: this material was to be deaccessioned.

The military collection of 26,000 pieces, spanning nearly five centuries of history, is the largest and most diverse in western Canada. As the collection is truly international in scope, we decided to deaccession only those objects which do not have provenance and for which there are better-quality pieces, as a way of focusing and upgrading this collection.

The cultural history collection reflects a broad spectrum of life in western Canada. The strength of this collection is the story it can tell about settlement in western Canada, therefore, provenance was the most important factor. Objects which were without provenance related to western Canada, as well as those which were of low quality or duplicates, were deemed suitable for deaccessioning.

By November 1992, nine international collections had been selected, which included approximately 3000 objects, or 0.13% of our collections, with an estimated value of $5 million. Deaccessioning was to proceed over a five-year period. The six strategies were approved by the board of governors a month later.

Implementation

In January 1993 staff began the intensive, detailed work combing source files for each object and compiling specific lists. In March, the first four collections were approved for deaccessioning. The museum was keen to keep them in Canada. Letters were sent to 92 Canadian institutions in June, offering them the opportunity to purchase items from the nine collections. There was a modest response, and some items sold. Various proposals for selling the collections were reviewed. In the autumn, the museum was granted cultural property export permits for the first two collections of natural history. By mid-September, the Canadian press picked up on the story, resulting in wide, and largely fair, media coverage.

Throughout the year there had been regular discussions with the provincial government which provides 45% of the museum's funding, but by the late summer the Glenbow's deaccessioning policy came to be seen as controversial. There was concern over the use of funds, and a suggestion that the collections should be donated to other institutions in Alberta. A formal presentation at the end of the year, however, removed these difficulties. The first major sale was held at Sotheby's in New York in April 1994; 32 natural history books were sold for Canadian $770,965, with a further sale in London later in the year. Other material went to auction in various cities in the USA, Australia and Canada. About 80 per cent of the Africa collection was donated to the Provincial Museum of Alberta. To date, the Collections Restricted Fund stands at $3.4 million.

Deaccessioning in context

Income from the Restricted Fund will be applied only to collections care and documentation. The fund itself will only be used for purchases for the collections.

Deaccessioning of collections is not about lowering standards. It is dependent on good judgement and responsibility, and on being true to core values and beliefs. These are the same attitudes which should guide our acquisitions. In the past, there has been a great deal of mindless collecting, along with poor documentation and care of public collections. Deaccessioning is about making difficult but realistic decisions in the interests of the museum and its community. Stewardship means being entrusted with the management of another's property, and preserving that inheritance. It does not mean keeping everything in a collection for all time. To quote Sir Roy Strong: 'How can museums function properly if they are going to carry on collecting from here to eternity?' He goes on: 'What we should be doing instead is assessing our collections, refusing some, closing others, and even more important, putting what we have in good order.'[1] We no longer have the resources for the proper long-term care and management of collections not germane to our purpose. Through deaccessioning, Glenbow believes it is ensuring the prudent application of its resources and maintaining public confidence.

Collections are not absolute entities. By continuing to add to them, we change their character and emphasis. As the demographics of communities change, museums must reconsider and refocus their collections. Museums must continue to refine and collect in areas appropriate to their core mandate in order to maintain the vitality of the museum. Deaccessioning and disposal are direct consequences of acquisition. Museums can neither stop collecting nor continually expand facilities or staff to accommodate new collections.

Museums cannot be static, fixed institutions. They must be dynamic and respond to our changing environment. At Glenbow, for example, staff have learned a great deal about our First Nations collections in recent years. As museum professionals, we now handle and care for sacred material in storage, in ways that were unheard of even five years ago. We have also placed sacred material on long-term loan in non-traditional environments with First Nations individuals who have the spiritual rights to this material.

Work on the deaccessioning strategy will be ongoing until 1997. It has given the museum a much more closely defined international scope to its collections, and focused these, to provide a better overall direction for the core collections. It has also guaranteed a level of care and maintenance for the core collections in the future through establishing the Collections Restricted Fund.

---

1   R. Strong. *Museums: Two Contributions Towards the Debate* (London: Art Documents, 1985), 4.

23 Collecting live performance

James Fowler

Providing the national record of stage performance in Britain is a problematic role for the Theatre Museum. Formed in 1974 as a branch of the Victoria & Albert (V&A) Museum, the Theatre Museum has run its own site in Covent Garden, London, since 1987, and attracts well over 100,000 visitors each year. It has of late been radically revising its collecting policy to put greater emphasis on recording contemporary performance, and to open up new opportunities for access and interpretation.

The performing arts are almost as difficult to define as performance itself.[1] Their significance depends on the social, religious or theatrical contexts in which they occur.[2] Tragedy as performed in Ancient Greece, for example, was a mix of dance, music, scenic spectacle and spoken text, more opera than what we might term theatre today. Documenting the history, craft and practice of the live performing arts is a very wide brief. Far from being fixed entities, the performing arts have an astonishing capacity to combine with one another, or evolve new forms (such as performance art), or reinvent themselves (such as pantomime), or change radically in response to shifts in taste and fashion. The Cirque du Soleil, for example, have replaced traditional animal acts, which attract social disapproval, with a magical fusion of acrobatics, physical theatre, music, song, mime, costume and lighting.

It has been suggested that many people now reared on television, cinema and live music, 'are uncomfortable with the suspension of disbelief required by stage plays'. Traditional theatre, it is claimed, is really as 'dead as a doornail' with an 'audience that has been dying off for years'.[3] Such trends and developments in the performing arts need to be documented but, with limited staffing and finances, the museum is compelled to devote

---

1   M. Carlson, *Performance: a critical introduction* (London: Routledge, 1996).
2   J. Adshead, *The Study of Dance* (London: Dance Books, 1981), 4–6.
3   A. Smith, 'How to get rave reviews?', *The Sunday Times*, 11 February 1996.

most of its collecting energy directly to theatre, dance, musical theatre and opera, and less than it would like on live performance of popular music. The need for a 'new centralised museum designed to promote our musical heritage' has already been identified.[4] Since it already covers many forms of stage music, the museum would be, subject to adequate funding, well placed to document concerts. Such a role would logically extend that of the V&A, which holds the national collection of musical instruments, and complement the coverage given by the recently acquired Arts Council archive. Given sufficient resources, the Theatre Museum could fulfil its purpose by covering the live performing arts equally well.

The museum's greatest challenge, however, is in collecting performance. Fugitive in nature, and created through time via interaction with an audience at a particular venue, it does not survive as an object with a life of its own. One must gather instead records and artefacts generated by, or associated with, live performance and its processes and contexts. This documentary material ranges from video and sound recordings, programmes, reviews, photographs, prompt-books, posters and archives to designs, models, costumes, properties, puppets, paintings, prints, drawings and items of stage technology, as well as a library of over 100,000 playtexts, journals and books. Collecting and making accessible such a profusion of evidence requires the Theatre Museum to be a museum, a library and an archive.

When collecting items associated with performance, much depends on the virtue of association. Personal scrapbooks compiled by performers as records of their careers are usually worthwhile additions, unlike other more personal effects. As James Fenton notes: 'there are limits ... to the attention we can lavish on the old socks and stockings of someone else's heroes and heroines.'[5] The museum owns the boots of the great eighteenth-century actress Sarah Siddons. How acceptable these are as objects depends on how well they are interpreted. By themselves they may appear slightly absurd as personal relics. But in a display about footwear on stage they can have a real story to tell. The late Beryl Reid, for instance, was well known for buying shoes which gave her a feel for the characters she played.

---

4   K. Arnold-Forster and H. La Rue, *Museums of Music: A Review of Musical Collections in the United Kingdom* (London: HMSO, 1993), 68.

5   J. Fenton, 'The Cherry Orchard Has to Come Down', *The New York Review of Books,* 43(6) (4 April 1996): 16–17.

Another problem is filling the ever-present gap between the surviving record or artefact and the associated performance. In the study of stage design, for example, photographs of sets and costumes tell only part of the story. As John Gielgud observes: 'In spite of the accuracy of photography, one is rarely given a very successful impression of the effect of stage decor on an audience. Drawings by the designers and, in some cases, the survival of models, as well as the actual costumes, give one a far more fascinating record of past productions.'[6] And yet the 'authenticity' of such objects can mislead when they are divorced from the processes and contexts that were their *raison d'être*, especially when treated as discrete works of art. As David Hockney says of stage design: 'there is no fixed work of art in the theatre; every work has to be brought to life by the people doing it.'[7]

If live performance is one of the great uncollectables, how has the Theatre Museum risen to the challenge? Initially, the collection grew along traditional museum lines around a nucleus of programmes, reviews, photographs, playtexts and ephemera amassed from the late nineteenth century onwards by private collector Gabrielle Enthoven. Her collection focused on the London stage, which was so dominant then that no actor merited a biographical 'first appearance' file until they had trodden the boards of a London theatre.[8]

Despite campaigning in the press for a 'museum of theatre arts' in 1911, it took Enthoven thirteen years to persuade the V&A to accept her collection, and she continued to update it, largely at her own expense, until her death in 1950. Being part of a decorative arts museum inevitably conditioned the development of her theatre collection. As a documentary wing of the V&A's Department of Engraving, Illustration and Design, Enthoven bought stage designs, prints and drawings in line with that department's collecting policy. Other V&A departments occasionally acquired theatre material. The National Art Library, for example, which already held rare David Garrick correspondence, William Charles Macready acting copies and Elizabethan

---

6   A. Schouvaloff, *Theatre on Paper* (New York: The Drawing Center, 1990) 1, 221.

7   Ibid.

8   Systematic coverage of regional theatre began in earnest when the Theatre Museum came into being in 1974. Today, programmes are continuously gathered from over 250 British venues, and reviews cut from seven daily newspapers to provide an overview of the performing arts across the country.

playtexts in the Dyce and Forster bequests, also bought theatrical books which mostly dealt with stage art and design. But no attempt was made to acquire costumes, properties or similar artefacts.

The Theatre Museum came into being not by uniting performing arts material held in other V&A departments – which they still retain to this day – but by combining the Enthoven collection with the holdings of two external organisations – the British Theatre Museum Association and the Friends of the Museum of Performing Arts which had bought many outstanding Diaghilev Ballets Russes costumes and backcloths at auction in the late 1960s for a projected dance museum. The backcloths, which include the Picasso-designed act-drop for *Le Train Bleu* (1924), are the biggest and amongst the most valuable objects in the Theatre Museum. Measuring up to 10 metres by 11 metres or more, they are difficult to store, conserve and display. The prospect first of 'being landed with a lot of costumes' and then of having to 'display the Picasso curtain'[9] caused some consternation within the V&A – not unjustifiably, since the museum still lacks the facility to do so. The adoption of costumes and backcloths for the new Theatre Museum was a major breakthrough in collecting policy which raised awareness of how diverse documentation of the performing arts needs to be.

In collecting terms, however, a holistic approach poses a real challenge. It demands a breadth of expertise greater than that found in most museums, and a readiness to use new technology – video recording, for example – to maintain the necessary balance of evidence regarding the various elements of performance and its processes. Problematic in this respect is stage technology such as the lighting control equipment, lamps and sound effects machines which the museum acquired in the 1970s and 1980s. Historic, and in some cases unique, such material falls more within the ken of the Science Museum than the V&A, since it is neither decorative nor artistic, and often unwieldy. The Theatre Museum's current policy in this area is a compromise. It aims to cover the subject primarily through paper documentation but collect three-dimensional items of a modest size where these are especially important and can be displayed.

The museum's collecting policy underwent a sea change from 1990 when Margaret Benton – an ex-BBC television producer and former deputy of the National Museum of Film, Photography and Television in Bradford –

---

9   R. Buckle, *In the Wake of Diaghilev Autobiography 2* (London: Collins, 1982), 230–31.

became its head. Officially recognised as the National Museum of Performing Arts, the museum became less hidebound by the traditional materials-based, object-centred thinking of its parent museum. It actively began to acquire important collections instead of waiting for them to turn up, and undertake proactive documentation of the contemporary stage. A drive to forge stronger links with the theatre profession and improve the museum's public face resulted in major acquisitions. These include over 60,000 playtexts and books from the former British Theatre Association which now form an important source for play revivals. Archives, such as those of former West End producer H.M. Tennent, impresario Sander Gorlinsky, the English Shakespeare Company, Kenneth Branagh's Renaissance Theatre Company and the Arts Council of Great Britain (which documents the state-subsidised arts since the Second World War) have been gathered. One recent acquisition alone comprised over 9000 plans from the firm of Frank Matcham.

As a result, professional theatre organisations are beginning to see the museum as a resource and not simply a repository and exhibitor of records and artefacts. The Association of British Theatre Technicians, for example, now uses the museum to conduct public interviews with backstage celebrities which the museum records on video for posterity.

The biggest breakthrough, however, has come with the video-recording of contemporary productions for the new National Video Archive of Stage Performance. This began in 1992, and centres on a unique agreement with the Federation of Entertainment Unions which allows recordings to be made for archival purposes without payment of fees to the artists. Permission from each member of the company involved is also required, and recordings are strictly confined to museum premises. Tapes can be viewed by individuals in the study room or by educational groups, and more recently it has become possible to show clips in the galleries. The initiative was long overdue in Britain; the Lincoln Center in New York and the Netherlands Theatre Institute in Amsterdam have recorded stage performance on video for over twenty years.

As an Arts Council report observed in 1992, it would be perverse to ignore what video offers:

> We should not have forgiven our ancestors if they had had the opportunity to record Mozart playing the piano or to film David Garrick acting and had neglected to do so. With all the technology at our disposal, it would be equally unforgivable if we did not create a record in sound and vision of the evolution

of the performing arts. For non text-based art, such as mime and live art, performance is the history: without a record of the performance, the history disappears.[10]

Over seventy recordings have been made to date and an experienced video producer appointed. The policy is to record shows demonstrating innovation, excellence, rarity, cultural diversity, educational potential, or which are typical of their genre or feature new plays of the work of a distinguished company, performer, designer or director. Productions range from London's West End and fringe to documentary drama in Stoke-on-Trent, pantomime in Birmingham and new opera such as Harrison Birtwistle's *The Second Mrs Kong* at Glyndebourne.

Productions are shot during a normal performance in the theatre as faithfully as possible, without altering the lighting or disrupting the audience. Up to three cameras are used: one to give a wide view of the whole stage, others for closer shots. While one camera may serve in a small venue or of necessity when money is scarce, the best compromise from an artistic and cost point of view is two cameras. Because VHS or Super VHS tape is archivally unstable and deteriorates markedly in quality when copied, the museum now records to broadcast standard using Beta, and hires in professional crews of specialist director, camera operator and sound recordist. Good sound quality has been found to be particularly vital. Costs reflect the high standards and range from almost £2000 per recording on one camera to around £9000 using three.

The museum's recently appointed Contemporary Performing Arts Curator consults external advisers to help decide which productions to video. The aim is to set up a panel in due course, and document each choice more fully. Working formally by committee, however, could prove cumbersome, as it takes a week to set up a simple recording, and much longer for a multi-camera operation – which may be too long for shows that slip in and out of town. If the museum's current Lottery bid for £2.1 million is successful, it will make a further 200 recordings over the next four years, 20% of which will be in the regions. Dance, opera and other performing arts will also be fully represented, and appropriate methods of recording developed for them. The video recordings are available (by appointment) in the museum study room. Soon it is hoped that visitors will also be able

---

10   Arts Council of Great Britain, *Towards a National Arts and Media Strategy*, (London, 1992), 111.

to view video extracts plus associated documentation onscreen in the galleries. To maximise access, the feasibility of regional viewing centres and remote access is also being explored.

Video has been described as doing 'little more than mummify the theatrical event it seeks to conserve'.[11] Some directors see it as unequal to their work on stage, which cannot be translated into another medium. Certainly, it does not serve all aspects of production equally well: the actors' performance itself generally fares better than other elements such as stage design. Nevertheless, most practitioners feel that some living record is better than none at all. Simon Callow found it 'incomprehensible' that the original production of David Edgar's play *Mary Barnes* was never filmed:

> It was a unique combination of people, and the inter-action with the audience had produced an extraordinary intensity. It should have been recorded then. It's all gone now. It'll never be like that again. One feels a little sad about the evaporation of all one's work ...[12]

The National Video Archive of Stage Performance has attracted widespread support from theatre professionals. Some have been quick to realise the value of video as a showcase which may have important spin-offs. Several producers and backers have bought or supported overseas tours or film versions of productions after seeing museum videos of them.[13] Video recordings add a vital dimension to the museum's other records while greatly increasing useful contact with the theatre profession. For curators of such an elusive subject, it is satisfying to make history out of something that would otherwise vanish. Video has enormous potential not only for the individual researcher but also in its capacity to enliven exhibitions for the general visitor. Educationally, it enables young students, who may find it difficult to attend live performance, to compare productions of a play. The museum already runs various workshops where acting styles on video are contrasted. A group will act and discuss a scene from a play, then watch the same scene from a professional production on video before performing the scene again, taking into account the interpretation in the recording.

---

11 S. Trussler, *The Cambridge Illustrated History of British Theatre* (Cambridge: Cambridge University Press, 1994).

12 S. Callow, *Being an Actor* (London: Methuen, 1984.), 81.

13 B. Nightingale, 'Here's wonders we made earlier', *The Times*, 5 July 1996; J. Thaxter, 'Memory lane', *The Stage*, 25 July 1996.

Video looks set to drive Theatre Museum collecting policy increasingly in the future, since the aim is to gather designs, artefacts and other documentation relating to productions recorded. This in-depth coverage will complement the reviews and programmes already being gathered from across the country so as to provide the best possible national overview of the performing arts in Britain.

24 Redefining collecting

Tomislav Sola

First, museums were nothing but visitable collections. Museums as we know them were only to appear through slow progressive change over a period of two hundred years. But is the modern museum the final and only answer to the set of needs which created it? Today, we are witnessing both an unprecedented flourishing of museums and their deepest conceptual crisis. An investigation of the tradition to which museums belong may help us understand the motives for their formation and the institutional consequences we know today. It may also help us make decisions about the future of museums and collections, and therefore collecting itself.

Vincent Wilcox wrote recently: 'Growth is an inherent part of the mission of most museums.'[1] Ten or more years ago, the physical growth of collections appeared less of a problem. Museums were following a valid tradition, and museology predicted for them an increasingly important cultural role. Museology, which had evolved as a discipline alongside the expansion of the museum sector, had produced a new perspective which questioned tradition and the pursuit of simple novelty. However, museums are complex organizations, and not all the outcomes of change (no matter how well informed) are predictable.

One by-product, of both continued acquisition and the birth of museum communication, was the 'reserve collection'. It had appeared that museums could continue as an expression of their inherent acquisitiveness, but they could not. It had seemed that they could limit themselves to the function of credible three-dimensional collective memory, but this is now inconceivable. We have touched the ceiling of growth, both physically and financially.

Museums do make sense, however, as part of the 'mega-brain' that we are creating as a product of civilisation. Consequently, their mission cannot be

---

1   U.V. Wilcox, 'Detached storage: the Smithsonian Institution's museum support centre', *Museum International*, 47(4) (1995), 18–22.

defined simply as that of memory, which, to continue the analogy, is but one function of the brain.[2] Nor can it be defined as, or confined to, science or education. Museums must define themselves in terms of quality,[3] that is responsibility and wisdom.

Much of what we have in our museum collections is, by nature, subjective and haphazard – collected in pursuit of different ambitions and hardly capable of meeting contemporary needs. Art treasures were used to finance wars,[4] others arose as war booty, some were partly restituted and others irreversibly damaged. The collected material remnants of history in constant making can rarely claim the continuity and coherence that historians and others might wish. From rich amateur collectors of the sixteenth century to modern-day tycoons, museum collections often embody the spirit of the few rather than a set of collective values. They perhaps reflect socialised possessiveness or greed for power. No financial or political hegemony is able to resist the temptation of also dominating spiritual values.

Museums are also expressions of collective conquest formed by equally zealous scholars and army leaders. Museums contain the evidence of our conquests, but seem not to expose that which we have yet to conquer.[5] Collections have been forced into obvious and factual frames of reference; museums became cultural or political mechanisms for the public relations of those in control. Academic objectivity, itself but a servant, has presented a different world history in every national museum. All cherish the representation of life through evidence of official excellence and perfection. This may tell us a lot about the aspirations of those societies which created these institutions, but little about the richness and variety of life itself.

Museums have been living witnesses to dying cultures and societies, seeing the whole fine infrastructure collapse and degenerate. They appeared on the scene as fetishistic souvenir hunters – doing their best to

---

2　'A great memory does not make a mind, any more than a dictionary is a piece of literature', Cardinal John Henry Newman.

3　T. Sola, 'Beyond the sharing of knowledge; an introduction to quality in museums', a paper presented at Sharing the Knowledge, the Annual Conference of the Museum Association of Canada, 1995.

4　J.M.A. Thompson, ed., *Manual of Curatorship* (Oxford: Butterworth Heinemann, 1992).

5　E. Mendis, *Museums and the New Technology* (Sydney: Museums Association of Australia, 1980).

save the hat of a drowning man. Museum 'collectibles' rarely suggested the slowly appearing museum mission of serving a developing society, let alone a sustainable one. 'Sustainable' is a useful word for museums, implying a process which is harmonious and continuous, such as using the past as a source of survival wisdom. Relatively early in their history, museums possessed an unconstrained belief in the value of the object; 'But, objects do not make a "museum", they merely form a collection.'[6] The failure to include everyday objects removed life from museums and for a long time blurred the vision of those who might give them a new purpose.

Corrupted by a perverted sense of quality many museums pursued 'giantism', that quantitative monster always there when responsibility is scarce. 'Hudson's law' in museology links large collections to bad collection care.[7] Growth is a universal problem[8] with a Pandora's box of consequences. It appears innocuous but in fact presents a deep conceptual crisis which endangers the museum's mission and its position in contemporary society. Never having fully succeeded in forming a profession, museum people also might be an endangered species;[9] professionals have certainly began to talk about 'dying museums'.[10] Apparently drawing lifeblood from their acquisitiveness, it is suggested that they die when they stop adding to their collections or when they have no collecting policy. But perhaps what museums perceive as an organ is really a cancer.

Experience suggests, for example, that only 10% of collections can be preserved (well),[11] despite 60% of museum budgets being focused on collection care.[12] Until recently no one asked 'What is the cost of collecting?' Today, the question is posed by numerous governments (in the UK, France,

---

6   J.C. Dana, *A Plan for a New Museum* (Woodstock, Vermont: The Elm Tree Press, 1920).

7   A reference to Kenneth Hudson.

8   J.T. Wilson quoted in J. Whitman, 'More buttons, buzzers and bells', *Museum News*, September/October, (1978), 47.

9   T. Sola, 'Museum professionals – the endangered species', in P.J. Boylan (ed), *Museums 2000* (London: Museums Association/Routledge, 1992).

10   M. Jaoul, 'Why reserve collections?', *Museum International*, 47(4) (1995).

11   Words of the president of the Conservation Committee at the General Conference of ICOM, The Hague, Netherlands, 1989.

12   G.F.L. MacDonald, 'L'avenir des musées dans le village global', *Museum*, 155 (1987), 214.

the Netherlands, Sweden). If some museums are moving towards an unknown future at the growth rate of 7%,[13] their collections will double in a decade. The philosophy is one of acquire now, think later. But dying of bulimia or anorexia is not entirely a problem of added or lost physical substance. It is also a deficiency of mind. Why should museums be any different? Museology embodies the transfer of professional experience, self-analysis, self-criticism, policy creation and professional development, but it fails to recognise the paradoxical role of collections as both blessing and curse.

What matters is knowing the ends which collections and their governing institutions are destined to serve. From this perspective, one can create responsible and realistic policy which would have the solid (if not unanimous) support of taxpayers.

Blame for museum failings is easily assigned to professional ineptitude, but this is an oversimplification. The true cause lies much deeper in museum philosophy. The current debate, which places fetishism for originals in opposition to objects in the virtual realm, is an example of the way questions concerning the quintessence of objects and ideas have been put aside. The older literature is full of evidence suggesting how the collection is 'all-important',[14] 'the predominant reason for many a museum's existence'.[15]. Doyens of the profession have proclaimed that museums had to concentrate upon collections (and not simply for the purposes of producing knowledge).[16]

But a few were able to discern the true problem. It must be the inescapable divine request of Eunomia, one of the Horae, deity of order, that museums come down with an addiction to the quantitative dimension of reality – to constantly count everything (arithmomania). Or perhaps it is by the mother of the Muses, Mnemosyne, that the misunderstanding of her gift was to cause still another illness, hypermnesia, an astonishing memorising of the most insignificant details: more and more about less and less. It certainly did not mean the trivial quotidiana, in spite of the timely,

---

13   B. Lord, et al., *The Cost of Collecting* (London: HMSO, 1989).
14   A.M. Heath, 'The training of education officers', in *Museum Education Training* (Sydney: Museum Education Association of Australia, 1977), 5–9.
15   E.P. Alexander, *Museums in Motion* (Nashville: American Association for State and Local History (AASHL), 1979), 119.
16   G. Lewis, lecturing at the Commonwealth Institute, London at the international seminar Museums in Education, 1982.

sane voices which urged 'conservation of everyday life artefacts, rather than great monuments of antiquity'.[17] In pursuit of scientific perfection, curators often purged the passion and personal touch of great collectors from their collections. They did it by adding, filling gaps, making the collections objective and exhaustive, and even by deaccessioning. By demonstrating such a disregard both for the life of the collection and for the story it tells by its very composition, they were also ignoring life itself.

Obsession with the three-dimensional object is ultimate proof of the difficulties of understanding the true purpose of museums. The museum object, collected, researched, exposed and interpreted, is not the final product of the museum working process. If eternity was a possibility, it would not be achieved by infinite survival of physical substance alone. Material culture may be instructive, but only as a means for understanding non-material culture. The latter, as the aggregate of the values, norms and knowledge of a society, is a cultural structure of ideas more than a physical entity. It explains and makes us aware of values and meanings, and thus provides arguments for continuity and survival. The capacity of the mental or spiritual far excels that of the physical.

The meaning of museums is not to study the past, but how we relate to it. As such, the museum has become the mediator between users and the past, amplifying and decoding, stimulating, assisting. But the museum does not generate identity, it is not a 'generator of culture'.[18] As I have written elsewhere (because I find it a precise metaphor), it is neither the heart itself, nor the machine to stand in its place, but a pace-maker to help it function.

Any museum object is polysemous, but when classified and interpreted from a discriminative point of view, its rich interpretive capacity is lost as it emits only a narrow and misleading fragment. Users should not have to think about the frustrations and partitions of individual fields of study when forced to reconstruct the former whole. Users do not need isolated, specialist, decontextualized knowledge. The method – essentially academic analysis – should not claim the status of the product.

Museum hypermnesia is a process of fighting the invented enemy: the natural process of forgetting; the oblivion of filtered, selected knowledge.

---

17   G.P. Marsh, *Man and Nature* (Cambridge, Mass.: Harvard, 1965 [1864]) (ed. D. Lowenthal).

18   As was claimed by the title of the General Conference of ICOM, The Hague, Netherlands, 1989.

Any human being performs this natural process constantly, as perfect recall would transform us all into neurotics. And, curiously, it is in pursuit of this that new technology is being used. Oblivion is as natural and as important as memory. To forget is to create hierarchies and classifications by importance, need and potential. In order to filter and extract the wisdom needed to move, develop and continue, traditional cultures (of which we keep the physical remnants in our darkened stores) used ritual, myth and art, themselves the products of abstraction and sublimation capable of transcending the factual nature of their former reality. What we require from this mega-machine[19] with its immense reservoirs of knowledge is the product of simple, common wisdom.

Cultures cannot be preserved in collections, just as the museum tiger has little chance of contributing to the continuation of its species. Preservation of a sort only happens when there is a danger of deterioration, degeneration and decadence; when fieldwork rescues things and values from extinction. If the disease is acculturation or 'desertification' of cultures (due to internationalisation), one would imagine that the enemy should be neutralised where it performs its crime: the real world. Reality is our primary collection, of which we need to preserve the essence of its richness and variety. One means to achieve this is in the museum collection: like a gland in a body, it should help society function and grow harmoniously. Anything that restores balance and fights the forces of pauperisation of the world is legitimate and good. So collections have to return to their origins. Of course, the profession will tackle physical obstacles first; the problem is, however, quite conceptual in its essence.

Recent professional testimonies provide us with a lot to think about: 'The lifeblood of museums is in their collections ... The museum, if it is not a collection, is nothing.'[20] Acceptable, but only if we redefine both the museum and the collection. The wide but only reasonable denomination of the (true) museum collection is that it is reality itself – past, present and future. But on a map, a scale of one to one cannot be represented: reduction and concentration are necessary whilst still maintaining the credibility of the information preserved. In similar fashion, the museum is an artificial mechanism for the preservation of developmental codes whose existence is

---

19   An expression taken from L. Mumford, *Mit o Masini* (Zagreb,1986).

20   N. Cossons, 'Class, culture and collections', in G. Kavanagh, ed., *The Museums Profession* (Leicester: Leicester University Press, 1991), 24.

endangered by entropy. Amongst those that perform this best are the non-institutionalised museums of individuals, groups and communities which represent life itself.

It required no special museological intuition to know some ten years ago that collection growth would fill all available space.[21] The solution to the problem was postponed; its root, hyper-acquisitiveness or the 'museumisation' of the world, remained untackled. The new reserve stores of the Musée National des Techniques in Paris, at Saint Denis, or the Museum of London's dislocated storage, or Smithsonian Institution's futuristic new reserves in Maryland, will not solve the problem, but give it more time to grow without the interference of museological philosophy. The bright and revolutionary example of Sweden's Samdok organisation, rooted in co-operation in the very process of collecting, is little exploited and feebly praised.

An awareness of the limited logic of quantity and an understanding of the social role of museums has been present in the profession for a long time.[22] We are now in an era of quality, when heritage-centred institutions have to redefine their mission through this long-neglected optic.

Increasing numbers of museums derive their collections from the participation of the community they serve. Many eco-museums did this, but others less easily defined also did so, such as the Museum of the Romanian Peasant in Bucharest, which encouraged peasants to visit the museum, give objects and receive a certificate. The Finnish Forest Museum, started *ex nihilo*, assembled the entire collection from gifts, offering in return a certificate, a year's free entrance, and the donor's name in the book at the entrance. The Workers' Museum in Copenhagen embodied a similar philosophy: 'Exhibitions were based on the material people had given us, that is to say, on those very objects which they perceived as their history.'[23] It is perhaps unlikely that museums such as these will accumulate in their reserves so much as to be unable to show more than 10 or 20%. The quality difference lies in the motives for collecting: for academic study (user-

---

21 T. Sola, lecture entitled 'Museum centres – cornerstones of an international network', Rikstutstalningar, Stockholm, 1987; The initiative for centralised storage for the museums of Zagreb, first proposed in 1982; 'Slovenianum', the project of a new, central Slovenian museum institution, Ljubljana, 1988.

22 Dana, op. cit.

23 P. Ludvigsen, 'A Workers' Museum in Copenhagen', *Museum International*, 47(4) (1995), 41

compromised), or for the user (science-compromised). This latter approach changes the character of the collection (partly) into an interpretive inventory. This is, of course, the Trojan horse which we started to fill long ago with so-called 'secondary material'. But the fortress had to be opened and remain so.

Information technology is shifting museums' emphasis,[24] making possible transparency in their working processes, opening up collections to users, creating truly interdisciplinary networks and greater participation. Technology enables wider professional and social communities to take possession of their heritage, and for heritage itself to become a force within society.

A fairly recent development has been to make collection outposts visitable by CD-ROM or the Internet. But using this interface these institutions could be anywhere, and indeed are new institutions. This cloning is hardly a sensible solution to anything, but corresponds perfectly well to the way all big issues are handled. If the answer is not part of the solution, it must be part of the question.

An alternative and more genuine innovation was the development of loan services earlier in the century. This occurred particularly in North American art museums, where the tax benefits of purchasing works of art for non-profit organisations obliged their public use. There was a specific American responsibility towards the taxpayer which inspired a belief in making art available. Art rental was typical of aims to make art accessible to as many people as possible. In Canada, the Gallery of Art in Ontario established this service in 1965. Art Bank Canada came into existence in 1972 with the aim of distributing contemporary Canadian art to any interested party. Their reserve was a virtual museum, and in the early 1980s 60% of the collection was always on loan.

Participation in conservation is also possible, as the example of the British National Library shows: some ten years ago, it launched a campaign offering for adoption books in need of conservation. A contribution of over £200 entitled the benefactor to put their name in the book to mark their involvement.

Alternatively, users can be involved in the museum by participating in its foundation and running. Only then does it become part of living. But such

---

24   T. Sola, 'How museology perceives information technology', Commet Conference, Swansea/Barcelona, 1995.

ı raises a host of professional issues and difficulties which have
y resolved.

...seums are entitled to profit immensely from the upsurge in
hypermedia. Properly used, they will provide for the extension of collecting
(by adding pictorial information in profusion), interpretation (by providing
integrated contextual information) and participation (by leaving open
channels of exchange with users). As a consequence, the traditional
collection might change, perhaps by becoming smaller and less expensive
to maintain. The original three-dimensional resource would become a kind
of gold reserve guaranteeing the value of the communicative currency
issued by the museum. But this currency could also be issued by others and
remain valid – we know that a museum can exist without holding a
collection; the collection of the Museum of Jewish Diaspora in Tel Aviv, for
example, is scattered all over the world. The 'hypermuseum' then exhibits
practically no original objects, but the information is original and genuine,
composed to tell a story which is both accurate and convincing.

So what matters is that a museum preserves the values for which it was
created. It can do this by hoarding physical remnants of the past or by
ensuring that credible messages are created. When appropriated by the
majority, and integrated into their changed behaviour, these assure the
continuation and survival of that identity the museum was set to protect.
This is the only true reason to collect.

This all may mean that the Malraux's vision of an imaginary museum
becomes possible in the form of the hypermuseum, cybermuseum or
virtual museum.

The traditional collection claims to be identity itself: it both represents
identity and stands in its place. It is composed of originals, but in truth the
only original is the complex whole of which individual objects form a part.
We attempt to regain a lost reality through the fragments we have
collected. Aware of this, we add further pieces, regardless of where they
come from, in order to complete the jigsaw. Thus the concern we assign to a
collection stored in a museum can be extended to things over which the
museum can never have complete control and which may indeed only exist
in a virtual world. Leopold Senghor said that with any old man who dies in
Africa, an entire library passes away. One might replace 'library' with
'museum', as everyone is also a rich source of memories and filtered
experiences assembled as a consequence of one's life. Everyone
unconsciously creates a kind of mental museum in response to their

environment. The use of hypermedia might make this concept of a museum attainable.

The hypermuseum as an idea offers considerable flexibility in the way information can be manipulated and delivered. Interactive media, digitised images and virtual environments create new possibilities for communication,[25] but also for collecting. The hypermuseum becomes a flexible information space capable of reaching specific user groups, and even individuals.

There is no reason, however, to believe that collecting will cease or slow down; the pressure for quantitative perfection is still too strong. The current trend for new museums will also not disappear overnight, but there will be a reactive process looking at alternatives and rationalising collections. Perhaps this will involve the redistribution of collections. The Matchstick Museum in Jonkoping, Sweden, for example, has material placed in local schools where it enjoys a level of care beyond that which the museum could afford. This material is also a token of partnership. Relationships such as this can be based on education, but equally on prestige, research, industry and so on. Could private individuals participate in this kind of arrangement? Or is this simply heresy? There are both psychological and ethical benefits. The bond between a museum and its community would be strengthened. The alternative might be museums suffocated and imprisoned by their collections. Of course, such ideas require massive revision of professional thinking and perfectionist aims. Perfectionism is a barrier to corruption, but also to common sense.

Many museums will turn into corrective mechanisms[26] – a means of fighting growing entropy. They have got to move towards sustainable development, and to view their collections philosophically as filtered human experience which has to reach the quality of wisdom. 'To attain knowledge, add things every day. To attain wisdom, remove things every day' (Lao Tse). In the search for past experiences, museums can furnish perfect examples of material evidence. But museums should participate in the everyday battle for sane solutions against social, cultural and environmental devastation. To do differently and claim a distinctive role in

---

25 For example, computer holography offers many possibilities such as in the reconstruction of the Cosquer cave in France presented at Imagina 1996 at the Institut National de l'Audiovisuel.

26 T. Sola, 'The prologue to the cybernetic museum', paper presented at the conference 'Museums and Sustainable Development', 1992.

ld be a mere demagogy. Preserving species diversity is one area
1seums are finding a role, but equally, they can mitigate, to
...egree, the loss of language, custom, oral tradition, and so on. In such
cases, these collections should express the dynamics of what is happening
and communicate this so that the public can understand the purpose of
collections and collecting.

It is possibly true that most museums could reduce their collections to a
minimal size without seriously harming their value.[27] But, to achieve this,
the profession will need a new level of maturity and to question possessive
self-sufficiency or the sanctity of collections.

There are three basic functions of a museum: collecting, research and
communication. These three aspects are equally subject to the consequences
of excessive growth. Once established, they have a natural tendency to
separate and form an independent existence. This was quite obvious some
ten years ago, even before the development of dislocated storage, exhibition
centres and research institutes. There is a centrifugal tendency constantly
pulling the institution apart. But there is also the centripetal tendency
which is trying to keep the whole together. In the modern age, this pull
might be supplied by integrated action and informatics.

Whatever we might be doing to find solutions, it remains the thing to
impress fellow professionals and quite another to impress that far more
important jury, the customer (or indeed our taxpaying owners). One starts
to wonder, though, how long will it take before our customers start telling
us how bad we are at what we do. Or perhaps they will just walk away.

---

27   J. Glusberg, *Hladni i vruci muzej* (Zagreb, 1986), 36.

Index